TONGU]

MW00774245

*A Bible of
the Non-Christian World*

COMPILED BY

GRACE H. TURNBULL

. . . And there appeared unto them cloven
tongues like as of fire, and it sat upon each
of them.

And they were all filled with the Holy Ghost
and began to speak . . . as the Spirit gave
them utterance.   ACTS II. 2–4

BALTIMORE

THE JOHNS HOPKINS PRESS

1941

PREFACE

A collection of extracts from the religious scriptures of the pagan world would be utterly incomplete without some representative passages from the literature of that nation which through its philosophers and poets has contributed most perhaps to the deeper thought of mankind, strangely lacking though it be in any formal canon of so-called sacred scripture corresponding to the Indian Vedas or the Jewish Bible. Around the figure of Socrates almost as much as about that of Buddha or Mohammed have centered the highest aspirations of an entire race and epoch, and his name, like theirs, has been passed down the centuries with almost equal veneration. Plato and Plotinus soar to as lofty spiritual heights as Zoroaster or Lao-Tzu, and may almost be said to have founded a religion. Epictetus' teachings are as indispensable to as large a proportion of the world as are the Laws of Manu or the Canon of Confucius. Nor could the Roman philosophers be left without representatives in an anthology of this kind. Seneca received the appellation "Saint Seneca" from the early Christian Church, and Marcus Aurelius was a glowing example of the Christianity of Nature: the Emperor Diocletian prescribed a distinct ritual for him as one of the gods, and the reverent devotion of the ages has made of his Meditations sacred scriptures indeed. Beside the reflections of this truly royal Roman the Edicts of the Indian King Asoka deserve a place, officially repudiating as they do the Law of Force and adopting in its stead the Law of Piety as the constitution of the land. The moral precepts of the ancient Egyptians, too, though they do not fall within the category of strictly sacred scripture, are interesting not only in themselves, but as the prototypes of Proverbs and Ecclesiastes. Readers of this volume will trace between it and the Hebrew Bible innumerable other parallelisms, a few of which have been referred to in footnotes. Their interest will be increased if one remembers that in the majority of cases the pagan passages *precede* the Jewish and Christian equivalents.

It would be interesting to inquire into the causes of that great tidal wave of religious thought and aspiration which swept the world about the sixth century B.C. enriching it in India by the Upanishads and Buddha himself, in China by Confucius and Lao-Tzu, in Greece by Thales, Anaximander, Anaximenes, Xenophanes, Pythagoras and Socrates, in Persia by Zoroaster; and of that second lesser wave about the first century which left in its wake in India, Rome and Greece the Bhagavadgita and the Laws of Manu, Seneca and Epictetus, in Palestine the Supreme Light of the World.

It is worth while to wonder, too, why so many details of the life and legend of Buddha are echoed in those of Christ—the Immaculate Conception, symbolic star, and angelic choir; the renouncing of an earthly kingdom, the fasting and temptation in the wilderness; the sending forth of the disciples, the earthquake and darkness following upon the death.

But it seems best to lay before the reader without delay the sacred texts themselves and let him answer for himself the questions they evoke. If at a first reading they seem arid and lacking in the beauty of the Hebrew Scriptures, let him remember that this is partly due to the fact that they are not, like the Bible, a tradition of our race, part of the very stuff and structure of our minds, absorbed in babyhood and ringing in our ears like old familiar tunes. One must reread them many times before one can absorb the mood of an alien race and think in its peculiar terms. Then, too, of this Bible of the Pagans we are not so fortunate as to possess a King James version with its rare simplicity and fitness of form and phrase.

I wish to acknowledge here my immense obligations to the many authors and translators, dead as well as living, whose works are listed in the Bibliography; without the free use of these the present volume could not have been compiled. To the Clarendon Press of Oxford who have graciously given me permission to make copious extracts from the authoritative translations of the Sacred Books of the East, my debt is peculiarly heavy. Also I want to express my deep gratitude and thanks to the various friends and scholars who have generously given me of their expert assistance and advice by reading my work in manuscript and making criticisms and corrections: the late Dr. Maurice Bloomfield, formerly Professor of Sanskrit and Comparative Philology at Johns Hopkins University, who very kindly looked through my selections from the Buddhist Scriptures; Dr. A. V. Williams Jackson, Professor of Indo-Iranian Languages at Columbia and an eminent authority on early Zoroastrianism, who read the extracts from the Avesta; Dr. Frank R. Blake, Associate Professor of Oriental Languages at Johns Hopkins University, who looked over the Assyrian and Chaldean Penitential Psalms; that prominent son of India, Mr. Dhan Mukerji, who read the extracts from the Bhagavadgita; Dr. William Norman Brown, A.B., Ph.D., Professor of Sanskrit at the University of Pennsylvania, who revised those from the Vedic Hymns and Upanishads; Dr. George Boas, Ph.D., Associate Professor of Philosophy at Johns Hopkins University, who revised the Enneads of Plotinus, and Mr. T. Y. Wang, Director of the Fengtien Mission of Education, who made a careful checking-up of the proper names occurring in the Chinese Classics and rendered them by one uniform system of transliteration.

I have made no attempt to present here the full and logical development of any religious or philosophical system; instead, I have chosen those passages which seem to have the greatest beauty and spiritual appeal, leaving it to the reader to enter on his own account into a more intensive study of that religion which interests him most: to this end he may find useful the Bibliography subjoined to this book.

I should esteem it a favour to be informed of any errors which may have slipped my attention, as also of any texts of notable beauty which should obviously have been included in a collection of this kind; though being necessarily restricted within very definite bounds, this anthology can make no claim to being inclusive, and represents in the last analysis the personal choice of the compiler. I hope it may lead others to compile Bibles of their own to supply the lack which may be felt in this: for it is a great pleasure to commune with the great ones of heaven and earth, and why should we deny ourselves this delight?

G. H. T.

223 Chancery Road,
Baltimore, Md.
March, 1928.

CONTENTS

ix

TO
THE UNKNOWN GOD

Thee, self begotten, who, in ether rolled
Ceaselessly round, by mystic links dost blend
The nature of all things, whom veils enfold
Of light, of dark night flecked with gleams of gold,
Of star-hosts dancing round thee without end.

—Fragment 593, Euripides (480-406 B.C.)

THE UNKNOWN GOD

I AM unknown to him who saith he knoweth Me, but to him who knoweth that he knoweth Me not, I am known.
Inscription on an idol in India.

I AM all that was, and is, and is to be, and my veil no man hath lifted. *From the shrine of Neith at Saïs.*

I HAVE kindled the light, I have woven the star-strewn path. *Egyptian Book of the Dead.*

THE concealed spirit, a mystery for him whom He hath created, is Amon, the ancient of days, who is from the beginning, the Creator of Heaven, the earth, the depths, and the mountains. *Inscription at Thebes, Egypt.*

HE cannot be sculptured in stone. He cannot be seen. Service cannot be rendered to Him. Gifts cannot be presented to Him. He is not to be approached in the sanctuaries. Where He is is not known. He is not to be found in inscribed shrines. No habitation can contain Him.
From Hymn to Hapi, by an Egyptian Scribe of the 18th Dynasty.

O LORD, no god is equal to Thee! Heaven beareth Thy spirit, earth Thine image, and the depth is furnished with Thy mysteries! *To Osiris-Serapis, in an early Papyrus of the Dead.*

HOMAGE to Thee! Goodness itself, Lord of Time, who conductest eternity! *Papyrus 3292, Louvre MSS.*

THE great and living Aton, ordaining life, my Father, my Rampart of a million cubits, my Remembrancer of eternity, Lord of fate!

There is no poverty for him who hath set Thee in his heart; such a one cannot say, O that I had! When Thou bringest life to men's hearts by Thy beauty, there is indeed life!   *Akhnaton, King of Egypt, 1375-1358* B.C.

THE heart of a man is his own god.
                                     Egyptian inscription.

THAT God, the All-Worker, the Great Soul, ever seated in the heart of His creatures, is framed by the heart, by the thought, by the mind; they who know that, become immortal.   *Shvetashvatara Upanishad, 4th Adhaya.*

THE Inseparable Companion.
              Ajatasatru, King of Benares; Brihad-
              Aranyaka Upanishad.

THALES was asked, What God was: That, he said, which hath neither beginning nor end. Of all things, the oldest is God. All things are full of God. The mind of the universe is God.   *Aet. Plac. i. 8, Dox. 307.*

GAZING up into the broad expanse of heaven, Xenophanes declared, The One is God!
              Aristotle, Metaphysics, I. 5, 986b 23.

GOD is one, supreme among both gods and men, resembling mortals neither in form nor in thought.

He is all eye, all thought, all hearing. Without toil He ruleth all things by the purpose of His mind, and evermore doth He abide in the same place, moving not at all.
       Fragments 23-26, Xenophanes, 628-520 B.C.

KNOW God, who is Number and Harmony!
              Pythagoras, 580(?)-500 B.C.

God fulfilleth every purpose, even as He desireth, God that not only overtaketh the winged eagle, but surpasseth the dolphin on the sea, and bendeth many a proud mortal beneath His sway, while to others He giveth glory that knoweth no eld.

Surely the great mind of Zeus doth pilot the destiny of those whom He doth love.

Pythian Odes II. 49, and V. 122,
Pindar, 522-443 B.C.

WE cannot bring God nigh to us, that we should see Him with our eyes; nor can we lay hold of Him with our hands, the two highways by which faith entereth into the heart of man.

For He hath no human head fitted to bodily members; nor do arms spring from His shoulders; He hath no feet, no swift knees. He is only a sacred and unutterable Mind with fleet thoughts flashing through all the world.

Fragments 133, 134, Empedocles,
492-432(?) B.C.

GOD is a Geometrician (God continually geometrizes).

Attributed to Plato by Plutarch.

THE Measure of all things (referring to Protagoras, who taught that man was the measure of all things).

Plato, 429-347 B.C.

THERE existeth Something which doth impart motion without Itself having motion imparted to It![1] Something which is eternal. And the Prime Mover imparteth this motion. Upon such a principle do heaven and earth depend.

God's life is like that of which we catch a transient glimpse when our life is at its best. Thus indeed His life always is, for His very self-activity is bliss.

[1] *Primum mobile immotum. Actus purissimus.*

The principle of life is in God; for energy of mind doth constitute life, and God is this energy. His joy is in the exercise of His essential energy. He is eternal and perfect, without parts and passions, indivisible and unchanging.   *Aristotle, Metaphysics XI. vii.*

JUST as in a chorus, when the leader giveth the signal to begin, the whole chorus joins in song, mingling in a single studied harmony their varied voices, so too is it with the God that ruleth the world.

For at the signal given from on high by Him, the stars and the whole heaven move, and the sun doth travel forth on his double course whereby he divideth day and night.

And in their due season the rain, the wind and the dews are produced by the First Primæval Cause; the flowing of the rivers, the swelling of the sea, the ripening of fruits, the nurturing and the prime and decay of all things.

That this Force is unseen standeth in the way neither of its action nor of our belief in it. For the spirit of intelligence whereby we live, though invisible, is yet seen in its operations.

Thus too we must think of God, who in might is most powerful, in beauty most fair, in time immortal, in virtue supreme. For all that happeneth in the air, on the earth, and in the water, may truly be said to be the work of God, who possesseth the universe.

For God is to us a Law, impartial, admitting no correction or change, and better and surer than those engraved on tablets.

God being one yet hath many names. He is called the Son of Kronos and of Time, for He endureth from eternal age to age. He is God of Lightning and Thunder, of the Clear Sky and the Ether, of the Thunderbolt and Rain.

After the fruits He is called the Fruitful God; He is the God of Birth and the God of our Fathers. He is God of Comradeship and Friendship and Hospitality, and in very truth the Saviour and God of Freedom.

I think also that God and nought else is meant when we speak of Necessity, which is as it were invincible being; and Fate, because His action is continuous and He cannot be stayed in His course; and Destiny, because all things have their bounds and nothing which doth exist is infinite.   *De Mundo, VI, VII,*
Aristotle, 384-322 B.C.

THE God that ruleth the city is Love.
Attributed to Zeno, the Stoic, 362-264 B.C.

GOD is the helping of man by man, and this is the way to eternal glory.   *Pliny, quoting the Stoic philosopher*
Posidonius (?), 136-51 B.C.

I AM grateful to Nature, not so much when I see her on the side that is open to the world, as when I am permitted to enter her shrine. Then one may seek to know of what stuff the universe is made, who is its author and guardian, what is the nature of God.

Here at last the soul comes to learn what it has long sought, it begins to know God. But what is God? The universal Intelligence. What is God? did I say? All that you see and all that you cannot see.

His greatness exceeds the bounds of thought. He is all in all, He is at once within and without His works. In us the better part is spirit, in Him there is nothing except spirit.

He is wholly Reason: though the eyes of mortals are so sealed by error that they believe this frame of things to be but a fortuitous concourse of atoms, the sport of chance. Yet than this universe could aught be fairer, more carefully adjusted, more consistent in plan?[2]

Seneca, Preface to Quæstiones Naturales.

NOR is it for man that God has made all these things. How small a portion of His mighty work is entrusted to us! But He who directs them all, who established and laid the foundations of the world, who has clothed Himself with creation, and is the greater and better part of His work, He is hidden from our eyes. He can be perceived only by thought.[2]

Quæstiones Naturales, Bk. VII. xxx.

THE ancient sages recognized the same Jupiter as we do, the Guardian and Ruler of the universe, its soul and breath, the Maker and Lord of this earthly frame of things, to whom every name of power is appropriate.

If you prefer to call Him Fate, you will not be wrong. He it is on Whom depend all things, the Cause of causes.

If you prefer to call Him Providence, you will still be right; for He it is by whose counsel provision is made for the world that it may pursue its orderly course and unfold the drama of its being.

If you prefer to call Him Nature, you will make no mistake; for He it is from whom all things derive being, and by whose breath we live.

---

[2] After the translation by John Clarke.

If you prefer to call Him the World, you will not err,
for He is everything that you can see. He is wholly in-
fused in all His parts, self-sustained through inherent
power.[2]

Quæstiones Naturales, Bk. II. xlv,
Seneca, 4 B.C.-69(?) A.D.

THE general inclinations which are naturally implanted in my soul to some religion, it is impossible for me to shift off; but there being such a multiplicity of religions in the world, I desire now seriously to consider with my self which of them all to restrain these my general inclinations to. And the reason of this my inquiry is not that I am in the least dissatisfied with that religion I have already embraced; but because 'tis natural for all men to have an overbearing opinion and esteem for that particular religion they are born and bred-up in. That, therefore, I may not seem biased by the prejudice of education, I am resolved to prove and examine them all; that I may see and hold fast to that which is best.

That I may make diligent and impartial inquiry into all religions and so be sure to find out the best, I shall for a time look upon myself as one not at all interested in any particular religion whatsoever; but only as one who desires, in general, to serve and obey Him that made me, in a right manner, and thereby to be made partaker of that happiness my nature is capable of.

Bishop Beveridge, 1636-1707.

INTRODUCTION

Is it less idolatrous to worship few gods than many? Is it less idolatrous to worship one god than several if that one be but a fragment of the veritable God, the fetich set up by a very fallible human fancy, the imagination of but a small portion of the race of man?

There are idols made by hands, and idols manufactured in men's brains. Are the idols of men's minds less idols than those made with hands if they represent but a partial and unworthy view of God? Shall we set up the idol of our own race and epoch as the sole God to worship for all times to come? Others have done the same. And who shall judge between?

The only God whom man can worship without idolatry is the Unknown God—that Supreme Power who "is not a Mind, but something higher than a Mind; not a Force, but something higher than a Force; not a Being, but something higher than a Being; something for which we have no words, something for which we have no ideas."

The Mohammedans consign to the first circle of Hell the wicked of their own faith; to the second, the Jews; to the circle lower still the Christians, "because they dare to associate another with God; for the Christians say: The Merciful hath taken to Himself a Son." Mohammedan damns Christian, Christian condemns Mohammedan, Mohammedan and Christian unite in dubbing the heathen idolatrous. The Athenians, pointing to Socrates, cry: That is the atheist who says that there is only one God! And the early Christians in their turn were called by the heathen atheists.

The expression of the divine element, the glory in nature, as found in the Vedic and Egyptian Hymns, the stress which Buddha places on the inevitability of Cause and Effect, which Zoroaster lays on the conflict of the

Good and Evil Powers; Confucius' calm insistence on decorous virtue, the impassioned pleadings of the inspired Prophet of Islam—all have met some inner need of man. Unto each and all of these seers appeared "tongues like as of fire . . . and they were all filled with the Holy Ghost." The paths by which men climb from the shadows of the mountain's base toward its towering summit, start from widely divergent points. As they mount, their ways converge. Once on the cloudless peak, they all see at last the selfsame God. St. Augustine quotes a heathen of his day as saying: "Under different names we adore the only Divinity whose eternal power animates all the elements of the world." Amon or Ormazd, Ishtar, Indra or Osiris, Jupiter or Jehovah, God or Goddess—the names do not greatly signify; the divinities they designate equally answer to the deep human need, as they all embody the most prized ideals of man. "Whensoever piety languisheth, and impiety doth prevail, I create Myself. I am born age after age for the preservation of the righteous, the destruction of evildoers, and the establishment of virtue. . . . Whatever god a worshipper may seek in earnest faith, that selfsame faith in his own god do I confirm. . . . However men may come to Me, thus even serve I them."

If the readers of this book should by it be led to a deeper understanding of the alien races who, like them, have sought and are seeking still, the one true God, though interpreted in different ways; if it should bring about a greater sympathy and charity between all countries, sects and times and creeds, it shall not have been compiled in vain.

There is a tendency in all religious belief not only to become obstructed with graven images interposed between man and God, but to become encrusted too with myth and legend and with stock and stone of out-worn phrase and dogma which distort the truth and leave the worshipper insensible and cold. By the unfamiliar then he may be shocked once more to life; by the many-sidedness of the ideal of God as held by the several nations of old he can be made to realize the relativity of the Absolute and the fluidity of Truth; and to see man's various conceptions of his Creator as but "a dome of many-coloured glass" with which he stains "the white radiance of eternity." And so from dogmatism and intolerance he may advance to receptiveness and universality, to an abhorrence of rigid creeds, to a ready acceptance of all that is best in the thought of all sects and nations, to a religion as comprehensive, as all-embracing and all-sustaining as God Himself, to sympathies that reach down the ages to all men and times.

In the earliest existing documents there already comes to light the ceaseless searching after God if haply He might be found; and the unanimity of this quest all down the ages is the surest evidence of man's need of Deity. Whatever this straining after God may signify, whether He can be expressed in human terms or not, whether He is but the projection of our own highest ideals, no study is more uplifting than the tracing through the centuries of man's eager, often crude attempt to overtake His Creator and portray Him in all His blinding glory to our mortal eyes.

As far into the remote reaches of existence as we can penetrate, we find too the persistent idea of holiness and righteous living, however that ideal may vary from age to age. Strange, how this notion of holiness (*wholeness*) first entered human thought! Yet there it is, voicing itself in admonitions and aspirations very like our own, in prayers that might have been written yesterday, in lives that approach the Christian ideal if not that of Christ Himself!

If man's conception of God be but the projection of his own highest ideal, then he has cause for deepest humility in that this his ideal has not grown consistently in spiritual beauty throughout the ages. The ancient potters and builders of Egypt long before Isaiah's day conceived of the Highest as Xnum (Potter or Builder). His manifestation was through Thoth (the Word) ages before St. John saw that the "Word was God." Amon was the Ancient of Days who "wipeth away tears from all eyes" centuries before the God of Daniel was conceived or the God of Revelation. "Thy love is in the south, Thy grace is in the north, Thy beauty taketh possession of all hearts," sang the old Egyptian to his God hundreds of years before we learned that "God is Love." "Recompense evil with good," said Lao-Tzu six hundred years before Christ proclaimed the Golden Rule, and two hundred years before the Sermon on the Mount had been pronounced the Law of Manu had admonished man to bless when he is cursed.

Lessons of the beauty of love and self-sacrifice, and of the horror of war, as well as conceptions of the infinity of God and the grace of the life of the spirit fall with double force from the lips of pagan prophets, and we cannot but be touched by the sublimity of the ideals of these old philosophers, preachers and poets too far from Christ in time and place to have ever touched His garment or known the virtue that went out from Him.

And if the nations who profess the teachings of Brahman and Buddha, Mohammed, Confucius and Zoroaster have fallen immeasurably below the models set by them, that the so-called Christian nations have been falser yet to the standards of Christ is evidenced by the gross materialism of their civilizations and their participation in recent times in the most criminal and bloody war that the world has ever staged. They need not scorn to read Asoka's appeal for peace engraved on the living rock of India, nor to join in the prayer of Aristophanes that "from the murmur and subtlety of suspicion" with which we vex one another "we may be given rest."

> Oh Thou that makest wars to cease in all the world,
> Make war and tumult now to cease . . .
> Make a new beginning,
> And with some finer essence of forbearance
> Temper our mind.

Thus prays the pagan satirist. And beside this living, loving God of Greek and Egyptian and old Chinese seer we might well hesitate to place the sometimes passionate, revengeful God of the early Hebrews. But the Jehovah of the primitive tribes of Israel gradually evolved till in their prophets He became at last the very tender God of Mercies, feeding His flock like a shepherd, gathering the lambs in His arm.

On the whole the book which we have been wont to call *the* Scriptures, the Word of God, is perhaps the most sublime creation known to man. What heathen work can touch it? But that it is possible to place at its side other holy scriptures, other Bibles of inspired words, Bibles of the pagans, can be shown by the present collection culled from the non-Christian sacred scriptures of the ancient world. And there are yet other Bibles possible, the Bibles of the present, slowly forming now all unknown to us; and the Bibles of the future, the Bibles of the man of science; for revelation is not closed.

Could we shake ourselves free from prejudice of ancient root and emerge for a moment from narrow dogmatism and cherished sectarianism into the light of that broad day where men of very various lives and faiths in various ways are seeking Truth, we could learn much from the natural Christianity of the heathen, and recognize more easily the often vain profession of the Christian, the false science of the man of religion as well as the sincerity of the religion of the man of science. The latter has to teach us that the power of the mysterious Force which men name God is more miraculously manifest in the eternal regularity of Nature's laws than in any infringement of them which we call miracle, and that the study of those laws is the channel through which can come the richest revelation.

"The new statement is always hated by the old, and to those dwelling in the old comes like an abyss of scepticism." But Buddha had the strength to see that the Law which he enunciated was but a "raft"—a thing to be abandoned for something better when it had touched the farther shore of truth.

"Where the Spirit of the Lord is, there is liberty";

nor should we fear to let fall a flood of light upon the greatest of man's problems—his relation to the Universe and to the Spirit—sure, no matter to what lengths research may lead us, that beyond our searching and our science, receding ever, but abiding still, the unexplored, unending Mystery waits, as Terrible and Beautiful as before.

THE BOOK OF GENESIS

EARLY CONCEPTIONS OF THE GENESIS
OF THE WORLD

Whence are we born? Whereby do we live and whither do we go? O ye who know Brahma, tell us at whose command we abide here, whether in pain or pleasure. Should time, or nature or necessity, or chance or the elements be considered as the cause, or He who is called Purusha, that is, the Supreme Spirit?

Shvetashvatara Upanishad 1.

*Principio caelum ac terras camposque liquentis
lucentemque globum Lunae Titaniaque astra
Spiritus intus alit, totamque infusa per artus
mens agitat molem et magno se corpore miscet.
Inde hominum pecudumque genus, vitaeque volantum,
et quae marmoreo fert monstra sub aequore pontus.
Igneus est ollis vigor et caelestis origo
seminibus, quantum non noxia corpora tardant,
terrenique hebetant artus moribundaque membra.*

Virgil, *The Æneid* VI. 724ff.

TONGUES OF FIRE

THE BOOK OF GENESIS [1]

THEN was there neither aught nor naught. No sky nor anything above it. What covered all, and where, by what protected? Was it water or deep darkness?

Death was not there, nor immortality; nor confines of day and night. But that One breathed calmly alone; other than the One existed nothing which since hath been. Darkness was concealed in darkness in the beginning; indistinguishable water was all this universe.

But the living force which lay enveloped in the husk at length burst forth from fervent heat. Through desire, the primal seed of mind, arose creation; desire known to the wise as the bond of being and non-being.

Who knoweth, and who shall in this universe declare, whence and why this manifold creation sprang? Who can penetrate the secret of its rise? Who knoweth whence this varied world arose, or whether it doth uphold itself or not?

He who in highest heaven is the Ruler of this universe, He knoweth, or haply knoweth not!

Rig-veda X. xi. 129 [2]

IN the beginning there was the mere state of being, one only without a second. It willed, I shall multiply and be born. It created heat. That heat willed, I shall multiply and be born. It created water. The water willed, I shall

---

[1] For other early endeavors to solve the problem of the genesis of the world, see in this volume Psalm XXXV; the ''Book of Lao-Tzu,'' pp. 159, 160; the ''Book of Plato,'' p. 303; the ''Book of Epictetus,'' p. 357.
[2] See p. 45.

multiply and be born. It created aliment. Therefore, whenever rain doth fall, much aliment is produced.

That being willed, Entering these three divinities in a living form, I shall develop names and forms. Then that being entered into those three divinities with his living self, and revealed names and forms.

Chandogya Upanishad [3] *VI. ii iii.*

THIS world, which is the same for all, neither any god nor man hath made; but it was always, is and ever shall be ever-living fire, kindling by measure and dying out by measure.

All things are exchanged for fire, and fire for all things; as all goods are exchanged for gold, and gold for all goods.

God is day and night, winter and summer, war and peace, satiety and famine. He changeth as fire when it is mingled with different kinds of incense, and is named as each man listeth.

From all cometh one and from one cometh all.

Heraclitus, [4] *Fragments 20, 22, 36, 59.*

HARDLY can these things be seen by the eyes or heard by the ears of men, so hardly grasped by their mind! But, O ye gods, hallow these lips of mine and make a pure stream flow from them!

There is no coming into being of aught that perisheth, nor any end for it in baneful death. Mingling and separation of the mingled,—that is all; birth is but a name men give to these.

For it cannot be that aught can arise from what in no way is, and it is impossible and unheard of that what *is*

---

[3] See p. 29.

[4] Heraclitus of Ephesus (536-475 B. C.), the most original of the pre-Socratic philosophers, was the inventor of the Logos, from which the science of logic is named, and on which the Christian doctrine of the Word is based. He set up as his Absolute a universal fire. He was the author of the pithy aphorism; Man's character is his fate. (Fragment 121.)

should perish; for it will always *be,* wherever one may keep putting it.

Come hearken to my words, for learning addeth strength to thy mind. At one time things grew to be one alone out of many; and then again fell asunder so that there were many from the one,—fire and water and earth and the endless height of the air; and, apart from these, baneful Strife, and in their midst Love.[5]

Let thy mind's gaze rest upon her. It is she who awakeneth thoughts of love and fulfilleth the works of peace. No mortal man hath searched her out.

When Strife had fallen to the lowest depth of the vortex, and Love had come to be the center of the whirl, all things came together in Love so as to be one only.

But many things unmixed remained, alternating with the things that were mixed, as many as Strife retained in its grasp; for it had not yet retired altogether to the outermost boundaries of the circle.

But just in proportion as it was continuously rushing out a gracious and divine impulse of blameless Love kept ever coming in.

And straightway things grew mortal that were wont to be immortal before, and things before unmixed were mixed. And from these as they were mingled the countless tribes of mortal creatures poured forth, fashioned in all manner of forms, a wonder to behold.

Empedocles, Fragments 2, 4, 8, 12, 17, 35.[6]

ALL things were together infinite both in number and smallness, for the small too was infinite. Air and æther prevailed over all things, both of them being infinite.

Fragment 1.

[5] The forces which Empedocles names *Love* and *Strife* may be rendered in modern scientific terminology, *Affinity* and *Repulsion.*

[6] Greek philosopher living in Sicily (about 492-432 B. C.) ''than whom,'' says Lucretius, ''Sicily hath produced nothing holier, more marvellous, or more dear.'' He was popularly believed to work miracles and to possess divine power.

NOR is there a least of what is small, but there is always a smaller. But there is also always something greater than what is great, and it is equal to the small in amount.

Fragment 3.

AND we must suppose that there are contained many things and of all sorts in the things that are uniting, seeds of all things, with all sorts of shapes and colours and savours, and that men have been formed in them and all animals that have life, and that these have inhabited cities and cultivated fields as with us.

And that they have a sun and moon and other heavenly bodies as with us and that their earth bringeth forth for them many things of all kinds. Thus much have I said with regard to separating off, to show that it will not be only with us that things are separated off, but elsewhere too.

But before they were separated off, when all things were together, not even was any colour distinguishable; for the mixture of all things prevented it, of the moist and the dry, and the warm and the cold, and the light and the dark, and of much earth that was in it, and a multitude of innumerable seeds no one like another.

And these things being so, we must hold that all things are in the whole.

Fragment 4.

AND all things will be in everything, nor is it possible for them to be apart, but all things will have a portion of everything.

Fragment 6.

As these things revolve [they] [7] are separated out by the force and swiftness. And the swiftness maketh the force. Their swiftness is not like the swiftness of any of the things that are now among men, but in every way many times as swift.

Fragment 9.

[7] The beginning of Frag. 9 is lost, and in the original what remains does not make a complete sentence: . . . *as these things revolve and are separated out by the force and swiftness.*

ALL other things partake in a portion of everything, but Nous [8] is infinite and self-ruled, and is mixed with nothing, being alone, Itself by Itself.

For It is the thinnest and purest of all things, and It hath all knowledge about everything, and the greatest strength; and Nous hath power over all things, both greater and smaller, that have life.

And Nous had power over the whole revolution, so that it began to revolve in the beginning; but the revolution extendeth over a larger space, and will extend over a larger still.

And all things that are commingled and separated off and differentiated are known by Nous.

And Nous set in order all things that were to be, and that were but are not now, and that are; and directed too this revolution in which now revolve the stars and the sun and the moon, and the air and the æther that are separated off.

And this revolution caused the differentiation, and the rare is differentiated from the dense, and the warm from the cold, the light from the dark, and the dry from the moist. *Fragment 12.*

AND when Nous began to set things in motion, there was differentiation of all that was in motion. And as things were set in motion and separated, the revolution caused them to be separated much more. *Fragment 13.*

AND Nous, which ever is, is certainly now there also where all other things are, in the surrounding mass, and in what has been united with it and separated off from it. *Fragment 14.*

THE dense and the moist and the cold and the dark collected where the earth is now, while the rare and the

[8] *Nous*, Greek for Mind, Reason, Intelligence, Spirit.

warm and the dry and the bright went out toward the further part of the æther.

Fragment 15.

From these as they are separated off earth is solidified; for from mists water is separated off, and from water earth. From the earth stones are solidified by the cold, and these rush outwards more than water.

Fragment 16.

We Greeks follow a wrong usage in speaking of coming into being and being destroyed; for nothing comes into being or is destroyed, but there is mingling and separation of things that are.[9] So they would be right to say, instead of *origin,* commingling; instead of *destruction,* dissolution.[10]   *Anaxagoras,*[11] *Fragment 17.*

The universe first existed only in darkness, imperceptible, undefinable, undiscoverable, and undiscovered; as if immersed in sleep.

Then the self-existing Power, undiscovered Himself, but making the world discernible, with the five elements and other principles, appeared in irresistible power, dispelling the gloom. He whom the mind alone can perceive, whose essence eludeth the external organs, who hath no visible parts, who existeth from eternity, even He, the soul of all beings, shone forth of His own will.

He having willed to produce various beings from His own divine substance, first with a thought created the waters, and placed in them a productive seed.

[9] I. e., *seeds* or *sperms.*
[10] The fragments are given according to Diels' enumeration, and are taken with minor changes from Burnet's *Early Greek Philosophy.* Adam & Black.
[11] Greek philosopher, exponent of Atomism, living about 500-427 B. C. He invented two of the most important conceptions in philosophy, *Nous,* the Cause of the cosmos, and *telos,* Its end or purpose in bringing order and harmony from chaos. Banished from Athens because he taught theories about "the things on high," Anaxagoras settled at Lampsacus, which upon his death erected an altar to his memory dedicated to the Mind and Truth.

The waters are called *nara*, because they were the production of Nara, or the spirit of God; hence He is called Nara Yana, or *moving on the waters*.[12]

From the supreme soul He drew forth mind, existing substantially though unperceived by sense, immaterial; and from mind, or the reasoning power, He produced consciousness, the internal monitor, the ruler.

And from them both He produced the great principle of the soul, or first expansion of the divine idea; and all the vital forms endued with the three qualities of goodness, passion, and darkness, and the five organs of sensation.

Then, pervading with emanations of the supreme spirit the minutest atoms of existing things, He formed all creatures.

When that Divine One waketh, then doth this world stir; when He slumbereth tranquilly, then the universe doth sink to sleep.

First Book of the Laws of Manu.[13]

Know first that heaven and earth and ocean's plain,
The moon's bright orb, and stars of Titan birth
Are nourished by one Life; one primal Mind,
Immingled with the vast and general frame,
Fills every part and stirs the mighty whole.
Thence man and beast, thence creatures of the air,
And all the swarming monsters that be found
Beneath the level of the marbled sea;
A fiery virtue, a celestial power,
Their native seeds. retain.

Virgil,[14] *Æneid VI. 723ff.*

BEFORE the sea and land and all-covering heaven appeared, there was one aspect over the whole of nature. All was rude, unelaborated, a mass called Chaos.

---

[12] Comp. Genesis I. 2.   [13] See page 247.   [14] Virgil (70-19 B. C.).

It was inert weight, the atoms of things in disorder and
confusedly intermingled; no sun as yet gave light to the
world, nor did the moon by increasing recover her horns
anew; no earth as yet hung in the surrounding air,
balanced by its own weight, nor did the ocean as yet
embrace the continents with its mighty arms.

This conflict of the elements God and benign Nature
pacified, distinguishing each from each, solid from fluid,
earth from air.

Whoever that God was, He distributed all things, sending each to its place.   *Ovid,*[15] *Metamorphoses I, 4ff.*

At the beginning all things were in the mind of Wakonda. All creatures, including man, were spirits. They
moved about in space between the earth and the stars.
They were seeking a place where they could come into
a bodily existence.

They ascended to the sun, but the sun was not fitted for
their abode. They moved on to the moon and found that
it also was not good for their home. Then they descended
to the earth. They saw that it was covered with water.

They floated through the air to the north, the east, the
south, and the west, and found no dry land. They were
sorely grieved. Suddenly from the midst of the water
uprose a great rock. It burst into flames and the waters
floated into the air in clouds.

Dry land appeared; the grasses and the trees grew. The
hosts of spirits descended and became flesh and blood.
They fed on the seeds and grasses and the fruits of the
trees, and the land vibrated with their expressions of
joy and gratitude to Wakonda,[16] the Maker of all things.
           From the Ritual of the Omaha Indians.

---

[15] Ovid, 43 B. C.-17 (?) A. D.

[16] *Wakonda* stands for the mysterious life power permeating all natural
forms and forces and all phases of man's conscious life. Visible nature
seems to have mirrored to the Omaha mind the ever-present activities of
the invisible and mysterious Wakonda and to have been an instructor in
religion and ethics: "Wakonda causes day to follow night without varia-
tion, and summer to follow winter; we can depend on these regular changes

SEEKING, earnestly seeking in the gloom. Searching—yes on the coast line—on the bounds of night and day; looking into the night.

The night had conceived the seed of night. The heart, the foundation of night, had stood forth self-existing even in the gloom. It groweth in gloom, the sap and succulent parts, the life pulsating, and the cup of life. The shadows screen the faintest ray of light.

The procreative power, the ecstasy of life first known, and joy of issuing forth from silence into sound. Thus the progeny of the Great-Extending filled the heaven's expanse; the chorus of life rose and swelled into ecstasy, then rested in bliss of calm and quiet.

Maori Poem of Creation.[17]

Io dwelt within the breathing-space of immensity. The universe was in darkness, with water everywhere. There was no glimmer of dawn, no clearness, no light.

And He began by saying these words, that He might cease remaining inactive: Darkness, become a light-possessing darkness!

He then repeated these selfsame words in this manner, that He might cease remaining inactive: Light, become a darkness-possessing light! And again an intense darkness supervened.

Then a third time He spake, saying: Let there be darkness above, let there be darkness below, let there be darkness unto Tupua, let there be darkness unto Tawhito; a dominion of light, a bright light! And now a great light prevailed.

Io then looked to the waters which compassed Him about and spake a fourth time saying: Ye waters of

and order our lives by them. In this way Wakonda teaches that our words and acts must be truthful so that we may live in peace and happiness with one another.'' This definition of Wakonda and the transcription of the fragment of the Ritual are from the article by Alice C. Fletcher, 27th annual report of the American Bureau of Ethnology.

[17] From J. C. Andersen's *Maori Life in Ao-tea.*

Tai-kama, be ye separate, heaven be formed! Then the sky became suspended.

Bring forth, thou Tupua-hono-nuku! And at once the moving earth lay stretched abroad.

Maori chant.[18]

HE abideth, Taaroa by name, in the immensity of space. There was no earth, there was no heaven, there was no sea, there was no mankind.

Taaroa calleth on high; He changed Himself fully. Taaroa is the root, the rocks, the sands; Taaroa stretcheth out the branches; Taaroa is the light; Taaroa is within; Taaroa is below; Taaroa is enduring, Taaroa is wise. He created the land of Hawaii, Hawaii great and sacred, as a cruse for Taaroa.

O foundations, O rocks, O sands! Here, here, brought together, press together the earth, press, press again! Stretch out the seven heavens, let ignorance cease. Create the heavens, let darkness cease. Let anxiety cease within. Fill up the foundations, fill up the rocks, fill up the sands!   *Tahitian Hymn of Creation.*[19]

[18] Journal of the Polynesian Society, XVI.
[19] From *The Polynesian Race*, by A. Fornander. This and the two preceding selections are quoted in *Primitive Man as Philosopher*, by Paul Radin.

THE EGYPTIAN BOOK OF WISDOM

BEING SELECTIONS FROM THE TEACHINGS OF KAGEMMA,
PTAH-HETEP, KING KHATI, AMEN-EM-
APT AND ANI

*God findeth His satisfaction in truth;
and He findeth His pleasure in the
most perfect purity. God hath purity
dearer than millions of gold and silver
offerings.*

Inscription on the doors of
the Temple of Edfu.

THE EGYPTIAN BOOK OF WISDOM

Selections from the Teaching of Kagemma

The Teaching of Kagemma or Ke'gemni [1] (*I have found a soul*), *the oldest book of Egyptian moral precepts, composed during the Third Dynasty, after 3000 B.C. To be found in the Prisse Papyrus together with the Precepts of Ptah-hetep.*

The innermost chamber openeth unto the humble man, and a wide seat is given to him that is gentle of speech; but sharp knives are set against one that would wrongfully force a way.

If thou sit at meat with a company, restrain thine appetite, gluttony is an abomination. A cup of water quencheth the thirst, a mouthful of melon stayeth the heart.

Be not haughty because of thy might in the midst of thy fellows. Beware of making strife; man knoweth not what shall happen, nor the things that the God will do when He punisheth.

Selections from the Precepts of Ptah-hetep

The Precepts of Ptah-hetep, [1] the Friend of God; *the Governor of the city of Memphis, written for his son about 2600 B.C. when he was one hundred and ten years old, during the Fifth Dynasty, in the reign of Assa,*

[1] Breasted says that Kagemma and Ptah-hetep were sages of the 3rd and 5th Dynasties into whose mouths the wisdom of the 12th Dynasty was put; but that some of the precepts attributed to Ptah-hetep are doubtless older than the collection itself. The various estimates of the dates of the Egyptian Dynasties differ by centuries, many scholars adopting lower figures than those given here. Most of the Egyptian names are also variously rendered; their consonants only being known, to make them pronounceable the vowel sounds must be supplied.

King of Upper and Lower Egypt. With the Instruction of Kagemma it is contained in the Prisse Papyrus and constitutes the oldest book in the world, being composed more than two millennia before the Hebrew Proverbs and Hexateuch were compiled.

Be not puffed up because of that which thou knowest; but hold converse with the ignorant man as with the sage; for there are no bounds to knowledge, and no craftsman hath attained to all the excellencies of his art. Good words are more rare than emeralds found by slave-maidens in rocks of pegmatite.

If thou find a disputant while he is hot, get not into a passion with him. Thou hast the advantage if thou keep silence when he is uttering evil words. Despise him not because thou art not of the same opinion.

If thou be a leader, as one directing the conduct of the multitude, pursue thou a course that is wholly excellent, that thine own conduct be without reproach. Truth is great, and enduring in virtue; since the time of Osiris, it hath not been moved. He who departeth from its laws is sorely chastised. There is great power in truth; the good man saith: It was a possession of my father.

Cause not fear among men, for God punisheth the like. Live, therefore, in the house of kindliness, and men shall come and bring gifts of themselves.

If thou have known a man of none account that hath been advanced in rank, be not haughty toward him by reason of that which thou knowest concerning him; but honour him that hath been advanced according to that which he hath become.

Follow thy heart as long as thou livest; diminish not the time of following the heart, for it is abhorred of the soul that its time of ease be taken away. Spend not the day in labour beyond what is necessary to maintain thy house. When riches are gained, follow the heart; for riches are of none avail if one be weary.

If thou be among people, make for thyself love, the beginning and end of the heart. The man who is great of heart is one of God's men. He hearkeneth unto the command of his heart, his enemy becometh his possession.

If thou be a leader, be gracious and hearken unto the speech of the suppliant. Stop not his word until he hath poured forth all he hath in his heart to tell thee, but be desirous of removing his injury. A fair word coloureth the heart.

If thou desire that thy conduct be good and preserved from all evil, keep thyself from every attack of covetousness. It is a fatal malady that cannot be conquered. It setteth at variance the father-in-law and the kinsmen of the daughter-in-law; it turneth the kindly friend into the bitter enemy, it driveth away the trusted servant from his master, it sundereth husband and wife.

It is a treasure-house of every kind of evil and the girdle of all wickedness. The man who hath Truth for his towline walketh whither it leadeth his steps and acquireth an habitation; but the avaricious possess not so much as a tomb.

Let not thy heart be extortionate when a division of property is made, and what is thy due shall come to thee.

If thou wouldst be wise, provide for thine own house and love the wife that is in thine arms. Anoint her, gladden her heart in the time that thou hast; she is an estate conferring great reward upon her lord. Be not harsh to her, for gentleness mastereth her more than force. So shalt thou keep her in thy house. If thou resist her will, it is ruin to thee. Open thine arms to her and show her thy love.

Satisfy thy hired servants out of such things as thou hast, for it belongeth to them that God hath favoured so to do. Peace dwelleth not in that town wherein are servants in distress.

Repeat not extravagant speech, neither listen thereto; it is a thing which hath escaped a hasty mouth. When such speech is repeated unto thee, hearken not thereto, look to the ground. Speak not regarding it, that he who is before thee may learn wisdom. Cause that which is just to be done, cause it to triumph.

If thou be a man of high rank who sittest in the council of thy lord, direct thy thought entirely to that which is good. To hold thy peace is better for thee than the teftef flower. Speak only when thou knowest a matter and canst make it manifest.

If thou be powerful, make thyself to be honoured for knowledge and for gentleness. Command only to direct; to be absolute is to fall into error. Exalt not thy heart, that it be not brought low.

The man that reckoneth accounts the whole day long passeth never a glad moment; he that gladdeneth his heart all the day long provideth not for his house. The bowman hitteth the mark, as the steersman reacheth his goal, now letting alone, now pulling. He that obeyeth his heart shall command.

After a violent quarrel, be at peace with him that is hostile unto thee, his opponent. It is such souls that make love to grow.

If thou have become great after being of none account, and have gotten riches after squalor, being foremost in thy city, and have knowledge so that promotion is come unto thee, swathe not thy heart in thy hoard; thou art only the steward of the good things of God. Put not behind thee thy neighbor who is as thou wast. Be to him as were he thine equal.

If thou wouldst seek out the nature of a friend, ask it not of any one; go to him, pass the time with him alone, that thou injure not his affairs. Debate with him after a season; test his heart in an occasion of speech. Be not reserved with him when he openeth speech, neither answer him after a scornful manner.

Let thy face be bright what time thou livest. That which goeth into the storehouse must come out therefrom, and bread is to be shared. It is a man's kindliness that is remembered of him in the years after his life.

If thou hearken to these things which I have said unto thee, thy wisdom shall be advanced. Apart from the truth that belongeth to them, the memory of them shall never depart from the mouths of men by reason of the beauty of their phrasing.[2] Every word shall pass current as a thing that cannot perish out of the land, and it shall be made a pattern whereby the princes and the nobles shall speak well.

It is the Teaching a man should hand on to those that come after him, that they also may hear. Thereby he becometh a master-craftsman in speech.

He that obeyeth becometh one obeyed. It is good indeed when a son obeyeth his father; and his father that hath spoken hath great joy of it. Such a son shall be mild as a master.

Let that which thou speakest implant true things and just in the life of thy children. Forsooth, a good son is the gift of the God; he doeth more than is enjoined on him, he doeth right and putteth his heart into all his goings.

Be thy heart overflowing, but refrain thy mouth![3]

SELECTIONS FROM THE TEACHING OF KING KHATI

The Teaching of King Khati written nearly three thousand years before Christ as instruction for his son Merikara.

SHOW thyself to be a speaker of the truth before God. The heaven of a man is a good disposition.

[2] Ptah-hetep has put ''the words of the counsel of the men of old'' into rhythmic form which allows of neither omissions nor variations.

[3] Compiled from renderings by Philippe Virey, E. A. Wallis Budge and F. Ll. Griffith.

Make thyself a craftsman in speech, for the tongue of a
man is his weapon, and speech is mightier than the
sword.

Those who do not know cannot seize the man who knoweth, and where he is no evil taketh place.

Good is graciousness. Let thy loving sympathy stand
as a memorial of thee. Multiply thy benefits in the city.
The people will give thanks to God therefor, they will
praise thy goodness, and pray for thy health in years
to come.

It is a good thing to work for those who are to come
after. Pay honour to a life of work.

Speak what is true in thy house, and the princes who
are on earth shall reverence thee.

Do right and thou shalt continue upon the earth. Make
the weeper to cease from his plaint, and fleece not the
widow woman.

Make no distinction in thy behaviour towards the son
of a man of rank and the son of humble parents, but
attach to thyself a man by reason of what his hands have
effected.

Remember the Assessors in the other world who judge
wrong-doers. Know thou, they will not be lenient on
the day of judgment of wretched man. It is a terrible
thing for a man who knoweth his sin to be accused
thereof.

Fill not thy heart with hope because of length of years,
for they regard a lifetime as a single hour. There in
the other world existence is everlasting. A fool is he
who hath put the remembrance of it away from him.
The man who attaineth to that place without wrongdoing
hath an existence like that of God; he steppeth boldly
like the Everlasting Lords.

Pay honour to God, and say not: He is poor in spirit.

Drop not thy hands in idleness, but work with all thy
will. Indifference destroyeth heaven.

Work for God and He will in like manner work for thee. The man who worketh for Him God knoweth full well.

Keep order among men and women, who are the flocks and herds of God. He made heaven and earth for their pleasure; He dissipated the darkness of the waters; He made the breezes of life for their nostrils.

They are images of Him, who came forth from His members. He made the daylight for their pleasure; when they weep He hearkeneth. God knoweth every name.[4]

Selections from the Teaching of Amen-em-apt

The Teaching Concerning Life, written probably in the second half of the second millennium, possibly around 1000 B.C. Amen-em-apt as Grain Scribe of Upper and Lower Egypt controlled the produce of the harvests and held besides many other important offices.

I pray thee lend me thine ears, and hearken to the things that will be said. The setting of them in thy heart will be advantageous unto thee. They will enable thy heart to right itself when a gale of words beateth hard upon it.

Thou wilt find my words a treasure-house of life, and a source of strength and safety upon the earth.

Guard thyself against plundering the poor man, and from treating with harshness the destitute.

Accept not a bribe from a man of power and authority if he would have thee treat wrongfully for him the poor man in distress.

Thou shalt not inflict an injury on him that hath attacked thee; show thyself friendly to the man for whom thou hast antipathy.

Work the steering oar, we must give a passage to the man in evil case! May not we ourselves become like

---

[4] This and the following two selections are after the rendering by E. A. Wallis Budge in *The Teaching of Amen-em-apt*, Martin Hopkinson & Co., London.

unto him? Set him up on his feet, extend thy hand to him gladly. Satisfy him to the full with bread-cakes of thy providing; commit him unto the hands of the God.

Drive not thy furrows through the lands of another. Better is one apt [5] of land which the God hath given thee than five thousand apts which thou hast gotten by fraud.

Acquire not the habit of passing the day in the eating-house, nor of tasting one pot of beer upon another. Those who thus pass their time become tomorrow merely victuals.

Hanker not greedily after the things of the man whose food is dainty and spiced. Now the food that is dainty and spiced is as a storm in the gullet.

Better are bread-cakes of flour and water with a loving heart than rich meats that carry with them bickering and quarreling.

Better the beggar in the hand of God than the rich at ease in a comfortable habitation.

Better the praise with the love of men than riches laid up in a treasure-house.

Fashion not thy heart in such wise that it hankereth after the things of wealth, nor abandon thyself to material things.

Accustom thyself to direct to Aton thy sincere prayer, saying: Grant me, I beseech Thee, strength and health! He will give thee the things that are necessary for life. Thou shalt be safe from anxious care.

Put thyself for safekeeping into the hand of the God. Cast thyself into the two arms of the God. To thy silent meditations add prostrations on the ground.

Show thou affection to people of humble condition.

I beseech thee to spread with the tongue the report of only that which is good upon the earth; as for reports of evil, hide them in thy bosom.

[5] About 6 ft.

God hateth the man who uttereth frivolous, lying speech; and the man who nourisheth enmity is an abomination unto Him.

Do the thing that is right and thou wilt attain to a true state of being.

Make not the balance to swerve through thy falsification of the weights.

If thou seest another stumble from time to time, go with him to enable him to continue on his way.

Bring not to an end in slumber the early hours of the day. Say not: Today is even as tomorrow morning! For tomorrow hath yet to come, today hath yet to pass away.

Accustom not thyself to lie in bed whilst the dawn is breaking in awful beauty. To what can the break of the day and the dawn be compared? The man who hath no knowledge of the dawn, to what can he be likened?

Whilst the God is employed in His works of beneficence, man indulgeth in slothfulness! On one hand the chatter of men, on the other the works that the God doth perform!

Let all thy plans and behaviour have a sound foundation.

Be weighty in thy mind, consolidate thy heart, accustom not thyself to shape thy course by thy tongue. Though the tongue of a man be the steersman of the boat, it is the God of All who is the watcher in the bows.

Though a man mix the mud and straw, it is God who is the builder. It is He who throweth down, it is He who buildeth up. It is He who maketh one man to oversee a thousand.

Man liveth his hour of life. Rejoice, and be glad. It is God who maketh him to arrive in the other world; he is safe in the hands of God.

The love of God is more precious and estimable than to be honoured of the nobleman.

Now God is established upon Truth. He giveth it to the man who loveth Him.

The man of God [6] is like a large leafy tree planted in fertile ground. It blossometh, it doubleth its yield of fruit in the summer. It hath its place before the face of its lord. Its foliage is sweet, the shadow thereof is pleasant, and it is carried at its end into the groves of God. [7]

SELECTIONS FROM THE MAXIMS OF ANI

Written by the Scribe Ani for his son Khensu-hetep under the XXIst or XXIInd Dynasty.

THE occasion having come and gone, one seeketh in vain for another.

The House of God abominateth overmuch speaking. Make thou thy prayer with a loving heart, and let thy words be hidden. God will do what is needful for thee; He will hear thy petitions and accept thine oblations.

Be friendly, and associate thyself with one who is just and true after thou hast observed the manner in which he doth act.

Let thine eye be open, that thou come not out as a beggar. The man who is slothful and weak will never come to honour as will he who hath marked out the course of his life.

Fill not thy heart with love for the possessions of another; as for him that is in want, let him have his fill in his house; be thou his girdle wall.

If thou journey on a road made by thy hands each day, thou wilt at last arrive at the place where thou wouldst be.

---

[6] *Ger Maa*, the Silent True One: but it is possible that the phrase has a very special meaning of a religious character which Egyptologists have so far failed to discover. Compare this verse with Psalm I, of the Old Testament.

[7] Adapted from a rendering by E. A. Wallis Budge.

Let not thy heart be exalted before the flatterer. One word spoken in haste, if it come from thy mouth, being repeated, will make thee bitter enemies. Take good heed that thou do not thyself give rise to thine own ruin.

The heart of a man is the storehouse of a granary full of all manner of answers; therefore choose thou those that are good and utter them, and those that are evil keep closely confined within thee. A violent answer is like the brandishing of weapons; but speak with the graciousness of affection and thou shalt be beloved forever.

Make double the bread-cakes that thou givest to thy mother, and carry her as she carried thee. For she bore thee long beneath her heart as a heavy burden; and when thy months were accomplished she brought thee forth and set thee like a veritable yoke upon her back, and gave thee her breast to thy mouth.

Afterwards she placed thee in the house of instruction, and whilst thou wast being taught the writings she came to thee there day by day with meat and drink from her house. Now thou art come to man's estate; thou art married and hast a house. Let it not happen that she hath cause to reproach thee; may she not lift up her hands to God in complaint!

Eat not thy bread whilst another standeth by an hungered and thou dost not stretch out thy hand to him. It hath never been surely known when a man will come to want. One man hath riches, another is poor. He who was prosperous a year gone by doth serve this year in the stalls.

Seek silence for thyself.[8]

[8] Adapted from the translation by E. A. Wallis Budge.

SELECTIONS FROM
THE UPANISHADS

Whate'er exists within this universe
Is all to be regarded as enveloped
By the great Lord, as if wrapped in a vesture . . . .
There is one only Being who exists
Unmoved, yet moving swifter than the mind:
Who far outstrips the senses, though as gods
They strive to reach Him; who Himself at rest
Transcends the fleetest flight of other beings;
Who like the air, supports all vital action.
He moves, yet moves not; He is far, yet near;
He is within this universe, and yet
Outside this universe; whoe'er beholds
All living creatures as in Him, and Him—
The universal Spirit—as in all,
Henceforth regards no creature with contempt.

Isa Upanishad, translated by
Sir Monier Williams.

" . . . *the most rewarding and the most elevating read-*
ing which there can possibly be in the world. It has been
the solace of my life and will be of my death."

Schopenhauer, on *The Upanishads.*

THE UPANISHADS

The Upanishads (Sessions under a Teacher), *mystic teachings forming the philosophical portions of the early Indian Vedas, and called by the Hindus the* Shruti, *or* revealed literature, *are among the most astounding productions of the human mind in any age or country. Somewhat preceding perhaps that remarkable period of philosophic and religious thought about the 6th century* B.C., *when Pythagoras, Confucius, Buddha and Zoroaster dawned upon the world, in them is found the earliest serious attempt to deal with the mighty problem of the great unseen Powers and the meaning of this world and life. Their fundamental tenet is monism; they find the ultimate verity of the All of existence in Atman (Soul or Self), and Self is Brahma, and the self in man is continuous with this highest Self. The following selections are given in the probable order of the original composition of the Upanishads from which they are taken.*

BRIHAD-ARANYAKA UPANISHAD

FROM the unreal lead me to the real! From darkness lead me to light! From death lead me to immortality!

I. iii. 28.

ONE seeth the Atman not, for It doth not appear as a whole. When It doth breathe, It is called breath; when It speaketh, It is called voice; when It seeth, eye; when It heareth, ear; when It thinketh, mind.

All these are but the names of Its acts. He who worshippeth It as the one or the other of these, hath not knowledge. One should worship It as the Self, for in It all these become one.

This Self which is nearer to us than anything, is dearer than a son, dearer than wealth, dearer than aught else. He who thus knoweth, *I Am Brahma*, becometh this All. Even the gods have not power to prevent his becoming thus, for he becometh their Self. *I. iv. 7-10.*

WHEN Yajnavalkya was about to enter upon another stage of life, he said: Maitreyi, I am about to wander forth from this my house. Behold! let me make a final settlement between thee and Katyayani.[1]

Then said Maitreyi: My Lord, if this whole earth, full of wealth, were mine, should I be immortal thereby?

Nay, said Yajnavalkya: As the life of the rich even so would thy life be. But there is no hope of immortality by reason of wealth.

Then said Maitreyi: That by which I cannot become immortal, what can I do with that? But what my Lord knoweth, tell that to me.

Then said Yajnavalkya: Thou who wast dear to me, hast by this become increasingly so. Come, I will expound it to thee.

Verily, a husband is not dear, for love of the husband; but for love of the Atman is a husband dear. A wife is not dear for love of the wife, nor are sons, nor the worlds, nor all creatures. All is not dear for love of all, but for love of the Atman is all dear.

Verily, it is the Atman that should be seen, hearkened to, pondered on, O Maitreyi! When we have seen and heard and understood the Atman, then the universe is known.

Just as when a lute is being played, one cannot seize the sound; but by grasping the lute itself, the sound is also seized, so from the Atman are all these things breathed forth.

As all waters find their centre in the sea; all sounds in the ear; all precepts in the mind; all knowledge in the

---

[1] Before going to be an anchorite, he would make a settlement between his two wives.

heart; as a lump of salt, cast into the water doth dissolve so thou canst not seize it again, but wherever thou tastest it is salty, thus verily this Great Being, infinite, limitless, is compact of knowledge. *II. iv. 1-12.*

HE who dwelleth in the earth, yet is other than the earth, whom the earth knoweth not, who directeth the earth from within, He is thy Soul, the Ruler within, the Immortal.

He who dwelleth in the waters, in the fire, in the air; He who dwelleth in the sun, moon, and stars, who dwelleth in space, in darkness and light; who dwelleth in all beings; in the breath, in the eye, in the ear, in the mind; in all things, yet is other than all things, whom all things do not know;

The unseen Seer, the unheard Hearer, the unthought Thinker, the unknown Knower; He is thy Soul, the Ruler within, the Immortal. There is no other seer, no other hearer, no other discerner, no other knower than He. *III. vii. 3-23.*

YAJNAVALKYA came to Janaka, King of Videha. So now the King asked him: What is the light of man?

Yajnavalkya answered him: The sun, O King! For with the sun indeed as his light, man moveth around, goeth about his labour, and returneth.

But when the sun hath set, Yajnavalkya, what then is the light of man?

The moon, indeed, is his light; for with the moon as his light, man moveth about and performeth his labour.

When the moon hath set, Yajnavalkya, what is the light of man?

Fire, indeed, is his light, by the fire he performeth his labour.

When the sun hath set, and the moon hath set, and the fire is gone out, what then is the light of man?

The soul, indeed, is his light; for with the soul as his light, man moveth about, performeth his labour and returneth.

And there are for the soul two states, one here in this world and one in the other world; and betwixt them the state of sleep when it seeth both those states together.

Having subdued by sleep all that belongeth to the body, sleepless itself, it looketh down upon the sleeping senses.

Leaving its lower nest in breath's protection, and upward from that nest immortal soaring, wherever it listeth it doth roam about immortal, the golden-pinioned only swan of spirit. It moveth in a dream-state up and downward, divinely assuming many shapes and forms.

Then, as a falcon, or an eagle, having flown about in space, exhausted foldeth its wings and is borne to its nest; so doth the spirit haste to that state in which, asleep, it feeleth no desire and dreameth no more dreams.

This, indeed, is its true form, free from desire, free from fear. For as one embraced by a beloved woman wotteth not of anything without or within, so also the soul in the embrace of the Self knoweth naught without or within.

Then is a father not a father, a mother not a mother, the worlds not worlds, the gods not gods. He is not followed by good, not followed by evil, for then he hath passed beyond all the sorrows of the heart.

Verily, while he doth not there see with the eyes, yet he is seeing. For sight is inseparable from the seer, because it cannot perish.

Verily, while he doth not taste, speak, hear, think, touch, know, yet he is tasting, speaking, hearing, thinking, touching, knowing. For taste, speech, hearing, thought, touch, knowing, are inseparable from the seer; for they cannot perish.

An ocean is that one seer without any duality; this is the Brahma world, O King! (Thus did Yajnavalkya instruct him). This is his highest goal, this is his highest success, his highest world; this is his highest bliss. All other creatures live on a small portion of that bliss.

IV. iii. 1-32.

As a goldsmith, taking a piece of gold, reduceth it to a new and more beautiful form, just so this soul, striking down this body and dispelling its ignorance, maketh unto itself a new and beautiful form like that of Brahma.

According as one acteth, according as one conducteth himself, so doth he become. The man of good deeds becometh good. The man of evil deeds becometh evil. One becometh pure by virtuous action, bad by bad action.

They who know the breathing of the breath, the seeing of the eye, the hearing of the ear, the thinking of the mind, they have comprehended the ancient, primeval Brahma. *IV. iv. 4, 5, 18.*

PRAYER OF A DYING PERSON

THE face of the Real is covered with a golden disk.[2] That do Thou, O God, uncover for one whose law is to see the Real.

O Nourisher, the sole Seer, O Controller, O Sun, spread forth Thy rays and gather them! The light which is Thy fairest form, I see it. He who is yonder, I myself am He.

My breath to the immortal wind, then this my body to ashes! *V, xv.*

CHANDOGYA UPANISHAD

VERILY, this whole world is Brahma. Tranquil, let one worship It as that from which he came forth, as that into which he will be dissolved, as that in which he doth breathe.

He who consisteth of mind, whose body is life, whose form is light, whose conception is truth, whose soul is space, containing all works, all desires, encompassing

---

[2] The Sun.

this whole world, smaller than a grain of millet or the kernel of a grain of millet, greater than the earth, the atmosphere, these worlds.

This is the Soul of mine within the heart, this is Brahma. Into Him I shall enter on departing hence.

Now verily, man is a creature of will. According to what his will is in this world, so will he become when he departeth hence. Let him therefore form for himself a purpose!   *III. xiv. 1-4.*

UDDALAKA ARUNI said to his son Svetaketu: Of this great tree, my dear, if one should strike at the root, it would bleed, but live. If he should strike at its trunk, it would bleed, but live. If he should strike at its top, it would bleed, but still live. Being pervaded by the living Self it continueth to stand, eagerly drinking in moisture and rejoicing.

But if the life leave one of the branches thereof, it drieth up; if it leave a second branch, that withereth; if it leave the whole, the whole withereth.

Even so, Know, said he, when the living Self hath left it, this body dieth; the living Self dieth not. That which is the subtile essence, the whole world hath that as its soul. That is Reality. That is Atman. That art thou, Svetaketu!

Do thou, Sir, cause me to understand even more.

So be it, my dear, said he. Bring hither a fig! Here it is, Sir. Divide it. It is divided, Sir. What dost thou see there? These rather fine seeds. Of these, break one. It is broken, Sir. What dost thou see there? Nothing at all!

Then said he to him: That subtile essence which thou dost not perceive, verily, my dear, from that subtile essence this great Nyagrodha tree doth arise. Believe it, my son, that which is the subtile essence, the whole world hath that as its soul. That is Reality. That is Atman. That art thou, Svetaketu!

Do thou, Sir, cause me to understand even more.

So be it, my dear, said he. Place this salt in water; in the morning come unto me. The son did so. Then Uddalaka said to him: That salt thou didst place in the water last evening, bring it hither! Then he grasped for it, but found it not, for it was dissolved. The father said: Take a sip from this end; how is it? Salt, said he. Take a sip from the middle; how is it. Salt! Take a sip from that end; how is it? Salt!

Then Uddalaka said unto his son: Thou dost not perceive Being here, but verily, it is here. That which is the subtile essence, the whole world hath that as its soul. That is Reality. That is Atman. That art thou, Svetaketu!

Do thou, Sir, cause me to understand even more.

So be it, my dear, said he. As one might lead away from the Gandharas a person with his eyes bandaged, and then abandon him in a place where no man was; as there he might turn either to the east, to the north, or to the south, since he had been deserted with his eyes bandaged;

As, if one released his bandage and told him, In that direction are the Gandharas; he would, by asking from village to village arrive home; even so, here on earth one who hath a teacher knoweth; I belong here only so long as I shall not be released from the body. Then shall I reach home!   *VI. 11, 12, 13, 14.*

He who knoweth the Soul crosseth over sorrow.
                                         VII. i. 3.

As far, verily, as extendeth this world-space, so far extendeth the space within the heart. Within it, indeed, are contained both heaven and earth, both fire and wind, both sun and moon, lightning and stars, both whatever is and what will be; everything here is contained within it.
                                         VIII. i. 2.

TAITTIRIYA UPANISHAD

THAT, verily, whence beings here are born, that by which when born they live, that into which they enter at their death, that try to understand. That is Brahma!

III. 1.

KENA UPANISHAD

How can one teach concerning Brahma? He is neither the known nor the unknown.

That which cannot be expressed by words, but through which all expression cometh, this know thou to be Brahma. That which cannot be thought by the mind, but by which all thinking cometh, this know thou as Brahma. That which cannot be seen by the eye, but by which the eye beholdeth, is Brahma.

If thou thinkest that thou canst know It, then in truth thou knowest It very little. To whom It is unknown, he knoweth It; but to whom It is known, he knoweth It not.

I, II.

KATHA UPANISHAD

INTO the heart of Naciketas, while still a boy, faith entered. Unto him said Death: Whatever desires are difficult to attain among mortals, ask for them according to thy wish.

Choose the wide abode of the earth, and live thyself as many harvests as thou desirest. Choose wealth and long life. Be king, Naciketas, on the wide earth! I make thee enjoyer of all desires. These maidens fair with their chariots and their lyres, such as indeed are not to be obtained among men, be waited on by these whom I bestow on thee!

Naciketas said: These things last only till tomorrow, O Death. The vigour of all the powers they wear away. Even the whole of life is short indeed. Keep thou thy chariots, thy dance and song! Not by wealth is man to be satisfied. Shall we choose wealth when we have seen thee? Shall we live so long as thou shalt rule?

What mortal here below, having come into their presence, and knowing the freedom from decay enjoyed by the Immortals, would delight in a long earthly life? Naciketas chooseth as his boon none other than that which causeth him to enter into the hidden world!

I know that what is called a treasure is transient, for the eternal is not obtained by things which are not eternal.
I. 23-29; II. 10.

THE knowing Self is unborn, It dieth not; eternal, primeval, everlasting, It is not killed though the body be killed. The slayer thinketh he slayeth, the slain believeth himself destroyed; the thoughts of both are false; the Soul surviveth, It doth not kill, nor doth It die.

Subtler than the subtlest, greater than the greatest, is the Soul set in the heart of creatures here. Though sitting still, It proceedeth afar; though lying down, It goeth everywhere; though among bodies, It is bodiless.

This Soul is not to be obtained by intellect nor by learning. The wicked never can know It. Whom the Soul chooseth as Its own, to him is It revealed. *II. 18-24.*

KNOW thou the Self as riding in the chariot, the body as the chariot, the intellect as the charioteer, the mind the reins. The senses they call the horses, the objects of the senses are their roads.

He who hath no understanding and whose mind is never firmly held, his senses are unmanageable, like vicious horses of a charioteer.

But he who hath the understanding of a charioteer, and who controlleth with the reins of his mind his senses like good horses, he reacheth indeed that place from whence he is not born again; yea, he reacheth the end of his journey, the highest place of Vishnu!

The sharp edge of a razor is difficult to pass over; thus the wise declare the path to the Self is hard.

He who hath perceived that which is without sound,
without touch, without form, without decay, eternal,
without beginning, without end, beyond the Great, and
unchangeable, is freed from the jaws of death.

III. 3-9, 14, 15.

As pure water poured into pure becometh the very same,
so becometh the soul of the seer who hath understanding.

IV. 15.

HE, the Highest, who waketh in us while we sleep and
shapeth one lovely sight upon another, He alone is the
Bright, Immortal One; He is Brahma. All worlds are
contained in Him, and no one goeth beyond.

As the one fire entering the world, though one, differeth
according to that it doth burn; thus the one Self in all
things becometh different according to that It doth enter,
and It existeth also without.

As the sun, the eye of the whole world, is not sullied by
impurities seen by the eyes, thus the one Self within all
things is never sullied by the misery of the world, being
external to it.

There is one Ruler, the Self within all things, who
maketh His one form manifold. The wise who perceive
Him within, to them belongeth eternal peace, to others
not.

There is one eternal Thinker who though one, fulfilleth
the desires of many. The wise who perceive Him within,
to them belongeth eternal peace, to others not.

The sun shineth not there, nor the moon and the stars,
nor these lightnings, and much less this fire. When He
shineth, everything shineth after Him; by His light are
all these lit.[3]

V. 8-15.

EVERY man that knoweth Him is liberated, and obtaineth
immortality.

[3] Comp. Rev. XXI. 23: And the city had no need of the sun, neither
of the moon to shine in it; for the glory of God did lighten it, and the
Lamb is the light thereof.

His form is not to be seen, none may with his eye behold it. He is imagined by the heart, by wisdom, by the mind. Those who know this are immortal.

Not by speech can He be apprehended. How can He be apprehended otherwise than by saying: He is?[4]

VI. 8, 9, 12.

ISA UPANISHAD

THAT Self though changing not Its place is swifter than all thought. The senses never reach It, It goeth on before. Though standing still, It overtaketh them that run.

It moveth and It moveth not; It is far and likewise near: It is inside of all, outside of all.

When to the understanding man all beings have become the Self, what sorrow, what affliction can there be for him who hath once beheld that Unity?   *4-7.*

MUNDAKA UPANISHAD

As from a blazing fire sparks of like substance fly forth a thousandfold, so from the Imperishable, beings manifold are produced, and return thither also.   *II. i. 1.*

By truthfulness, indeed, right knowledge and abstinence must that Self be gained; the Self whom spotless anchorites gain is pure, and like a light within the body.

Truth alone conquereth, not untruth; by truth is the path laid out, the way of the gods on which the sages ascend to the highest place of the True One.

That true Spirit shineth forth, vast, heavenly, of unthinkable form, smaller than the small; He is farther than the far, yet near at hand; He is hidden in the secret place of the heart, among those who even here behold Him.

He is not apprehended by the senses, nor by austerity nor good works. When a man's nature is purified by the serene light of knowledge, then, meditating, doth he behold him who is without parts.

4 Comp. Ex. III. 14.

Whatever state a man whose nature is purified imagineth, whatever desires he desireth, that state he conquereth and those desires obtaineth.   *III. i. 5-10.*

As flowing rivers are resolved into the sea, losing their name and form, so the wise, released from name and form, pass into the Divine and Highest Spirit. He who knoweth that Supreme Spirit, becometh very Spirit. Freed from the fetters of the heart, he becometh immortal.   *III. ii. 8, 9.*

SHVETASHVATARA UPANISHAD

WHAT is the cause? Whence are we born? Whereby do we live? And on what are we established?   *I. 1.*

BEYOND the darkness I know Him the great Spirit, shining as the sun; knowing Him is immortality; there is none other path by which to go. Than Whom there is naught higher, naught smaller, naught so great.

As a tree He standeth in the heavens firmly rooted; His spirit filleth all the universe. Without form, sorrowless is the Supreme. Pervading all things, He dwelleth within; He the Lord whose countenance is in all places, the gracious One whose presence is everywhere. Within the heart, perceived by the heart and the mind, dwelleth He the inward soul of all. To know this is immortality.

Himself void of sensation, yet reflecting the qualities of all the senses, Lord of all, of all Ruler and Refuge. Though in the nine-gated city [5] embodied, back and forth to the eternal as a bird He hovereth.

Handless He holdeth, footless He speedeth; eyeless seeth He, earless He heareth. Knowing all, Himself unknown; yet known of man as the great primeval Spirit.

Yea, I know Him, the ageless Ancient of Days, birthless, eternal. He is God who lendeth hues to all this manifold

[5] Of the body.

world; the Beginning of all, the End in which all things
dissolve. May He give us understanding!

He is the Fire, the Sun, the Wind, the Moon; the Bright
One, the Creative Spirit. Yea, man art Thou, and woman,
boy and maiden; Thou the aged tottering on his staff.
Thou hast the lightning as Thy child. Thou art the seasons and the seas. Having no beginning, Thou dost abide
with immanence wherefrom all beings are born.

In seeing Him man cometh to unchanging Peace. May
He endow us with understanding! [6]   *III. 8; IV. 12.*

SEEKING my freedom I take my refuge in that God who
is the light of His own thoughts, who is without actions,
without parts, tranquil, without taint, the highest bridge
of immortality,—like a fire that hath consumed its fuel.
Only when men shall roll up the sky like a hide will there
be an end of misery unless God hath first been known.
VI. 18-20.

MAITRI UPANISHAD

LET a man strive to purify his thoughts! What a man
thinketh, that is he; this is the eternal mystery. Dwelling
within his Self with thoughts serene, he will obtain imperishable happiness.

If the thoughts of a man were so fixed on Brahma as
they are on the things of the realms of sense, who would
not then be free from bondage?

The happiness of a mind which by deep meditation hath
been purged from all impurity and hath entered within
the Self, cannot be told in words; it can be felt by the
inward power only.

Water in water, fire in fire, air in air, no one can distinguish these; likewise a man whose mind hath entered
until it cannot be distinguished from the Self attaineth
liberty.

[6] Shvetashvatara Upanishad III. 8, IV. 12 are after a rendering by
K. J. Saunders in *Lotuses of the Mahayana.*

Mind alone is the cause of bondage and liberty for men; if attached to the world, it becometh bound; if free from the world, it attaineth liberty. [7]   *VI. 34.*

[7] The text of the above selections from the Upanishads is an adaptation of renderings of Sir Monier Williams, F. Max Müller, Arthur A. Macdonell, Windischmann and Robert Ernest Hume (*The Thirteen Principal Upanishads,* by permission of the publishers, the Oxford University Press).

THE BOOK OF PSALMS

BEING SELECTIONS FROM THE VEDIC, GREEK, EGYPTIAN AND
JAPANESE HYMNS AND ACCADIAN AND BABYLONIAN
PENITENTIAL PSALMS AND HYMNS OF THE
AMERICAN INDIANS

What else can I do, a lame old man, but sing hymns to God?

Epictetus.

THE BOOK OF PSALMS

THE VEDIC HYMNS

Being Selections from the Hymns which, with the Brahmanas, the Upanishads and the Sutras, constitute the Indian sacred scriptures known as the Vedas (or wisdom). They are the earliest form of Indian literature, the hymns of the Rig-veda being the oldest and most esteemed, those of the Atharva-veda being the latest.

I

Hymn to Varuna, Rig-veda I. 25.[1]

WHATEVER laws of Thine we as men do violate day by day, O God Varuna, deliver us not to the deadly weapon of the furious, nor to the anger of the spiteful!

BY means of our hymns, O Varuna, we free Thy thought for mercy as a charioteer freeth a steed that is bound. Away in search of good they fly as birds of the air unto their nests.

Varuna, who knoweth the path of the birds that fly through the sky, who on the waters knoweth the ships; who establisheth the laws, who knoweth the track of the wind, the spreading and high and mighty wind, and knoweth those that dwell above:

He, the very Wise One, sitteth there to govern; from whence surveying all hidden things, He doth regulate what hath been and what will yet be done. Yearning for Him, the far-seeing, my thoughts move onward as kine move to their pastures.

[1] The date of these hymns from the Vedas is wholly uncertain, one scholar placing the earliest Vedic hymns as far back as 4000 B. C.; others think they were composed as late as 800-600 B. C.; a larger group, however, places them between 1500 and 300 B. C.

Now that I bring the sweet offering Thou lovest, while
Thou priestlike dost partake of it, let us converse together again; oh hear this my prayer, Varuna! Be merciful now to me! Longing for help, have I called upon
Thee. Thou, O wise God, art Lord of all heaven and
earth; do Thou listen as I make my sacrifice.

II

Hymn to Varuna, or Surya, the Sun, Rig-veda I. 50.

BEHOLD the rays of Dawn like heralds lead on high the
Sun, that men may see the great all-knowing God. The
stars slink off like thieves in company with Night
before the all-seeing Eye whose beams reveal His
presence, gleaming like brilliant flames, to nation after
nation.

With speed beyond the ken of mortals, Thou, O Sun,
dost ever travel on, conspicuous to all. Thou dost create
the light, and with it dost illume the universe entire;
Thou risest in the sight of all the race of men and all the
host of heaven.

Light-giving Varuna! Thy piercing glance doth scan in
quick succession all this stirring, active world, and pene-
trateth too the broad ethereal space, measuring our days
and nights and spying out all creatures.

Surya with flaming locks, clear-sighted God of day, Thy
seven ruddy mares [2] bear on Thy rushing car. With these
Thy self-yoked steeds, seven daughters of Thy chariot,
onward dost Thou advance. To Thy refulgent orb beyond this lower gloom and upward to the light would
we ascend, O Sun, Thou God among the gods.[3]

[2] The seven days of the week.

[3] Adapted from Sir Monier Williams' translation.

III

Penitential Psalm of a Singer of the Family of the Vasishthas to Varuna, Rig-veda VII. 86.

FIRM, verily, are the creations through the power of Him who held the two wide worlds asunder; who raised the large and lofty vault of heaven, the day-star too, and spread the earth out broadly.

With mine own heart do I hold converse thus: When shall I have communion with Varuna? Will He without a grudge accept mine offering? When may I joyous look and find Him gracious?

Fain to discover this my sin, I go to the wise and ask of them; one and the self-same thing the sages tell me: Varuna, the Lord, hath with thee hot indignation.

What was mine offence, Varuna, that Thou wouldst slay Thy friend who singeth to Thy praise? Tell me, infallible Lord; guiltless then would I appease Thee with adoration.

Loose us from the sins committed by our fathers; from those wrongs too which we ourselves have done. Loose us, take off Vasishtha's fetters!

It was not by mine own will, Varuna. Seduction was it, thoughtlessness, strong drink, or passion. An older man hath led astray a younger.

O let me purged of sin like a slave serve Him the merciful! The gracious God hath granted wisdom to the foolish. He leadeth to riches the wise, Himself than all more wise.

May this our song of praise, Varuna, sovereign Ruler, reach Thy heart! In rest and labour do Thou bestow well-being, protect us evermore with blessings!

IV

Hymn to Varuna, Rig-veda VII. 87.

VARUNA cutteth a pathway for the sun, and causeth the river-floods to hasten seaward; He hath made for the shining days their mighty channels, guiding them as a racer guideth his horses.

Thy breath, the wind, resoundeth through mid-air, like a wild beast that smiteth its prey in pasture; between the exalted heaven and the earth, Varuna, are Thy loved habitations.

Varuna's messengers sent forth upon their errand survey the well-fashioned worlds. Wise are they and holy, the furtherers of the praises of the prudent. The sapient God shall speak to teach the race that cometh.

The wise Varuna hath made in heaven that golden swing [4] to cover it with glory. Ruling in the depths and meting out the regions, great saving power hath He, the Governor of the world.

Keeping the ordinances of our mother Nature, before Varuna may we be without sin, before Him who sheweth mercy even to the sinner. Preserve us evermore with blessings.

V

Penitential Psalm to Varuna, Rig-veda III. 89.

LET me not yet, O Varuna, go down into the house of clay; have mercy, Almighty, have mercy!

I go along trembling, like an inflated skin; have mercy, Almighty, have mercy!

Through weakness of will, Thou bright and powerful God, have I gone wrong; have mercy, Almighty, have mercy!

Thirst came upon Thy worshipper, though standing in the midst of the floods of waters; have mercy, Almighty, have mercy!

[4] The sun.

Whenever we men, O Varuna, commit an offence before the heavenly host; whenever through thoughtlessness we break Thy law, have mercy, Almighty, have mercy! Do Thou, O Thou wise God, grant protection to him who prayeth to Thee.

VI

Hymn to Varuna, Rig-veda.

VARUNA doth dwell in all worlds as sovereign; indeed the worlds are embraced by Him.

The wind which resoundeth through the firmament is His breath. He hath placed the sun in the heavens and opened a boundless path for it to traverse.

He hath hollowed out the channels of the rivers. It is by His wise contrivance that, though they all pour their waters into the sea, the sea is never filled.

By His ordinance the moon doth shine in the sky, and the stars which are visible by night do disappear on the approach of dawn.

Neither the birds flying in the air, nor the rivers in their ceaseless flow can attain a knowledge of His power or His wrath.

His spies behold both worlds, He himself hath a thousand eyes. He performeth all the hidden things that have been or shall be done.

VII

Hymn to Soma, Rig-veda.

WHERE there is eternal light, in the world where the sun is placed, in that immortal, imperishable world, place me, O Soma!

Where King Vaivasvata doth reign, where the secret place of heaven is, where those mighty waters are; there make me immortal!

Where life is free, in the third heaven of heavens, where the worlds are radiant; there make me immortal!

Where the place of the bright sun is, where there is freedom and delight, there make me immortal!

Where joy and pleasure reside, where the desires of our desire are attained; there make me immortal!

VIII

A Funeral Hymn.

OPEN thine arms, O Earth, receive the dead with gentle pressure and with loving welcome; embrace him tenderly, even as a mother foldeth her soft vestment round the child that she doth love.

Soul of the dead, depart; take thou the path, the ancient path, by which our fathers have gone before. Thou shalt meet the fathers and receive the recompense of all thy stored-up offerings, above. Return to thy home no more; assume a glorious form!

And do Thou, O mighty God, entrust him to Thy guards to bring him to Thee, and grant him health and happiness eternal![5]

IX

Hymn to Indra, the Storm-god, Rig-veda II. 12.

HE who, chief God of lofty spirit by power and might surpassed the gods, before whose breath through greatness of His valour the two worlds trembled, He, O men, is Indra.

He who hath firmly established the quivering earth, and brought the quaking mountains to rest; who measured out the intermediate spaces of the air, who gave the heaven support; He, O men, is Indra.

He who is helper of rich and poor alike, and of the suppliant who singeth to His praise; who hath begotten the

[5] These and the above passages are quoted on pages 24 to 32, *Sanskrit and Its Kindred Literatures,* by Laura E. Poor.

sun and the dawn of the morning, who leadeth the water-courses; He, O men, is Indra.

Heaven and earth bow down themselves before Him, before His might the very mountains tremble. He, O men, is Indra.

X

Hymn to Indra, Rig-veda VI. 30.

INDRA hath grown great, He alone is without age, He alone hath riches to give. Indra hath extended Himself beyond earth and heaven; the half of Him is equal to both the worlds, so great is He, so high is His godly nature. What He hath established none can impair.

Today, even now, Thy work doth abide in that Thou hewest a pathway for the rivers. The hills bow down before Thee as were they friends; the wide spaces of the universe are knit together by Thee.

Thou didst free the waters, opening wide the doors; Thou didst break the stronghold of the mountains. Thou didst become the king of all the moving world, bringing to light the sun, the dawn and heaven.[6]

XI

Hymn to Parjanya, the Rain-Cloud, Rig-veda V. 83.

SALUTE the mighty One with these thy songs of praise; Parjanya laud, with reverence seek to win Him.

The trees He doth shatter and He smiteth the demons of the earth. The whole world feareth the Wielder of the mighty bolt.

Like charioteer with whip urging his horses hard, He causeth to bound forth his rainy messengers; from far away arise the lion's thunderings, what time Parjanya filleth the skies with rain.

[6] Translation by E. Washburn Hopkins.

The mighty winds break forth, the quivering lightnings flash and fly, the growing plants shoot up, the heavens stream with rain; for the whole world of being refreshment is produced, what time Parjanya quickeneth the earth with moisture.

Under whose law the broad earth bendeth lowly, under whose law hoofed creatures leap and frisk; under whose law the plants do grow diversely; even Thou, Parjanya, grant us Thy mighty protection!

Bestow on us, ye Storm-winds, rain from heaven; come hither with this Thy thunder, O Parjanya, shedding the floods, our heavenly Lord and Father.

Bellow and thunder Thou, the vital germ deposit; draw well Thy water-skin unloosened downward, let heights and hollows all alike be flooded.

Draw up the mighty vessel, pour it downward; and let the liberated streams flow forward rushing, moisten and drench the earth and heaven; may there be found good drinking for the cattle.

When Thou, Parjanya, bellowing and thundering, smitest evil-doers, the whole world doth exult, yea, everything upon the earth.

Rain hast Thou shed, Thou hast made passable the desert places. The herbs Thou hast begotten for man's sustenance, and from Thy creatures hast received a song of praise.[7]

XII

Hymn to Prajapati, Lord of Creatures (or Hiranyagarbha), Rig-veda X. 121.

In the beginning arose the Source of Golden Light. He was the only born Lord of all that is, who stablished the earth and sky.

[7] Compiled from translations by Macdonell, R. T. H. Griffith and Griswold (*The Religion of the Rig-Veda*. Kind permission to make use of the latter has been granted by the Oxford University Press). Compare with Psalms XXIX and LXV of the Old Testament.

Who is the god to whom we shall offer our sacrifice?
He who giveth life, He who giveth strength, whose bidding the bright gods revere; whose shadow is immortality, whose shadow is likewise death.

Who is the god to whom we shall offer our sacrifice?
He who by His might is King of all the breathing and awakening world; who governeth man and beast; whose majesty these snowy hills, this ocean with its rivers declare; of whom these spreading regions form the arms.

Who is the god to whom we shall offer our sacrifice?
He through whom the firmament is strong and the earth solidly planted; through whom the heavens were stablished; who measured out the clouds that fill the sky.

Who is the god to whom we shall offer our sacrifice?
He to whom heaven and earth, established by His will, look up with trembling, over whom there shineth the rising sun.

Wherever, let loose in space, the mighty waters have gone, depositing a fruitful seed and generating light, there He arose who is the breath and life of all the gods.

XIII

Hymn to Varuna, Atharva-veda IV. 16.[a]

THE mighty Guardian who ruleth above beholdeth these worlds as if from anear. Though a man think to move with stealth, glide he never so softly along, or lurk in dark recess, this the gods know. Though two sit together devising in private, King Varuna is there a third, and knoweth it.

His is this boundless earth, and His is yonder sky whose confines lie afar. These two oceans are His loins, yet in this shallow pool He is contained.

Though a man should flee beyond the heavens he could not be free from Varuna. His messengers descend from

[a] Comp. Psalm CXXXIX of the Old Testament.

His abode; with a thousand eyes do they survey the earth.

King Varuna discerneth what lieth betwixt the earth and the sky and all that is beyond. Yea, the winkings of men's eyes, He reckoneth them every one.

XIV

Hymn to Kala, Time, Atharva-veda XIX. 53, 54.

TIME, like a brilliant steed with seven rays, and with a thousand eyes, imperishable, full of fecundity, beareth all things onward. On him ascend the learned and the wise.

Time, like a seven-wheeled, seven-naved car, moveth on. His rolling wheels are all the worlds, his axle is immortality. He is the first of gods. We see him multiplied in various forms.

He draweth forth, encompasseth the worlds; he is all future worlds; he is their father; he is their son; there is no power like him. The past and future issue out of Time, all sacred knowledge and austerity.

From Time the earth and waters were produced; from Time, the rising, setting, burning sun; from Time, the wind; through Time the earth is vast; through Time doth the eye perceive; mind, breath, and name are comprehended.

All rejoice when Time doth arrive,—the monarch who hath conquered this world, the highest worlds, the holy worlds, yea, all the worlds, and ever marcheth on.[9]

XV

Hymn to Vishnu, the Supreme Being, from Raghu-vansa, by Kalidasa.

HAIL to Thee, mighty Lord, the world's Creator, Supporter and Destroyer, three in one! Unmeasured and

[9] Adapted from Sir Monier Williams' translation.

unmeasurable, yet Thou measurest the world; desireless, yet fulfilling all desire; unconquered and a conqueror; unmanifested, yet manifesting; uniformly one, yet ever multiform.

Though ever present in the heart, Thou art infinitely distant; full of all pity, yet Thyself untouched by misery; the ever ancient One, yet never growing ancient; knowing all, yet never known; unborn, yet giving birth to all; all-ruling, yet Thyself unruled; seeming asleep, yet ever vigilant.

The ways which lead to everlasting bliss, though variously distinguished in the Veda, converge to Thee alone, even as the streams of Ganges' waters to their ocean home. Thou art the only way, the only refuge of all whose hearts are fixed on Thee, whose acts are centred in Thee, and whose worldly longings, checked and suppressed, have passed away forever.

Naught is unattained by Thee, and naught is unattainable, yet love, and love alone for these Thy worlds moveth Thee to act, leadeth to Thine incarnations.[10]

About 57 B.C.

JAPANESE HYMNS OF MAHAYANA BUDDHISM

XVI

Hymn to Avalokitesvara, the Lord who looks in pity on the world, from the Saddharma-pundarika Sutra (Lotus of the Good Law) XXIV. 23.

O Thou whose eyes are clear and kind,
Whose loving eyes reveal a loving mind,
Lord of the lovely face, beloved eyes!
O pure and shining One,
Radiant as the great sun,
Radiant as fire dost Thou arise,
Illumining our darkling sight,
To drive away the mists of night.

[10] From Sir Monier Williams' translation.

Thy rain divine doth quench our fire,
Thy law doth banish our desire:
Rejoicing in compassion, lo
Our Refuge, Thou, from every foe! [11]

About the end of the 1st cent. A.D.

XVII

Hymn by Honen Shonin.

What though these fragile bodies melt away
Like dew, when Death hath laid us low;
Our souls abide, and in a gladder day
Meet in the Lotus-bed where all shall grow. [12]

1133-1212 A.D.

XVIII

Hymn by Shinran.

Eternal Life, Eternal Light!
Hail to Thee, Wisdom Infinite,
Hail to Thee, Mercy shining clear,
And limitless as is the air!
Thou givest sight unto the blind,
Thou sheddest mercy on mankind.
Hail, gladdening Light,
Hail, generous Might,
Whose peace is round us like the sea,
And bathes us in infinity. [12]

1175-1265 A.D.

XIX

Hymn by Nichiren.

Alas! we may not meet Him face to face!
Yet is He with us all in every place.
Lo! in the mystic stillness of the dawn
When no man stirreth is the vision born! [12]

1222-1282 A.D.

[11] From *Lotuses of the Mahayana* by Kenneth Saunders.
[12] *Idem.*

EGYPTIAN HYMNS

XX

The Song of the Harper that is in the Hall of the Tomb of the King of the South, the King of the North, Antuf, whose Word is Truth. Papyrus Harris 500.

O GOOD Prince, it is a decree, and what hath been ordained thereby is well, that the bodies of men shall pass away and disappear whilst others remain.

Since the time of the oldest ancestors who lie at rest in their sepulchres, the Masters and also the Shining Ones who have been buried in their splendid tombs, who have built sacrificial halls in their tombs, their place is no more. Consider what hath become of them!

I have heard the words of Imhetep [13] and Herutataf [14] which are treasured above everything because they uttered them. Consider what hath become of their tombs! Their walls have been thrown down; their places are no more; they are as if they had never existed.

Not one of them cometh from where they are. Who can describe to us their condition, who can describe to us their surroundings, who can give comfort to our hearts, and can act as our guide to the place whereunto they have departed?

Behold, a man is not permitted to carry his possessions away with him. Behold, there never was any one who, having departed, was able to come back again! [15]

11(?)th Dynasty.

[13] A high official of Tcheser, a king of the third Dynasty.
[14] A son of Khufu, the builder of the Great Pyramid (fourth Dynasty).
[15] Translated by E. A. Wallis Budge, *The Literature of the Ancient Egyptians*, p. 242.

XXI

From a Dialogue between a Man and his Soul, on a papyrus at Berlin.

DEATH standeth before me today, as when a sick man becometh whole, as when one riseth after a fall.

Death standeth before me today as the odour of frankincense, as when a man sitteth under a sail in a cool breeze.

Death standeth before me today as a well-trodden path when a man returneth home from a ship of war.

Death standeth before me today as when a man longeth to see his home once more after years in captivity!

12th Dynasty.

XXII

Hymn to Maa (Truth), and Invocation to the Sun, from the Tomb of Rekhmara.

O SUN, who dost possess the Truth, and livest and quickenest through the Truth!
O Sun, adored and loved in Truth!
O Sun, perfected and fulfilled by Truth!
O Sun, glorified in Truth!
O Sun, from the beginning one with Truth!

XXIII

To the Supreme God, the Sun, from the Tomb of Rekhmara.

THOU inspirest Truth in our hearts which cause it to reascend toward Thee.

Since I know that Thou quickenest by the Truth, that Thou art very Truth, I have been just, free from falsehood, committing not iniquity.

XXIV

Hymn to the Sun God [16] *Amon Ra, from the papyrus at Gizeh.*

HAIL to Thee, Amon Ra, who dwellest in the sanctuary of Karnak;
Prince of heaven, Heir of earth, Lord of all things that exist,
Maker of things below and of things above!
He illumineth the Two Lands of Egypt, He traverseth the sky in peace. Great One of valour, Lord of awe; the gods gather as dogs at His feet, they recognize His majesty as their Lord.
Great of soul, lordly in manifestations, acclamations to Thee who dost upraise the sky and lay down the ground! [17]   *17th Dynasty (?-1580* B.C.).

XXV

Hymn to Amon Ra from the papyri at Gizeh and at Cairo.

HAIL to Thee Ra, Lord of Truth, whose shrine is concealed! Lord of Lords, Ancient of heaven, Maker of men, supporting their works; who givest them life, distinguishing one from another;
Listening to the poor in distress, gentle of heart when one crieth to Thee. Who deliverest the timid from him of a froward heart, and judgest the cause of the weak and oppressed.
Lord of wisdom, whose precepts are wise, at whose pleasure the Nile overfloweth her banks; Lord of sweetness,

---

[16] The creation of light was the highest manifestation of divine force, and in the rising and setting sun, invoked under various names in different times and places, the Egyptians saw the evidence of the almighty power of the one Supreme God embodied in its most splendid form.
[17] After the translation by F. Ll. Griffith. Reprinted from the Library of the World's Best Literature. Copyright.

great in love, at whose coming men live, at whose goodness the gods rejoice! Thy love is in the south, Thy
grace is in the north, Thy beauty taketh possession of
all hearts.

One and only One, Maker of all that is, who causest the
herbage to grow (which maketh the cattle to live) and
fruit-trees for mankind; giving breath to that which is in
the egg, supplying the needs of the mice in their holes,
and bestowing life on the birds in every tree;

Hail to Thee for all these things, the One alone with
many hands, waking while all men sleep to seek out the
good of Thy creatures. Homage to Thee in all their
voices; salutations from every land, to the height of the
heavens, to the breadth of the earth, to the depths of the
great waters!

The gods bow down before Thy majesty; the spirits Thou
hast created worship Thee, who hast hung the heavens
and planted the earth. Sovereign of life, health and
strength, we worship Thy spirit by whom we are made;
we thank Thee that Thou hast given us birth!

Dweller in the Horizon, Horus of the East, the wilderness createth for love of Him silver and gold and lapis-
lazuli, myrrh and incense mixed from the land of the
Matoi.   *17th Dynasty (?-1580 B.C.).*

XXVI

A Hymn of Praise to the Living Horus of the Two Hori-
zons, the Giver of Life for ever and ever, by Akhnaton
the Lord of the Two Lands of Egypt, the King who liveth
in Truth, the Lord of the Breath of Sweetness; from the
tomb of Api at Tel-el-Amarna, with an addition from
the tomb of Tutu.

THOU risest gloriously, O Thou living Aton, Lord of
Eternity! Thou art radiant, beautiful and strong. Thy

love is mighty and great; Thy light, of divers colours, leadeth all faces captive.

Thou fillest the Two Lands with Thy love, O Thou self-created God, Maker of every land and of whatsoever there is upon it, men and cattle, beasts of every sort, and trees of every kind that grow.

Thou art the mother and father of all that Thou hast made; their eyes, when Thou risest, turn and gaze upon Thee; their hearts beat high at the sight of Thee, for Thou risest as their Lord; their hands are lifted up in adoration of Thy person.

Thou quickenest hearts with Thy beneficent acts which are life. Thou sendest forth Thy beams, all the creatures Thou hast made leap toward Thee, and there is jubilee in every land.

Singing men and women make joyful sounds in the House of the Benben Obelisk,[18] and in every temple in the city of Akhnaton, the Seat of Truth.

Thy honoured son rejoiceth, his heart is glad, O Thou living Aton, who appearest in heaven. I am Thy son, satisfying Thee and exalting Thy name. Thy strength and Thy power are established in my heart.

Eternity is Thine emanation. Thou Thyself art alone, but there are millions of powers of life in Thee to make Thy creatures live. Buds burst into flower, the plants that grow on waste lands send up shoots at Thy rising.

The beasts frisk on their feet; the feathered fowl rise up from their nests and flap their wings with joy, and circle round in praise of the Living Aton.[19]

About 1375-1358 B.C.

[18] The Sanctuary at Heliopolis. The especially sacred portion of the obelisk is the pyramidal apex (Benben) with which it is surmounted.

[19] After the translation by E. A. Wallis Budge.

XXVII

The Longer Hymn to Aton, ascribed to King Akhnaton,[20] *from the tomb of Ai, Overseer of the Horse to Akhnaton.*

THY dawning is beautiful in the horizon of heaven, O Living Aton, Beginning of life! When Thou risest in the horizon of the east Thou fillest all lands with Thy splendour; fair-shining art Thou and great and radiant, exalted above the earth.

Thy rays envelop the lands, even all which Thou hast made. Thou bindest them with Thy love. Thou Thyself art afar, but Thy beams are upon the earth. Thou Thyself art on high, but Thy foot-prints are the day.

When Thou settest in the horizon of the west, the world is in darkness like death. Men lie down in their chambers, the lions come forth from their lairs. Darkness reigneth; the world is in silence.

The earth becometh light when Thou risest in the horizon, when Thou shinest as Aton by day. Thou scatterest the darkness. When Thou sendest forth Thy rays the Two Lands make festival.

Men wake and stand upon their feet, it is Thou who raisest them up, their arms uplifted in praise at Thy dawning. Throughout the land they go about their labour.

[20] Because of his power to throw off the shackles of tradition, in Egypt so overwhelming, and to substitute for the national cult of Amon, with its mechanical agencies for securing justification, a world-religion in the worship of Aton, and a reliance on his fatherly solicitude alone, Akhnaton (1375-1358 B. C.) has been called by Breasted "the first individual in history," "a God-intoxicated man whose mind responded with marvellous sensitiveness to the visible evidences of God about him." The worship of Aton which developed under Akhnaton into an exalted monotheism originated in Heliopolis, the ancient On, where Moses became "learned in all the wisdom of the Egyptians," passing on to the Jews perhaps the memory of this hymn which anticipates by hundreds of years the 104th Hebrew Psalm: "Thou makest darkness, and it is night: wherein all the beasts of the forest do creep forth. The young lions roar after their prey, and seek their meat from God.

The sun ariseth, they gather themselves together, and lay them down in their dens. Man goeth forth unto his work and to his labour until the evening.

O Lord, how manifold are Thy works!"

The cattle rest upon the herbage, the trees and plants do flourish, the birds flutter in the marshes, their wings uplifted in adoration to Thee. The sheep frisk upon their feet, all things winged fly; they live when Thou hast shone upon them.

The barques sail up and down the river, every highway is open at Thy dawning. The fish in the river leap up before Thee, Thy rays are in the depths of the great waters.

O how manifold are Thy works! They are hidden from our face, O Thou sole God, whose powers none other possesseth. Thou didst create the earth at Thy will, Thou existing alone,—men and women, cattle large and small, all that go upon the earth, all that fly on high.

Thou settest each man in his place, supplying his necessities, the portion allotted to him; and his days are reckoned. Their tongues are divers in speech, their forms likewise and the colour of their skins.

Thou makest the Nile in the nether world; Thou bringest it hither at Thy pleasure to preserve the people in life, inasmuch as Thou hast made them for Thyself, O Lord of them all, who dost support them to the uttermost. O Lord of every land, who risest for them, O Sun of the day, Thou great One of majesty, Thou makest also their life.

Thou hast set a Nile in heaven that it may fall for them, making a flood on the mountains, like the great sea, watering their fields in their districts. How excellent are Thy ways, O Lord of Eternity!

Thou dost create the seasons to develop all things Thou hast made; the winter season to bring them coolness, the summer to bring them heat. Thou dost fashion the beauty of form through Thyself alone. For Thou art the Lord of the day at its zenith. And Thou art in my heart.[21]

About 1375-1358 B.C.

[21] After Breasted's and Davies' translations.

XXVIII

A Hymn of Praise from the Papyrus of Ani.

HAIL, Thou Aton, who risest on the horizon day by day!
Shine Thou with Thy beams of light upon the face of
Ani, the truth-speaker, who singeth hymns to Thee at
dawn, and adoreth Thee at eventide. Let his soul appear
with Thee in heaven, and let him cleave his way among
the stars that never vanish.

When Thou risest and sendest forth Thy beams upon
the lands of the North and the South, Thou art beautiful,
yea beautiful, and all the gods rejoice when they see
Thee, the King of Heaven.

I would come before Thee daily to be with Thee and to
behold Thy beautiful Disk. I am one that worshipped
Thee on earth; let me enter the Eternal Land in the
Everlasting Country! O my Lord, I beseech Thee to
decree this for me!

Thou passest over the heaven, every eye watcheth Thy
course, Thou Thyself unseen. Thy beams fall on every
face, Thy divers lights and colours cannot be numbered
and cannot be told.

May I go forward as Thou dost advance without pause,
and dost in a moment pass over untold leagues; and as
Thou dost sink to rest, even so may I!

Grant that I may come into the Everlasting Heaven and
the Mountain where dwell Thy favoured ones. Let me
join myself to those who are perfect and holy and appear
with them to behold Thy beauties at eventide!

I lift my hands to Thee in adoration when Thou the
Living One dost set. Thou art the Eternal Creator and
art adored at Thy setting in heaven. I have given my
heart to Thee without wavering, O Thou who art the
mightiest of the gods! [22]   *18th Dynasty, 1580-1350* B.C.

[22] After the translation by E. A. Wallis Budge in "Tutankhamen."

XXIX

Hymn of Praise to the Sun-God, comprised in the Book of the Dead. From the Papyrus of Ani.[23]

HAIL to Thee, O Ra, Thou art adored! Thy beauties are before mine eyes, and Thy splendour falleth upon my body. The stars which never stay hymn Thee, and the stars which never vanish glorify Thee as Thou dost sink to rest in the horizon. Thou art beautiful at morn and at eve, O Living Lord, the Unchanging One, my Lord!

O Thou divine Substance, from whence all forms of life have sprung! Thou sendest forth the word, and earth is flooded with silence, O Thou only One who didst dwell in heaven before ever the earth and the mountains came into being.

O Shepherd, O Lord, Creator of what is, Thou madest all that sprang from the waters, and Thou shootest up from them over the land of the pools of the Lake of Horus. Glorify my spirit, O Osiris, make divine my soul!

Thou art worshipped in peace, O Lord of the gods, Thou art exalted by reason of Thy wondrous works!

The royal scribe in truth who loveth Thee; Ani, victorious in peace.[22]   *18th Dynasty, 1580-1350* B.C.

XXX

Hymn to Osiris, comprised in the Book of the Dead. From the Papyrus of Ani.[23]

PRAISE unto Thee, O Osiris, Lord of Eternity, whose forms are manifold and whose attributes are majestic. Thou turnest Thy face upon the Land of the West,[24] and Thou makest the earth to shine as with refined copper.

[23] The Papyrus of the scribe Ani was found in a Theban tomb and dates from the 18th Dynasty; but the Book of the Dead which it reproduces in part goes still further back.
[24] Amentet, "a land of slumber and heavy darkness."

Those who have lain down in death rise up beholding Thee; they breathe the air and look upon Thy face when Thy Disk riseth on its horizon. Their hearts are at peace inasmuch as they are beholding Thee, who art Eternity and Everlastingness!   *18th Dynasty, 1580-1350* B.C.

XXXI

Hymn of a Departed Soul to Osiris, from the Book of the Dead, 183.

GLORY be to Thee, Osiris, Beneficent Being! Thou endurest for all eternity, Thou God of millions of years! O Dweller in the Land of Holiness, Thy face is beautiful. Life is with Thee.

Let me follow Thy Majesty as when I was on earth; let my soul be summoned, and let it be found near the Lords of Truth. I have come to the City of God, the region that is eternally old, with my soul to be a dweller in this land. Its God is the Lord of Truth, He giveth old age to him that worketh Truth, and honour to His followers.

I have come unto Thee, my hands hold Truth, and there is no falsehood in my heart. Thou hast set Truth before Thee; I know on what Thou livest.[25]

XXXII

Hymn of the Deceased to Ra, from the Book of the Dead.

HOMAGE to Thee, O Ra! O Thou only One, O Thou Perfect One, O Thou who art eternal, who art never weak, whom no mighty one can abase; none hath dominion over the things which appertain to Thee!

O Divine Youth, who art self-created, I cannot apprehend Thee. Thou art the Lord of heaven and earth, and didst create beings celestial and beings terrestrial. Thou art the One God who camest into being at the beginning of time.

[25] This and the following selection are from *The Book of the Dead,* by E. A. Wallis Budge, a pamphlet published by the British Museum.

Thou didst create the earth, Thou didst make the sky and the celestial river Hep; Thou didst fashion the great deep and give life to all that therein is. Thou hast knit together the mountains. Thou hast made mankind and the beasts of the field to come into being.

O Thou Divine Youth, Thou Heir of Everlastingness, self-begotten and self-born, Mighty Being, One, though of myriad forms and aspects, Lord of Eternity, Thou art unknowable, and no tongue can describe Thy similitude. Millions of years have passed over the world, I cannot tell the number of those through which Thou hast passed.[26]

XXXIII

Hymn to Osiris, Stele of Amen-em-ha.

HE judgeth the world. The circuit of the sun is under Him, the winds, the waters, the plants, and all growing things. He giveth all seeds and the abundance of the ground. He bringeth plentifulness and giveth it to all the earth.

All men are in ecstasy, their hearts in sweetness, their bosoms joyful; they are every one in adoration. Every man glorifieth His goodness; mild is His love for us; His tenderness encompasseth our hearts, great is His love in every bosom; sanctifying, beneficent is His name!

Both worlds are at rest, evil taketh flight, and earth becometh fruitful and peaceful under its Lord.

18th Dynasty, 1580-1350 B.C.

XXXIV

Hymn of Praise to Amon Ra.

VAST is His largeness without limit. Virtue supreme, in unfathomable forms! Soul mysterious! Author of His fearful power, life holy and strong, created by Himself,

---

[26] After the translation by E. A. Wallis Budge.

glorious, diffusing radiance, insufferably bright! Worker of the ages who hath designed the world! O Amon, with the holy transformations!

He whom no man knoweth, refulgent are His forms, His glory is a veil of light. Mystery of mysteries! Mystery unknown!

The breath of truth is in Thy secret sanctuary. Thou art worshipped upon the waters; the fertile land adoreth Thee; the spirits of the east rejoice with Thee when Thy light illumeth their faces!

XXXV

Hymn to Ptah-tanen.

HAIL to Thee, O Ptah-tanen, great God who concealeth His form, Thou art watching when at rest, the Father of all fathers and of all gods; Watcher, who traversest the endless ages of eternity.

The heaven was yet uncreated, uncreated the earth, the water flowed not; Thou hast put together the earth; what Thou hast found apart, Thou hast put into its place.

O God, Architect of the world, Thou art without a father, begotten by Thine own becoming. Thou drivest away the darkness by the beams of Thine eyes. Thou ascendest into the zenith of heaven, and Thou comest down even as Thou hast risen.

Thou sustainest the substances which Thou hast made. It is by Thine own strength that Thou movest; Thou art raised up by the might of Thine own arms.

The roaring of Thy voice is in the cloud; Thy breath is on the mountain-tops; the waters of the inundation cover the lofty trees of every region.

Heaven and earth obey the commands which Thou hast given; they travel by the road which Thou hast laid down for them; they transgress not the path which Thou hast prescribed, and which Thou hast opened to them.

Thou restest and it is night; when Thine eyes shine forth, we are illumined. O let us give glory to God who hath raised up the sky, and who causeth His Disk to float over the bosom of Nut;[27] who hath made the gods and men and all their generations, who hath made all lands and countries, and the great sea, in His name of Let-the-earth-be!

XXXVI

Hymn for the harp, to Hapi, the God of the Nile, by Enna; from papyrus Anastasi VII in the British Museum.

BRINGER of food! Great Lord of provisions, Creator of all good things! Lord of terrors and of chiefest joys! All are combined in Him. He filleth the granaries, enricheth the store-houses; He careth for the state of the poor. He causeth growth to fulfil all desires, He never wearieth of it. He maketh His might a buckler.

He cannot be graven in marble as an image bearing the double crown. He cannot be beheld; He hath neither ministrant nor offerings; He is not to be approached in sanctuaries; His abode is not known; He is not to be found in shrines with painted figures. No habitation can contain Him.

Unknown is His name in heaven; He doth not manifest His forms! Vain are all representations.

18th Dynasty, 1580-1350 B.C.

XXXVII

Prayer of Rameses II when Egypt was hard pressed by the Hittites and other foes.

WHO then art Thou, O my Father Amon? Doth a father forget a son? Surely a sorry lot awaiteth him who doth oppose Thy will; but blessed is he who knoweth Thee, for Thy deeds proceed from a heart full of love.

[27] The heavens.

I call upon Thee, Father Amon! Behold me in the midst of many peoples, unknown to me; all nations are united against me, and I am alone; no other is with me. My many soldiers have abandoned me, none of my horsemen hath looked toward me; when I called them, none listened to my voice.

But Amon is worth more to me than a million of soldiers, than a hundred thousand horsemen and ten thousands of brothers and sons, even were they all gathered together. The work of many men is nought; Amon will prevail over them.   *1290* B.C.

XXXVIII

Hymn of Praise to Amon from the Papyrus at Leyden.

HEAVEN is of gold, the waters of lapis lazuli, and the earth is o'erspread with malachite, when He ariseth therein. The gods behold and their temples stand open.

The trees stir at His presence; they turn them towards His eye, and their leaves unfold. The cattle frolic before His countenance, the birds dance with their wings; they are in His hand, sealed with His seal, and no god openeth them save His Majesty.

How Thou voyagest, Harakhti, and doest daily after Thy manner of yesterday, Thou who makest the years, and marshallest the months!

Days and nights are according to His march. All men turn their faces towards Him and say, Welcome art Thou! They sing to Him in every chapel, and every place possesseth His love.

He who purgeth away evil and dispelleth sickness, who rescueth whom He will, coming from afar before an instant hath passed to him who hath called upon Him. He speaketh the gentle word in time of turmoil. A pleasant breeze to them that appeal unto Him. Preserving the weary.

He delivereth the helpless one. He is better than millions to the man who hath set Him in his heart. One warrior who fighteth in His name is better than thousands. He is perfect and seizeth His moment.

His image is not spread out in books. He is too mysterious that His glory should be revealed, too great that men should question concerning Him, too powerful that He should be known; whose name is hidden, for that He is a mystery.[28]   *Time of Rameses II (about 1300-1234 B.C.).*

XXXIX

A Hymn from the Temple in the Oasis of El-Khargeh.

(O) THE mysterious names of the God who is immanent in all things, the soul of the breath to all the gods! He is the body of the living man, the Creator of the fruit-bearing tree, the Author of the inundation; without Him, Osiris, Giver of light, nothing liveth within the circuit of the earth, whether north or south.

He is the Creator of every beast; He loveth the scorpion in his hole; He is the god of the crocodiles who plunge in the water; He is the God of them that rest in their graves.

Amon is an image, Atmu is an image, Ra is an image; He alone maketh Himself in millions of ways. A mighty builder He, who was from the beginning, who fashioned His body with His own hands, in all forms according to His will.

Permanent and enduring, He never passeth away. Through millions of endless years He traverseth the heavens, He compasseth the nether world each day.

He is the moon in the night and the king of the stars, who maketh the divisions of seasons, months and years; He cometh living everlastingly both in His rising and His setting. There is none other like unto Him; His voice is

---

[28] After the rendering by Erman (trans. by Aylward M. Blackman), with one interpolation.

heard, but He remaineth unseen to every creature that doth breathe.

He strengtheneth the heart of the woman in labour, and giveth life to those who are born from her. He traveleth in the cloud to separate heaven and earth, and again to reunite them, permanently abiding in all things, the Living One in whom all things live everlastingly.

XL

Hymn to Amon from Ostrakon [29] *5656a, British Museum.*

O AMON, as the herdsman bringeth forth his herds to pasture in the morning, so dost Thou lead the suffering to food; for Amon is a herdsman, herding them that lean on Him.

The sun of him who knoweth Thee not goeth down, O Amon! But as for him who knoweth Thee, he doth shine.

The forecourt of him who assailed Thee is in darkness, while the whole world is in light. Whoso putteth Thee in his heart, O Amon, lo, his sun doth dawn!

O Amon, I love Thee and have filled my heart with Thee. Thou wilt deliver me out of the mouth of man on the day wherein he speaketh lies; for the Lord of Truth, He liveth in truth. I will not follow the anxiety of my heart, for that which Amon hath said shall come to pass.[30]

13th or 12th century B.C.

XLI

From a votive stele at Berlin, 23077.
Nebre, Painter in the Necropolis, hath written this in the name of Amon, Lord of Thebes; making for Him praises because of the greatness of His might, and offering prayers before Him on behalf of his son Nakht-Amon, when he lay sick unto death because of his sin. I

---

[29] A potsherd or flake of limestone, used for inscription.
[30] After renderings by Breasted and Erman.

found that the Lord of gods came as the north wind while sweet air went before Him, that He might save Nakht-Amon.

PRAISE to Amon! I make hymns in His name, I render to Him praise to the height of the heaven and the breadth of the earth. I tell of His prowess to him who saileth down-stream, and to him who saileth up-stream.

Be ye ware of Him! Tell it to son and to daughter, to great and to small; tell it to generation after generation yet unborn. Declare it to the fishes in the stream, to the birds in the sky; repeat it to him who knoweth it not, and likewise to him who knoweth it. Be ye ware of Him!

Thou, O Amon, art the Lord of the silent, who cometh at the cry of the poor. When I cry unto Thee in my affliction, then Thou comest and savest me; that Thou mayst give breath to him who is bowed down, and save me lying in bondage.

Thou, Amon-Ra, art He who saveth him that is in the nether world; when men cry unto Thee, Thou art He that cometh from afar.

Though the servant be used to commit transgression, yet the Lord is wont to be gracious. The Lord of Thebes spendeth not the whole day wroth. His wrath is finished in a moment, it remaineth not.[31]

13th or 12th century, B.C.

XLII

From a Hymn to Thoth, Papyrus Sallier I. 8.

THOU sweet Well for him that thirsteth in the wilderness; it is closed to him who speaketh; it is open to him who keepeth silence. When he who is silent cometh, lo, he findeth the well![31]

[31] After the translation given by Breasted, in *Religion and Thought in Ancient Egypt.*

ACCADIAN AND BABYLONIAN PSALMS

Trembling one, pursued by evil, dash thyself against the bosom of thy God!

XLIII

A Penitential Psalm of the Accadians. Like its archetype engraved and written, Palace of Asshur-bani-pal, King of Assyria.

THE transgression that I commit, my God knoweth it. The water of my tears do I drink. O my Lord, my transgression is great, many are my sins. O my God, my transgression is great, my sins many! The forbidden thing did I eat.

My Lord in the wrath of His heart hath punished me; God in the strength of His heart hath overpowered me. I lay on the ground, no man took me by the hand. I cried aloud, there was none that would hear me. I was in darkness and trouble, I lifted not myself up. To my God my distress I referred, my prayer I addressed:

How long, O my God, shall I suffer? O Lord, Thy servant Thou dost not restore. In the waters of the raging flood seize his hand! The sin that he hath sinned, to blessedness bring back; the transgressions he hath committed let the winds carry away; my manifold affliction do Thou like a garment destroy!

O my God, seven times seven are my transgressions. My transgressions they are before me. May Thy judgments give me life! May Thy heart like the heart of a mother return to its place! [32]

[32] After a rendering by A. H. Sayce.

The content of these psalms may date as far back as some three thousand years before Christ, though they were transcribed from the original Accadian during the reign of that great patron of literature, Asshur-banipal, in the 7th cent., B. C., thus preceding by hundreds, if not thousands

XLIV

Babylonian Penitential Psalm to Ishtar(?)

I, THY servant, sorrowful, cry unto Thee. The sinner's earnest prayer Thou dost accept; the man on whom Thou lookest liveth, Queen of humanity, merciful One, whose forgiveness is ready, who acceptest the sigh of the heart.

Priest: O God and Mother Goddess, he crieth to Thee, turn Thy face to him, take Thou his hand!

Beside Thee there is no god to guide me. Look in mercy on me, and accept my sigh. Say Thou: How long shall My heart be wroth? Let Thy face be turned to me! Like a dove, full of sighing, I mourn.

Priest: With sorrow and woe his soul is full of sighing. Tears doth he shed, he poureth out laments.[33]

XLV

Accadian Penitential Psalm.

THY servant hath sinned and in anguish he crieth to Thee; like a thundercloud he causeth his tears to rain; he is overpowered and causeth his eyelids to weep. Like a shrieking bird he uttereth troublous cries; with weeping he declareth his woe.

What can my Lord's servant say or devise? Sin hath

of years the like impassioned utterances in the Hebrew Psalms which they may have inspired; for during the Babylonian Captivity (586-538 B. C.) the Jews probably became familiar with these hymns. Compare the following expressions in the Hebrew Psalms:

Oh, God, Thou knowest my foolishness and my sins are not hid from Thee. (Ps. LXIX 5.) My tears have been my meat day and night (Ps. LXII 3.) I have cried day and night before Thee; my soul is full of troubles. (Ps. LXXXVIII 2 & 3.) I looked for some to take pity, but there was none. (Ps. LXIX 20.) How long wilt Thou forget me, O Lord, for ever? (Ps. XIII 1.) Deliver me out of the mire, and . . . out of the deep waters. (Ps. LXIX 14.) I acknowledge my transgressions: and my sin is ever before me. (Ps. LI. 3.)

[33] After renderings by Crawford Toy and Sayce.

been laid upon him; darkness of the face is his daylight; he lieth prostrate. At the gate of his sin his hands are bound.

Take his hand, forgive his sin; remove the madness and wasting that is on him. Address Thy servant favourably and bathe his disease in the river. Loosen his chain, undo his fetter; enlighten his face; entrust him to his God who created him.

Give life to Thy servant! Accept his gift, receive his ransom; in a land of peace may he walk before Thee! May he pour out the oil of Thy courts like water! May he offer Thee the odours of cedar, the finest of incense, the fatness of wheat!

Look down, O Lord, upon Thy servant who is full of grief; let Thy wind blow and deliver him forthwith; strike off his bonds; let him draw full breaths; declare his judgment, pity, pity his life.[34]

XLVI

Babylonian Penitential Psalm.

O my Lord, long-suffering and merciful, may Thy heart be appeased, may my sin be forgiven, may my transgression be cleansed! Let the yoke be unbound, the chain be loosed. May the seven winds carry my groaning away.

May I strip off my evil so that the bird may bear it to heaven! May the river bear it along; the waters of the river, may they cleanse me as they flow! Make me to shine like a mask of gold. As a goblet of glass may I be precious in Thy sight!

Burn up my evil, knit together my life, and let me be kept with Thee! Yea, let me enter into E-Sag-il, the palace of the gods, the temple of life.[35]

[34] After a rendering by Sayce.
[35] *Idem.*

XLVII

Babylonian Penitential Psalm to Ishtar.

O MOTHER of the gods, who makest the young grass to sprout; Queen of mankind and guide of every birth; Mother Ishtar, whose might no god doth approach!

A prayer I will utter, let her do unto me what seemeth to Her good. From the day when I was little, much am I yoked with evil. Food have I not eaten, weeping was my meat; water I have not taken, tears have been my drink. My heart hath not been joyful, nor my spirits glad. Many are my sins, sorrowful my soul!

O my Lady, make me to know my doing, establish for me a place of rest. Cleanse my sin, lift up my head. Turn Thy face graciously to me, let Thine eye rest graciously on me. Let Thy heart be gentle, Thy spirit mild! [36]

XLVIII

Babylonian Psalm to Ishtar.

GOOD is it to implore Thee, for grace is in the oath by Thy name. Thy beholding is favour, Thy command is light. Have mercy upon me, O Ishtar, command my being in prosperity. Faithfully behold me, and receive my supplication.

Since Thy song I have learned, may I possess peace of heart. I have borne Thy yoke, therefore bring me unto rest. I have heeded what might advantage Thee, may mercy come straightway. I have faithfully cherished Thy glory, let there be acceptance and favour!

I have sought Thy splendour, may Thy countenance be bright! I have taken refuge in Thy dominion, may it mean life and health! Command, and Thy words shall be heard.

[36] After renderings by Sayce and Crawford Toy (the latter from the Library of the World's Best Literature. Copyright).

The word which I speak, even as I speak it may it be
received! In health of flesh and joy of heart, yea, Thou
shalt lead me daily. Lengthen my days, grant unto me
life; I would live and contemplate Thy godhead.

Even as I sing may I obtain! May heaven rejoice for
Thee, may the sea shout to Thee! May the gods of the
universe draw nigh unto Thee, may the mighty gods
make glad Thy heart! [37]

XLIX

*Accadian Hymn to Ishtar. Like its archetype written and
published. Palace of Asshur-bani-pal, King of Assyria.*

THE light of heaven which blazeth like a fire art Thou,
Thou who art strong as the earth! The path of justice
approacheth Thee when Thou enterest into the house of
man.

By day, O Virgin, adorn the heaven; Thou who art set
as the jewelled circlet of moonstone, adorn the heaven!

Ishtar: In the resplendent heaven to cause enlightenment to prevail was I appointed. In the beginning was
My glory. Ishtar of the evening sky am I. Ishtar the
divinity of the dawn am I. Ishtar, the Opener of the
Bolts of the Bright Heavens, is My name of glory.

As Queen of heaven above and below may My glory be
addressed. My glory sweepeth away the mountains altogether. Thou art the mighty fortress of the mountains,
thou art their mighty bolt, O My glory! [38]

L

Babylonian Hymn to Shamash, the Sun-god.

O LORD, Illuminator of the darkness, who piercest the
face of the heaven! Merciful God, who settest up those
that be bowed down; who sustainest the weak!

[37] After a rendering by Stephen Langdon.
[38] After a rendering by Sayce.

For Thy light the great gods wait. The archangels of the abyss, every one, do contemplate Thy face. The language of their praise as one word Thou dost direct.

Like a bridegroom Thou risest joyful and gracious. In Thy light Thou dost reach afar to the utmost bounds of heaven. The banner of the whole wide earth art Thou. O God, the men who dwell afar do look upon Thee and rejoice! [39]

LI

Sumerian Psalm to Enlil.

THE exalted One is like a wind, the exalted One like a wind hath cast me down, even me; the exalted One, the Lord of lands, He of the far-seeing mind whose word changeth not, against whose commands there is no turning back, the utterance of whose mouth is unalterable.

My gardens are rent, my forests are despoiled of leaves. The thoughts of my heart He rendereth vain.

Like a lone rush reed, behold, the mighty One, like a lone rush reed hath brought me low, even me; the mighty One, Lord of lands, He of the far-seeing mind, He of the faithful word, against whose commands there is no receding, Enlil whose command is unalterable,

Like a thistle hath made me, like a thorn-bush hath made me, like a lone mulberry-tree by the river's bank He hath made me, like a cedar in the desert, like a lone tamarisk in the storm; behold the mighty One like a lone rush reed hath brought me low, even me! [40]

LII

Psalm to Enlil.

O EXALTED Lord of lands, may Thy heart be turned, be turned! O Lord of the word of life, may Thy heart be turned, be turned! O Shepherd of the dark-headed

[39] After a rendering by François Lenormant.
[40] After a rendering by Stephen Langdon.

people, O hero of self-created vision, strong Lord who
directest mankind, who causest multitudes to lie down
in peace, may Thy heart be turned, be turned!

O Lord divine, strong One in heaven and earth; great
Judge, may Thy heart be turned, be turned!

That Thy heart be turned, that Thy heart be turned, be
spoken unto Thee.

Of him who hath supplication, may the supplication be
spoken unto Thee.

And he who hath entreaties may speak them unto Thee;
Enlil at whose going forth the heavens are arrested, who
when He stretcheth forth His arm, the heavens are arrested, Father Enlil, Lord of lands, exalted Lord of
Nippur! [41]

GREEK AND ROMAN HYMNS

LIII

From Pindar, Fragment Thren. II; Ol.2.57; Thren. I.

By happy lot travel all unto an end that giveth them
rest from their toil. The body indeed is subject unto the
great power of death, but there remaineth yet alive a
shadow of the life; for this only is from the gods.

And while the limbs stir it sleepeth, but unto sleepers
in dreams discovereth oftentimes the judgment that
draweth nigh for sorrow or for joy.

The guilty souls of the dead straightway pay the penalty
here on earth. But ever through nights and ever through
days the same, the good receive an unlaborious life
beneath the sunshine. They vex not with might of hand
the earth or the waters of the sea for food that satisfieth
not, but among the honoured gods enjoy a tearless life.

They who have wholly refrained their souls from deeds
unjust, journey on the road of Zeus to the tower of
Cronos, where the ocean breezes blow round the island
of the blest, and flowers gleam bright with gold, some
on trees of glory on the land, whilst some the water

[41] After a rendering by Stephen Langdon.

feedeth; with wreaths whereof they entwine their arms and crown their heads.

For them shineth below the strength of the sun whilst in our world it is night; and the space of crimson-flowered meadows before their city is full of the shade of frankincense-trees and of fruits of gold.

And some in bodily feats, some in harp-playing have delight; and among them thriveth all fair-flowering bliss, and fragrance streameth ever through the lovely land as they mingle incense of every kind upon the altars of the gods. *552-443* B. C.

LIV

From Euripides, The Bacchae.

O Strength of God, slow art Thou and still,
    Yet failest never:
On them that worship the Ruthless Will,
On them that dream, doth His judgment wait.
Dreams of the proud man, making great
    And greater ever
Things which are not of God. In wide
And devious coverts, hunter-wise,
He coucheth Time's unhasting stride,
Following, following, him whose eyes
Look not to Heaven. For all is vain,
The pulse of the heart, the plot of the brain,
That striveth beyond the laws that live.
Is it so hard a thing to see,
    That the Spirit of God, whate'er it be,
The Law that abides and changes not, ages long,
The Eternal and Nature-born—these things be strong?
What else is Wisdom? What of man's endeavour
    Or God's high grace so lovely and so great?
    To stand from fear set free, to breathe and wait,
    To hold a hand uplifted over Hate;
And shall not loveliness be loved for ever? [42]
    480-406 B. C.

[42] From *Euripides*, by Gilbert Murray, published by George Allen & Unwin Ltd.

LV

Hymn from the Consolation of Philosophy by Boëtius.[43]

Undying Soul of this material ball,
Heaven-and Earth-Maker! Thou who first didst call
Time into being, and by Thy behest
Movest all things, Thyself alone at rest,
No outward power impelled Thee thus to mold
In shape the fluid atoms manifold,
Only the immortal image, born within,
Of perfect beauty! Wherefore Thou hast been
Thine own fair model, and the things of sense
The image bear of Thy magnificence!
Parts perfect in themselves, by Thy control,
Are newly wrought into a perfect whole;
The yokéd elements obey Thy hand:
Frost works with fire, water with barren sand,
So the dense continents are fast maintained,
And heaven's ethereal fire to earth restrained.
Thou dost the life of threefold nature tame,
To serve the parts of one harmonious frame,—
That soul of things constrained eternally
To trace Thy image on the starry sky,
The greater and the lesser deeps to round,
And on Thyself return. Thou too hast found
For us, thy lesser creatures of a day,
Wherewith Thou sowest earth,—forms of a clay
So kindly-fragile naught can stay our flight
Backward, unto the source of all our light!
Grant, Father, yet the undethronéd mind!
A way unto the fount of truth to find,
And, sought, so long, the Vision of Thy face!
Lighten our flesh! Terrestrial vapours chase,
And shine in all Thy splendour! For Thou art
The final rest of every faithful heart,
The First, the Last! of the expatriate soul
Lord, Leader, Pathway, and Eternal Goal! [44]

About 475-524 A. D.

[43] Roman philosopher and statesman.
[44] Translated by Harriet W. Preston. Reprinted from the Library of the World's Best Literature. Copyright.

HYMNS OF THE AMERICAN INDIANS

LVI

Song of the Earth. A Hozhonji-Song [45] *of the Navajo Indians.*

All is beautiful,
All is beautiful,
All is beautiful indeed!

Now the Mother Earth
And the Father Sky
Meeting, joining one another,
Helpmates ever, they.
All is beautiful,
All is beautiful,
All is beautiful indeed!

And the night of darkness
And the dawn of light,
Meeting, joining one another,
Helpmates ever, they.
All is beautiful,
All is beautiful,
All is beautiful indeed!

Life-that-never-passeth,
Happiness-of-all-things,
Meeting, joining one another,
Helpmates ever, they.
All is beautiful,
All is beautiful,
All is beautiful indeed!

Now all is beautiful,
All is beautiful,
All is beautiful indeed! [46]

[45] "The Hozhonji songs are holy songs given to us by the gods," say the Navajos. "They are songs of peace and blessing. They protect the people against all evil."

[46] This and the following two extracts are from *The Indians' Book* by Nathalie Curtis. Copyright 1907 by Nathalie Curtis, 1923 by Paul Burlin. Pub. by Harper and Brothers.

LVII

Hymn sung from the summit of the hills at dawn, by the old men of the Cheyenne Indians to one of their oldest melodies.

HE, our Father, He hath shown His mercy unto me.
In peace I walk the straight road.

LVIII

Mountain-Song of the Navajo Indians.

Homeward behold me faring,
Homeward upon the rainbow;
Homeward behold me faring.
Lo, yonder, the Holy Place!
    Yea, homeward behold me faring.

To Sisnajinni, and beyond it,
The Chief of Mountains, and beyond it.
    Yea, homeward behold me faring.

To Life Unending, and beyond it,
To Joy Unchanging, and beyond it,
    Yea, homeward behold me faring.

LIX

Night Chant of the Navajo Indians.

In Tsegihi,
In the house made of the dawn,
In the house made of the evening twilight,
In the house made of the dark cloud,
Where the dark mist curtains the doorway,
The path to which is on the rainbow,
Oh Thou Divine One!
With the dark thunder above Thee, come to us soaring,
With the shapen cloud at Thy feet, come to us soaring,

With the zigzag lightning flung high over Thy head,
   come to us soaring,
With the rainbow hanging high over Thy head, come
   to us soaring!
I have made Thy sacrifice.
My feet restore for me, my limbs, my mind, my voice.
Today take away Thy spell from me!
Away from me Thou hast taken it.
Far off from me it is taken.
Happily my eyes regain their power, my head becometh
   cool.
Happily my limbs regain their power, I hear again.
Happily the old men will regard Thee, the old women,
   the young men and women, the children, the
   chiefs.
Happily may their roads home be on the trail of peace.

In beauty I walk,
With beauty before me I walk,
With beauty behind me I walk,
With beauty below me I walk,
With beauty above me I walk,
With beauty all around me I walk.

It is finished again in beauty,
It is finished in beauty,
It is finished in beauty! [47]

LX

Mountain-ᴗong oᶠ the Navajo Indians.

In a holy place with a God I walk,
In a holy place with a God I walk,
On Pelado Peak with a God I walk,
In old age wandering with a God I walk,
In old age wandering with a God I walk,
On a trail of beauty with a God I walk.

[47] Transcribed by Washington Mathews.

LXI

Hymn from the Ritual of the Omaha Indians.

Toward the coming of the sun there the people of every kind gathered, and great animals of every kind. Verily all gathered there together, by what means or manner we know not.

Verily, One alone of all these was the greatest, inspiring to all minds, the great white Rock,[48] standing as high as the heavens, enwrapped in mist, verily as high as the heavens.

Thus shall my little ones speak of Me,
As long as they shall travel in life's path, thus shall they speak of Me, such were the words, it hath been said.

He! Aged One, ecka, thou Rock, ecka! He![49] I have taught these little ones, they obey, ecka! He! Unmoved from time without end, verily Thou sittest in the midst of the various paths of the coming winds, in the midst of the waters Thou sittest, ecka!

He! The small grasses grow about Thee, ecka, Thou sittest as though making of them Thy dwelling-place, Thy head decked with the downy feathers of the birds, Aged One, ecka!

He! This is the desire of Thy little ones, ecka; That of Thy strength they may partake, ecka; therefore Thy little ones desire to walk closely by Thy side, ecka, Venerable One!

Oh Aged One! I implore, Thy children being in sore distress, *I shall be with them as instructor,* Thou hast said, that in Thee they may take refuge, ecka! Oh, Thy children desire to arise by Thy strength, ecka, do not reproach them, but judge them rather by their ignorance, Aged One, I implore!

[48] Comp. Psalm LXI. 2, of the Old Testament, and the Christian hymn, "Rock of Ages."
[49] *He!* an exclamation involving the idea of supplication and distress; ecka: a refrain meaning, *I desire, crave, seek.*

Oh Aged One, ecka! Oh, Thou recumbent Rock, to Thee I shall pray, ecka! Oh Aged One, ecka, the great water that lieth impossible to traverse, in the midst of the waters Thou camest and sat, Thou of whom one may think; Whence camest Thou?

It is said that Thou sittest crying: *If one of Mine prayeth to Me properly, I shall be with him, farther along he shall go. All the impurities I shall wash away from them.*

It is said that Thou hast commanded us to say to Thee, Our Father, ecka!

Thou Water, ecka! Oh, along the bends of the streams where the waters strike, where the waters eddy, among the water-mosses, let all the impurities that gall be drifted, ecka. *Whosoever toucheth Me with face or lips, all the impurities I shall cause to be cleansed,* it is said Thou hast said, *And all within the body I shall purify.*

When in their longing for protection and guidance the people sought in their minds for a way, they beheld Thee sitting with an assured permanency and endurance; there exposed to the violence of the four winds Thou sattest, possessed with power to receive supplications, Aged One, ecka!

Where is His mouth, by which there may be utterance of speech? Where is His heart, to which there may come knowledge and understanding? Where are His feet, whereby He may move from place to place? We question in wonder. Yet verily, it is said Thou alone hast power to receive supplications, Aged One, ecka!

I have desired to go yet farther in the path of life with my little ones, without pain, without sickness, O hear! This is my prayer, though uttered in words poorly put together, Aged One, ecka! [50]

[50] Transcribed by Alice C. Fletcher in consultation with Francis La Flesche, a member of the Omaha tribe; 27th annual report of the American Bureau of Ethnology.

THE BOOK OF PRAYERS

BEING A COLLECTION OF ACCADIAN, BABYLONIAN, EGYPTIAN, GREEK, ROMAN AND INDIAN PRAYERS

*Let us invoke God Himself, not in mere form of
words, but by elevating our souls to Him in
prayer. And the only way truly to pray is to
approach alone the One who is Alone. To contemplate that One, we must withdraw into the
inner soul, as into a temple, and be still.*
                              Fifth Ennead, Lib. I; Plotinus,
                              205-264(?) A.D.

*Pray, pray thou!
Before the couch, pray!
Before the throne, before the canopy!
Before the dawn's light, pray!
By the tablets and the books, pray!
By the hearth,
By the threshold,
At the rising of the sun,
At the setting of the sun, pray!
When thou comest out of the city and when thou goest
        into the city, and when thou enterest into the house,
        pray!
On the street, in the temple, on the road, pray!*
                    Accadian Prayer, Cuneiform Inscriptions
                    of Western Asia, IV. 58, 59.

*When you have shut your doors, and darkened your
room, remember never to say that you are alone;
for God is within, and your genius is within, and
what need have they of light to see what you are
doing?*   Discourses of Epictetus, 60-120 A.D.

THE BOOK OF PRAYERS [1]

I

Prayer of King Asshur-nasir-pal I to Ishtar of Nineveh who nourisheth humanity on her breast.

THE matter which hath befallen me in words I will rehearse unto the exalted One, unto the Goddess of the world who determineth decrees, the Lady of heaven and earth who receiveth supplication; unto the compassionate Goddess who hearkeneth unto entreaty, who entertaineth prayer, who loveth righteousness.

I make my prayer unto Ishtar to whom all confusion is a cause of grief. To my words of lamentation let Thine ear be given! To my sorrowful conversation may Thy heart be opened! Turn Thy face unto me, that by reason of Thy reconciliation the heart of Thy servant may be strong!

I Asshur-nasir-pal Thy servant, the humble and afflicted, was created in the mountains which no man knoweth. I was without understanding, but Thou, O Ishtar, by lifting up Thine eyes didst teach me and didst take me from the mountains and call me for a shepherd of the peoples. [2]

Thou hast assured me a sceptre of sanctuaries [3] until the growing old of mankind. From Thy mouth went forth the command to repair the ruined temples of the gods, and so the tottering temples I have repaired.

---

[1] For other prayers see in this volume Psalms I, III, V, VII, VIII, XXVIII, XXXVII, XLI, XLIII, XLIV, XLVII, XLVIII, LII, Brihad-Aranyaka Upanishad, I, iii; and V. xv; Book of Zarathushtra, Yasna XXVIII, XXXIII, and LX, Yasna Haptanhaiti, and Atash Nyayish.

[2] Compare with the call of David, I Sam. XVI. 11-13.

[3] The meaning is probably, *a sceptre recognized by all the gods.*

Before Thy divinity I did walk uprightly; but as one who feareth not Thy divinity hast Thou afflicted me. Yet am I ever cast down, I am distressed, and have no rest.

From my royal throne I departed; to the feast I had prepared I came not nigh; as for the palace and the revelry, I am removed. From the pleasure and the joy of life I am excluded. Mine eyes are sealed that I behold not, I lift them not above the ground.

How long, O Lady, shall sickness cease not and my knees waver?

I am Asshur-nasir-pal the distressed, who feareth Thee; look upon me, for I would implore Thy divinity. Have mercy on me, may Thy soul be appeased, may Thy grace incline Thy heart toward me. Cause my sickness to depart and my sin to be removed!

By Thy command, O Queen, may there come to me repose. In after days I will extol Thy deity, and Thy sovereignty I will magnify in the assembly of the gods, the councillors of heaven and earth.[4]

About 1030 B.C.

II

Accadian Prayer.[5]

GOD, my Creator, stand by my side! Keep Thou the door of my lips, guard Thou my hands, O Lord of Light!

III

Accadian Prayers for a Soul.

LIKE a bird may it fly to a lofty place; to the holy hands of its God may it return!

The man who is departing in glory, may his soul shine radiant as brass! To that man may the sun give life! Grant him a happy habitation!

[4] Adapted from a rendering by Stephen Langdon.
[5] See note to Psalm XLIII in this volume.

IV

Accadian Prayer against the Plague.

THINE is the depth of the ocean. Thine are all human beings, all who breathe, all who bear a name and exist on the surface of the earth.

The whole of the four regions of the world, the archangels of the legions of heaven and earth, how many soever they be, these are Thine.

Thou art the Life-giver! Thou art the Saviour! The Merciful One among the gods! Cure Thou this plague! [6]

V

Babylonian Prayer for the City of Ur: like its archetype written and published.[7] *Tablet of Ishtar-shuma-eresh, Chief Scribe of Asshur-bani-pal, King of the Universe.*

FATHER NANNAR, Lord of the firmament, Lord of the gods, Merciful One, Begetter of the universe, who foundeth among living creatures His illustrious seat; Father, long-suffering and full of forgiveness, whose hand upholdeth the life of all mankind;

Lord, Thy divinity, like the far-off heaven, filleth the wide sea with fear; First-born, Omnipotent, whose heart is immensity, and there is none who may discover it.

Who dost march in glory from the horizon to the zenith, opening wide the doors of heaven, and establishing light in the world; the Ordainer of the laws of heaven and earth, whose command may not be broken; Thou holdest the rain and the lightning, Defender of all living things.

In heaven, who is great? Thou alone. On earth who is exalted? Thou alone. When Thy voice resoundeth in heaven, the very gods fall prostrate. When Thy voice resoundeth on earth, the spirits kiss the dust.

[6] After the rendering by Lenormant.
[7] See note to Psalm XLIII in this volume.

Thy will is seen in stall and stable; it increaseth all living things. Thy word hath created law and justice, so that mankind hath established law.

King of Kings, whose divinity no god resembleth, where Thine eye doth glance there cometh harmony; where Thou dost grasp the hand there cometh salvation; look with favour on Thy temple! Look with favour on Thy city Ur![8]   *Between 669(?) and 626* B.C.

VI

Prayer of King Asshur-bani-pal.

MAY the look of pity that shineth in Thine eternal face dispel my griefs. May I never feel the anger and wrath of the God. May my omissions and my sins be wiped out. May I find reconciliation with Him, for I am the servant of His power.

May Thy powerful face come to my help; may it shine like heaven, may it bring forth in abundance, like the earth, happiness and every sort of good!   *650* B.C.

VII

Prayer of Nebuchadnezzar II upon ascending his father's throne.[9]

O ETERNAL RULER, Lord of all that doth exist, grant to the king whom Thou lovest, whose name Thou hast proclaimed, that he be guided as seemeth good to Thee! Lead him in the path of right!

I am the prince obedient to Thee, the creature of Thy hand. Thou hast created me, and hast entrusted to me the sovereignty over multitudes.

According to Thy goodness, O Lord, which Thou dost bestow upon all, may Thy supreme rulership be merciful. The fear of Thy divinity implant in my heart. Give what

---

[8] Adapted from a translation by Sayce.
[9] Comp. Solomon's prayer, I Kings III. 6-9.

seemeth good to Thee, for Thou art He who hath granted
me life!   *604* B.C.

VIII

*Babylonian Prayer. In the month Nisan, on the second
day, two hours after nightfall, the priest must come and
take of the waters of the river and say this prayer:*

O BEL, who in His strength hath no equal! Blessed Sovereign, Lord of kings, Light of mankind, establisher of
faith! The wide heaven is Thy habitation!

O Lord, Thine is the revelation and interpretation of
visions, and the seeing of wisdom. O Lord of the world,
Light of the spirits of heaven, utterer of blessings, who
is there whose mouth doth not murmur of Thy righteousness, or speak of Thy glory, and celebrate Thy dominion?

O Lord of the world, who dwellest in the temple of the
Sun, reject not the hands that are raised to Thee; show
mercy to Thy city Babylon; grant the prayers of Thy
people the sons of Babylon!

IX

Babylonian Prayer to Ishtar.

O GODDESS of men, Goddess of women, Thou whose counsel none may learn, where Thy glance falleth, the dead
live, the sick are healed, the sore made whole, seeing
Thy face!

So I, Thy servant, in stress of sorrow sighing woe, cry
unto Thee! O my Lady, look on me, accept my prayer!

X

Egyptian Prayer from the Papyrus Anastasi.

THOU sole and only One, Thou God of the Horizon, like
whom there is none other, Protector of millions, Saviour
of hundreds of thousands, who shieldest him that crieth
to Thee, Thou Lord of Heliopolis!

Punish me not for my many transgressions. I am one
that knoweth not himself, I am a man without understanding. All day I follow after mine own dictates as the
ox followeth after his fodder.

13th or 12th cent., B.C.

XI

Prayer to Aton from the coffin of Akhnaton.

I INHALE the sweet breath that cometh forth from Thy
mouth, I behold Thy beauty every day. It is my desire
that I may hear Thy sweet voice, even the north wind,
that my limbs may be rejuvenated with life through love
of Thee.

Give me Thy hands, holding Thy spirit, that I may
receive it and live by it. Call Thou upon my name to
eternity, and it shall never fail.   *About 1358* B.C.

XII

Prayer from Œdipus the King, by Sophocles.

MAY it be mine, in every act and word of life, to preserve
the piety and purity ordained by those high laws of
which Olympus is the only Sire, whose birth was in the
sky above and nothing human gave them being. In them
is a divine power which groweth not old.

About 400 B.C.

XIII

Socrates' Prayer from the Phaedrus of Plato.

*Phaedrus and Socrates, seated beneath a spreading
plane-tree in a spot sacred to the gods, have been in rapt
discussion through the heat of the day.*

*Phaedrus: But let us depart, the rather as the heat of the
day is over. Socrates: Were it not better to offer up a
prayer to these gods before we go?*

BELOVED Pan, and all ye other gods that haunt this place,
grant me beauty in the inward soul, and that the out-

ward and the inward may be as one. May I esteem the wise to be the rich, and may I myself have that quantity of gold that a temperate man, and he only, can carry.

About 400 B.C.

XIV

Prayer for Peace by Aristophanes during the Peloponnesian War.

OH Thou that makest wars to cease in all the world, in accordance with Thine ancient name we beseech Thee, make war and tumult now to cease.

From the murmur and subtlety of suspicion with which we vex one another give us rest. Make a new beginning, and mingle again the kindred of the nations in the alchemy of Love, and with some finer essence of forbearance and forgiveness temper our mind! [10]

400 B.C.

XV

Lacedaemonian Prayer to Zeus.

GIVE us, O King Zeus, what is good, whether we pray for it or not; and avert from us the evil, even if we pray for it. *4th cent.* B.C.

XVI

Prayer to Zeus by Cleanthes the Stoic.

O THOU who hast many names, but whose power is infinite and uncommunicated! O Zeus, first of immortals, Sovereign of nature, who subjectest all to Thy law, I worship Thee; for man is permitted to invoke Thee.

Everything that lives or moves, everything mortal on earth is born of Thee, and of Thee but an imperfect image. I will address to Thee my hymns, and will never cease to celebrate Thee.

This universe expanded over our heads is obedient to Thee alone; at Thy command are its motions in silence

[10] Translation by Prof. Alex. Nairne.

performed. Thunder, the executioner of Thy will, is launched by Thine invincible arm. Endowed with immortal life, it strikes, and nature is appalled.

Thou directest the universal mind that animates the whole, and that exists in all thy creatures; so unlimited and supreme is Thy power, O King!

Nothing in heaven, on earth, or in the sea, is produced without Thee, except the evil that springs from the heart of the wicked. Thou bringest order out of confusion, and by Thee is the jarring of the elements composed.

O God! from whom all blessings descend, whom the storm and the thunder-cloud obey, preserve us from error; deign to inform our minds; attach us to that eternal reason by which Thou art guided and supported in the government of the world;

That being ourselves honoured, we may honour Thee, as becomes feeble and mortal beings, by celebrating Thy works in an uninterrupted hymn: for neither the inhabitant of earth nor the inhabitant of heaven can be engaged in a service more honourable than that of celebrating the Divine Mind which presides over Nature.

3rd cent. B.C.

XVII

Another Prayer by Cleanthes.

LEAD Thou me on, O Zeus! And Thou, O Destiny! Whithersoever Thou ordainest unflinching will I follow; but if from wicked heart I will it not, still I must follow!

XVIII

Prayer by Seneca.

WE worship and adore the Framer and Former of the universe; Governor, Disposer, Keeper; Him on whom all things depend; Mind and Spirit of the world; from whom all things spring; by whose spirit we live; the Divine Spirit diffused through all; God all-powerful; God al-

ways present; God above all other gods. Thee we worship
and adore.   *1st cent.* A.D.

XIX

Prayer by Simplicius the Neo-Platonist.

I SUPPLICATE, O Lord, that Thou wouldst wash away the
dust of our spirit-eyes, that we may know well both God
and man!   *About 529* A.D.

XX

Prayer by Mohammed, quoted by Muslim.

O GOD, I take refuge with Thee from laziness and from
the weakness of old age and from debt and from that
which causeth me to sin.

O God, verily I take refuge with Thee from the punishment of the fire and the calamity of the fire, and from the
calamity of the grave and the punishment of the grave,
and from the evil and seduction of riches, and from the
evil and affliction of poverty.

O God, wash my sins in snow-water and hail-water, and
purify my heart as a white garment is cleansed from
impurity, and place a distance between me and my sins
as Thou hast placed a distance between the East and the
West.   *About 632* A.D.

XXI

Aztec Prayer for A Chief.

O LORD, open his eyes and give him light; sharpen his
ears and give him understanding, not that he may use
them to his own advantage, but for the good of the
people he rules.

Lead him to know and to do Thy will, let him be a trum-
pet which sounds Thy words. Keep him from the com-
mission of injustice and oppression!

XXII

Prayer of the Ancient Peruvians.

O PACHAMAC, Thou who hast existed from the beginning and shalt exist to the end, powerful and pitiful, who createst man by saying: Let man be; who defendest us from evil and preservest our life and health; art Thou in the sky or in the earth, in the clouds or in the depths?

Hear the voice of him who implores Thee, and grant him his petitions. Give us life everlasting, preserve us, and accept this our sacrifice.

XXIII

Prayer of the Navajo Indians to the Mountain Spirit.

> Lord of the Mountain,
> Reared within the Mountain,
> Young man, Chieftain,
> Hear a young man's prayer!
> Hear a prayer for cleanness.
>
> Keeper of the strong rain,
> Drumming on the mountain;
> Lord of the small rain,
> That restores the earth in newness;
> Keeper of the clean rain,
> Hear a prayer for wholeness!
>
> Young man, Chieftain,
> Hear a prayer for fleetness,
> Keeper of the deer's way,
> Reared among the eagles,
> Clear my feet of slothness.
> Keeper of the paths of men,
> Hear a prayer for straightness!
>
> Hear a prayer for courage.
> Lord of the thin peaks,
> Reared amid the thunders;

Keeper of the headlands,
Holding up the harvest,
Keeper of the strong rocks,
Hear a prayer for staunchness!
Young man, Chieftain,
Spirit of the Mountain! [11]

XXIV

Prayer from the Omaha Ritual. When a child was born, on the eighth day after its birth, the priest took his place at the door of the tent in which it lay and intoned in a loud, ringing voice:

Ho! Ye Sun, Moon, Stars, all that move in the heavens, I bid you hear me! Into your midst hath come a new life. Consent ye, I implore! Make its path smooth, that it may reach the brow of the first hill!

Ho! Ye Winds, Clouds, Rain, Mist, all ye that move in the air, I bid you hear me! Into your midst hath come a new life. Consent ye, I implore! Make its path smooth, that it may reach the brow of the second hill!

Ho! Ye hills, Valleys, Rivers, Lakes, Trees, Grasses, all ye of the earth, I bid you hear me! Into your midst hath come a new life. Consent ye, I implore! Make its path smooth, that it may reach the brow of the third hill!

Ho! Ye birds, great and small, that fly in the air; ho, ye animals, great and small, that dwell in the forest; ho, ye insects that creep among the grasses and burrow in the ground, I bid you hear me! Into your midst hath come a new life. Consent ye, I implore! Make its path smooth, that it may reach the brow of the fourth hill!

Ho! All ye of the heavens, all ye of the air, all ye of the earth, I bid you all hear me! Into your midst hath come a new life. Consent ye all, I implore! Make its path smooth, then shall it travel beyond the four hills.[12]

[11] A re-expression of a Navajo prayer, by Mrs. Mary Austin.
[12] Transcribed by Alice C. Fletcher and Francis La Flesche, an Omaha Indian; 27th annual report of the American Bureau of Ethnology.

XXV

Prayer of a Winnebago Indian.

I PRAYED to Earthmaker. And as I prayed I was aware of something above me, and there He was! That which is called the soul, that is it, that is what one calls Earthmaker.

Now this is what I felt and saw. All of us sitting together there, we had all together one spirit and I was their spirit or soul. I did not have to speak to them and get an answer to know what had been their thoughts.

Then I thought of a certain place far away and immediately I was there; I was my thought. I would not need any more food, for was I not my spirit? Nor would I have any more use of my body. My corporeal affairs are over.[13]

[13] Crashing Thunder: *The Autobiography of an American Indian,* ed. by Paul Radin. D. Appleton & Co., New York.

THE BOOK OF ZARATHUSHTRA (ZOROASTER)

BEING SELECTIONS FROM THE PERSIAN AVESTA
AND THE DINA-I MAINOG-I KHIRAD

Now the Persians I know to have the following customs. They count it unlawful to set up images and shrines and altars, because as I suppose they have not conceived the gods to be of like nature with men, as the Greeks conceive them. But their custom is to ascend to the highest peaks of the mountains, and offer sacrifice to Zeus. . . . It is not permitted to him who sacrificeth to ask for good things for his own private use; but he maketh petition for good to befall the whole Persian people.

Herodotus, 490(?)-426(?) B.C.

Some call the better power God, and the other a daemon, as doth Zoroaster the Magus. And he affirmed, moreover, that the former did, of anything sensible, the most resemble light, and the other darkness and ignorance.

Plutarch, 50(?)-120(?) A.D.

We worship the rule and the guardian angel of Zarathushtra Spitama who first thought good thoughts, who first spake good words, who first performed good actions, who was the first priest, the first husbandman, the first prophet, the first who was inspired, the first who hath given to mankind nature and truth; who first praised the purity of the living creation and destroyed idolatry; who confessed the belief in Ahura Mazda. Through whom the whole true and revealed word was heard which is the life and guidance of the world, the praise of the righteousness which is the greatest, best, and most excellent. Through his knowledge and speech the waters and trees became desirous of growing; through his knowledge and speech all things created by the beneficent Spirit are uttering words of happiness.

Farvardin Yasht, Avesta.

THE BOOK OF ZARATHUSHTRA

The Avesta (Law or Revelation) is the Bible of Zara-
thushtra, an Iranian sage who lived about the sixth cen-
tury B.C.[1],—*a period which also gave to the world Con-*
fucius and Buddha and Socrates. It is the sacred book of
the Parsis, that is to say, of the few remaining followers
of the religion prevailing in Persia when the Sassanian
Dynasty was overthrown by the Mohammedans. Three
of its priests or Magi, the Christian gospel relates, were
among the first to offer homage to the Child Jesus in
Bethlehem.

The idea of God's attributes as His messengers sent to
the human soul to ennoble and redeem, and of the re-
wards of Heaven and punishments of Hell as FROM
WITHIN *had never till Zarathushtra came been uttered or*
conceived. But the great inspiration of Zoroastrianism
is its exaltation of Truth; and the follower of Zara-
thushtra was preëminent for truthfulness., all ancient
historians agree. Ahura Mazda (Ormazd) was the God
of Truth or Light, and the Evil Spirit, Angra Mainyu
(Ahriman) was the Demon of Lies.

I

WITH outspread hands in petition, O Lord, first of all
things I will pray for the works of the holy spirit, O
Thou the Right, whereby I may please the will of Good
Thought.

I who would serve Thee, O Omniscient Lord, do Thou
give through the Right the blessings of both worlds, the
bodily world and that of thought, which set the faithful
in felicity.

[1] Prof. A. V. Williams Jackson gives as the most probable dates of
Zoroaster 660-583 B. C., but other scholars have placed him as far back
as 1000, 1400, even 6000 B. C.

I who would praise Thee, as never before, Right and Good Thought, and Omniscient Lord, come Thou to my help at my call. I who have set my heart on watching over the souls of my people, in union with Good Thought, will, while I have power and strength, teach men to seek after Right.

Come Thou, give, O Lord, as Thy gift to Zarathushtra by Thy sure words, long-enduring help.

May we never provoke Thy wrath, we who have been eager in bringing Thee songs of praise.

The wise whom Thou knowest as worthy, for their right doing and their good thought, do thou fulfil their longing by attainment. For I know that words of prayer are effectual with Thee, when they tend to a good matter.[2]

Yasna XXVIII.

II

Zarathushtra standing before the sacred fire explaineth to the people the doctrine of the Good and Evil Spirits.

AND now I will proclaim, O ye who draw near seeking to be taught, the praises which are for Ahura and the worship of Good Thought and the exalted truth arising from these flames.

Hear ye then with your ears; with clear understanding perceive it! It is for a decision as to creeds, man by man, each for himself! Before the Great Consummation, awake ye all to our teaching!

Two Spirits primeval there were, each independent in action, to wit, the Good and the Evil, in thought, word, and deed. Between them may the wise distinguish aright!

When these twain at the first came together to make life and the absence of life, and ordain how the world hereafter shall be, to wit, for the wicked Hell, the Worst Life; for the righteous, Heaven, the Best Thought;

[2] Adapted from Moulton's version, *Early Religious Poetry of Persia*, University Press, Cambridge.

The Demon of Lies chose to do evil, but the Holiest Spirit, who doth clothe upon Himself the heavens as a robe, chose Righteousness.

Between these twain the Demons might not choose aright; for as they deliberated, Delusion came upon them, so that they chose the Worst Thought; and thereupon they rushed to Wrath that they might corrupt the life of Man.

And to Man came Sovereign Power, Good Thought and Righteousness,[3] and Aramaiti, Archangel of Earth, increasingly gave to him bodily endurance; of Thy creatures, when Thou camest with Thy creations, he was the first.

And when just vengeance shall have come upon the wicked, then shall Good Thought dispense for Thee Thy kingdom, shall fulfill it for those who shall deliver the Demon of the Lie into the two hands of Righteousness.

And may we be such as bring on this great renovation and cause this world to progress, and may Ahura Mazda and Righteousness lend us their aid, that our thoughts may there be set where true Wisdom abideth in her home.

Then shall the blow of destruction fall upon the Demon of the Lie; but swiftest in the happy home of Ahura and of Good Thought the righteous saints shall gather who proceed in their walk on earth in good repute.[4]

Yasna XXX.

---

[3] *Amesha-Spentas*: the Holy or Bountiful Immortals, Spirits of God; abstract conceptions, at first personifications of virtues and moral powers; but later each took a part of the world under his care. They were Righteousness, Good Thought, Sovereignty, Piety, Weal and Immortality. They were within the concept of God, not separate from it; the combination, therefore, has to be taken into account if we would realize what attributes were assigned to the Deity in Zoroastrianism. From these divine beings Zarathushtra received commands and injunctions which he was to convey to mankind.

[4] Compiled from the versions by Mills, Moulton, Haug and Jackson, the latter in the Library of the World's Best Literature. Copyright.

III

HE that in the beginning made through His inner light
the multitude of heavenly bodies, by His wisdom created
Right, which Thou dost glorify through Thy Spirit, O
Lord, who art evermore the same.

Therefore as the first did I conceive of Thee, O Lord!
As the One to praise with the soul, as the Father of the
Good Thought within us, when I beheld Thee with mine
eyes as the true Creator of Righteousness, as the Lord
of the actions of life!

Thine, O Lord, was Piety; yea, Thine was Understanding and the Spirit, when Thou hast made a path for her
guiding.[5]   *Yasna XXXI.*

RISE up for me, O Lord, through Piety give me strength,
through the holiest Spirit give might, through the Right
give mighty prowess, through Good Thought give the
reward.

As an offering Zarathushtra bringeth the life of his own
body, the choiceness of good thought, good action, and
speech unto the Lord.[6]   *Yasna XXXIII.*

WHAT reward Thou hast given to those of the same law
as Thyself, O Lord Omniscient, that give also to us for
this world and that beyond. May we attain to that,
namely, union with Thy purity to all eternity.[7]
Yasna Haptanhaiti

WE worship the Lord Omniscient, the righteous Master
of Righteousness. We worship the Holy Immortals, pos-
sessors of good, givers of good. We worship the whole
creation of the Righteous Spirit, both the spiritual and
the earthly, all that supporteth the welfare of the good
creation.

[5] Compiled from versions by Mills, Moulton and Haug.
[6] Adapted from Moulton's version.   [7] Spiegel's version.

We praise all good thoughts, all good words, all good deeds which are and hereafter will be, and we likewise keep clean and pure all that is good.

O Omniscient Lord, Thou righteous happy Being! We strive to think, to speak, and to do only what may best promote the life of body and of soul.

We beseech the Spirit of the Earth by means of our tilling of the soil to grant us beautiful and fertile fields, to the unbeliever as well as to the believer.[8] *Yasna XXXV.*

Thus we worship the Lord Omniscient, who created the Spirit of the Earth and Righteousness, and who created the good waters and trees, and the splendours of light, and the earth and all good things.

We worship Him with our bodies and our souls. We worship Him as being united with the spirits of righteous men and women.

We worship Righteousness, the all-good, all that is very excellent, beneficent, immortal, illustrious,—everything that is good.[8]   *Yasna XXXVII.*

IV

I announce and will complete my worship [9] of Ahura Mazda, the Creator, the radiant and glorious, the greatest and the best, the most beautiful, the wisest, the most firm; who attaineth His ends the most infallibly, because of His Righteous Order; to Him who disposeth our minds aright, who sendeth afar His joy-creating grace; who made us and fashioned us, hath nourished and protected us, who is the most bounteous Spirit!

I announce and complete my worship of Good Thought, of Righteousness the Best, of Sovereignty which is to be desired, of Piety the Bountiful, and of universal Weal and Immortality.

And I announce and complete my worship of these places and these lands, these pastures and these abodes with

---

[8] Adapted from Haug's version.   [9] *Yasna,* worship with sacrifice.

their springs of water, and of these plants and of this
earth and yonder heaven, and of the holy wind, and of
the sun, moon and stars,—the eternal stars without beginning, self-disposing; and of all the holy creatures of
the Holy Spirit.

If I have by thought, word, or deed offended Thee,
whether by act of will, or without intent, I earnestly
atone for this by praise to Thee.[10]   *Yasna I.*

V

THIS I ask Thee, O Lord! tell me aright, how in pleasing
Him may we serve the Supreme One of the better world;
yea, how to serve that Chief who may grant us those
blessings of His grace, for He, bountiful as He is, will
hold off ruin from us all, guardian for both the worlds,
O Spirit Mazda and Friend!

This I ask Thee, O Lord! tell me aright; Who in the
beginning was the creator and father of Truth? Who
shewed the sun and stars their undeviating way? Who
caused the moon to wax and wane, save Thee?

Who from beneath hath upheld the earth and the clouds
above that they should not fall? Who made the waters
and trees of the field? Who is in the winds and storms,
that they so quickly run? Who, O Great Creator! is the
inspirer of good thoughts?

Who as a skilful artisan hath made the light and the
dark? Who created sleep and the zest of the waking
hours? Who spread the Auroras, the noontides and mid-
night, that call the discerning to their duties?

This I ask Thee, O Lord! tell me aright: Who fashioned
Piety the Beloved? Who through his guiding wisdom
hath begot the love of father and of son?

Tell me aright that holy Faith which is of all things best,
and which going hand in hand with Thy people shall
render actions just. My heart desireth to know Thee, O

[10] Adapted from Mills' version.

Lord! How to these Thy worshippers may that Piety once and evermore approach? Yea, I beseech Thee, tell me this, who am known as the foremost of Thy servants.

Yasna XLIV.

VI

AHURA MAZDA *spake* unto Spitama [11] Zarathushtra, saying: Do thou proclaim, O pure Zarathushtra, the vigour and strength, the glory, the help and the joy that are in the souls [12] of the faithful, the awful and overpowering souls of the dead!

Through their brightness and glory, O Zarathushtra, I maintain that sky above, shining and seen afar, encompassing the earth.

It looketh like a palace, that standeth built of heavenly substance, firmly established, with ends that lie afar; it is like a garment decked with stars that Mazda putteth on; on no side can the eye perceive the end thereof.

Through their brightness and glory, O Zarathushtra, I maintain the wide earth that beareth the high mountains, rich in pastures and waters; upon which run the many streams and rivers; upon which the many kinds of plants grow to nourish men and beasts, to nourish the Aryan nations, to help the faithful.

Through their brightness and glory the waters flow from the never-failing springs; the plants grow up from the earth by the never-failing springs; the winds do blow, driving down the clouds towards the never-failing springs.

Through their brightness and glory, O Zarathushtra, I maintain in the womb the child that hath been conceived, so that it dieth not; and I develop in it the bones; through their brightness and glory the mothers bring forth in safety and become blessed with children.

---

[11] His clan name.

[12] *Fravashis:* the protecting powers that maintain all beings; the everlasting and deified souls of the dead, believed to be angels stationed everywhere by Ahura to preserve the good creation.

Through their brightness and glory a man is born who is a chief in assemblies and meetings, who listeneth well to the holy words, whom Wisdom holdeth dear.

Through their brightness and glory the sun goeth his way, the moon her way and the stars go on their path.[13]

Farvardin Yasht.

VII

I PRAISE, invoke and weave my hymn to the good, heroic, and bountiful souls of the saints.

And having invoked them hither, we worship the good, heroic souls of the Bountiful Immortals, the brilliant, of effective glance, the lofty, the devoted, the swift ones of the creatures of Ahura who are imperishable and holy.

And having invoked them hither, we worship the spirit and conscience, the intelligence and soul of those lofty men and women who early heard the lore and commands of God, and loved and strove after righteousness.[14]

Yasna XXVI.

VIII

PRAYER FOR A DWELLING

MAY the good and heroic and bountiful souls [15] of the saints come here, and may they go hand in hand with us with the healing virtues of their blessed gifts as widespread as the earth, as far-spread as the rivers, as high-reaching as the sun; for the furtherance of better men, for the hindrance of the hostile, and for the abundant growth of riches and glory.

May obedience conquer disobedience within this house; may peace triumph over discord here, and generous giving over avarice, reverence over contempt, truthful speech over lying utterance. May Truth gain the victory over the Demon of the Lie.

---

[13] Adapted from Darmesteter's version.
[14] Adapted from Mills' version.   [15] *Fravashis.* See note 12, p. 111.

In order that our minds may be delighted, and our souls be the best, let our bodies be glorified as well; and O Mazda, may we see Thee, and may we, approaching, come round about Thee, and attain to entire companionship with Thee! And we sacrifice to the Righteous Order, the best, the most beautiful, the bounteous Immortal! [16]

Yasna LX.

IX

ZARATHUSHTRA asked Ahura Mazda: O Omniscient Lord, most beneficent Spirit, Maker of the material world, Thou Holy One!

What of the Holy Word is the strongest? What is the most glorious and victorious? What is the most effective?

Ahura Mazda answered: Our name, O Spitama Zarathushtra! That is the strongest part of the Holy Word; that is the most glorious and victorious; that is the most effective.

Then Zarathushtra said: Reveal unto me that name of Thine, O Omniscient Lord!

Ahura Mazda answered unto him: My name is I AM,[17] O Holy Zarathushtra! My name is Perfect Holiness, Understanding, Knowledge. My name is He who produceth weal, the Unconquerable One, He who maketh the true account, the All-Seeing, the Healing One.

Worship me, O Zarathushtra, by day and by night, with offerings of libations well-accepted. I will come unto thee for help and joy, I, Ahura Mazda.

I am the Keeper; I am the Creator and Maintainer; I am the Discerner; I am the most beneficent Spirit.

My name is the Bestower of Health. My name is the Glorious, the Most Glorious. My name is the Word of Prosperity, the King who ruleth at his will.

These are My names.

And he who in this material world, O Spitama Zarathushtra, shall recite and pronounce these names of Mine

[16] Adapted from the rendering by Mills.   [17] Comp. Exodus III. 14.

either by day or by night; when he riseth up or when he layeth him down; when he layeth him down or when he riseth up;

That man, neither in that day nor night, shall be wounded by the weapons of the foe; not the knife, nor the cross-bow, not the arrow, nor the sword, nor the sling-stone shall reach and wound him.

But those names shall come in to keep him from before and behind from the evil-doer bent on mischief, and from that fiend who is all death, Angra Mainyu. It will be as if there were a thousand men watching over one.[18]

Ormazd Yasht.

X

WITH these words Ahura Mazda rejoiced the holy Zara-thushtra: Purity is for man, next to life, the greatest good, that purity which is procured by the law of Mazda to him who cleanseth his own self with good thoughts, words, and deeds.

As much above all other floods as is the sea, and as a great stream floweth swifter than a slender rivulet; as high as the tall tree standeth above the small plants it doth overshadow and as heaven is above the earth it doth encompass round, so high above all other utterances in greatness, goodness, and fairness, is this law, this fiend-destroying law.   *Fargard V, Vendidad.*

THE will of the Lord is the law of holiness.

Haptan Yasht.

ONE may heal with holiness, one may heal with the Law, one may heal with the Holy Word. This it is that will best drive away sickness from the body of the faithful; for this is the best of remedies.[19]   *Ardihehisht Yasht.*

THE Law of Mazda will not deliver thee unto pain. Thou art entreated for charity by the whole of the living

---

[18] Adapted from the rendering by Darmesteter. Comp. Ps. XCI, Old Testament.   [19] Comp. the doctrine of the Christian Scientists.

world, and she is ever standing at thy door in the person
of thy brethren in the faith; beggars are ever standing
at the door of the stranger begging bread. Ever will that
bread refused be burning coal upon thy head! [20]

Vishtasp Yasht.

XI

ZARATHUSHTRA asked Ahura Mazda: O Lord Omniscient,
most munificent Spirit, Maker of the material world,
Thou Holy One! When one of the faithful departeth this
life, where dwelleth his soul on that night?

Then said Ahura Mazda: It taketh its seat near the head,
singing and proclaiming bliss: Happy is he, happy the
man, whoever he be, to whom Ahura Mazda giveth the
full accomplishment of his wishes! On that night his soul
tasteth as much of joy as the whole of the living world
can taste.

At the passing of the third night, as the dawn appeareth,
it seemeth to the soul of the faithful one as if it were
brought amidst plants and scents; it seemeth as if a wind
were blowing from the region of the south, a sweet-
scented wind, sweeter-scented than any other in the
world.

And it seemeth to the soul of the faithful one as if he
inhaled that wind, and he thinketh: Whence bloweth that
wind, the sweetest-scented I ever inhaled?

And it seemeth to him as if there advanced in that wind
the shape of a maiden bright, white-armed, well-grown,
erect, noble, of glorious seed, as fair as the fairest things
in the world.

And the soul of the faithful one spake to her, saying:
What maid art thou, who art the fairest maid I have ever
seen?

And she answered him: O thou youth of good thoughts,
good words, and good deeds, I am thine own conscience!
Everyone did love thee for that greatness, goodness, fair-

---

[20] Adapted from Darmesteter's version.

ness, sweet-scentedness, victorious strength and freedom from sorrow, in which thou dost appear to me;

And so thou didst love me for that greatness, goodness, fairness, sweet-scentedness, victorious strength, and freedom from sorrow in which I appear to thee.

I was lovely and thou madest me lovelier still; I was fair and thou madest me yet fairer; I was desirable and thou madest me still more desirable through this good thought, through this good speech, through this good deed of thine.

The first step that the soul of the faithful man made, placed him in the Good-Thought Paradise; the second step placed him in the Good-Word Paradise; the third step placed him in the Good-Deed Paradise; the fourth step that the soul of the faithful man made placed him among the Eternal Lights.[22]   *Yasht XXII.*

LET us embrace and propagate the good thoughts, good words and deeds that have been done and will be done here and elsewhere, that we may be of the number of the good!   *Afrin Paighambar Zartusht.*

XII

HAIL unto Thee, Atar, son of Ahura Mazda! Give me, O Atar, fullness of life; knowledge, sagacity, holiness of soul, and the understanding that groweth ever and is not acquired through learning; and manly courage, firm-footed, unsleeping, quick to rise up from bed, ever awake.
                                        Atash Nyayish.

WE sacrifice unto the bright and glorious Ahura Mazda; we sacrifice unto Peace, whose breath is friendly, and who is more powerful to destroy than all other creatures. We sacrifice unto the heavenly Wisdom, made by Mazda; we sacrifice unto Mercy and Charity.

[22] Adapted from Darmesteter's version.

We sacrifice unto all waters, made by Mazda and holy; we sacrifice unto all plants, made by Mazda and holy. We sacrifice unto the bright, undying, shining, swift-horsed Sun. We sacrifice unto the true-spoken speech that maketh the world to grow. We sacrifice unto the beneficent, bounteous Wind. We sacrifice unto manly Courage. We sacrifice unto the shining Heavens. We sacrifice unto the bright, all-happy abode of the holy ones.

We sacrifice unto the Earth, a beneficent God; we sacrifice unto these places, unto these fields; we sacrifice unto all the mountains that are seats of holy happiness, of full happiness, made by Mazda.

We sacrifice unto the eternal and sovereign luminous space, we sacrifice unto the sovereign place of eternal Weal.[23]   *Sirozah II.*

Selections from the Dina-i Mainog-i Khirad, the Opinions of the Spirit of Wisdom (580-599 A.D.), one of the Persian scriptures based upon the Avesta, written in Pahlavi, the mediæval form of the Persian language.

Hɪᴍ who is less than thee consider as an equal, and an equal as a superior.

Indulge thee not in wrathfulness; for when a man indulgeth in wrath he becometh then forgetful of his duty and good works, of prayer and the service of the sacred beings; and sin and crime of every kind occur to his mind; and until the subsiding of his wrath, he may be said to be like Ahriman.

Suffer no anxiety; for he who is a sufferer of anxiety becometh contracted in body and soul, and regardless of enjoyment of the world and spirit.

Thou shouldst not be too much arranging the world; for the world-arranging man becometh spirit-destroying.

[23] Adapted from Darmesteter's version.

Thou shouldst not become presumptuous through much treasure and wealth; for it is necessary for thee to leave all in the end.

Thou shouldst not become presumptuous through great connections and race; for in the end thy trust is in thine own deeds.

Thou shouldst not become presumptuous through life; for death cometh upon thee at the last, and the perishable part falleth to the ground.   *Chapter II, 4-113.*

THE pleasures which are superior to all pleasures are health of body, freedom from fear, good repute and righteousness.   *Chapter XIV, 14.*

To live in fear and falsehood is worse than death.
        Chapter XIX, 3.

POVERTY which is through honesty is better than opulence which is from the treasure of others.   *Chapter XV, 3.*

THE sage asked the Spirit of Wisdom: How is it possible to make Ahura Mazda, the archangels, and the fragrant, well-pleasing heaven more fully for oneself?

The Spirit of Wisdom answered thus: When they make the spirit of wisdom a protection for the back, and wear the spirit of contentment on the body, like arms and armour and valour, and make the spirit of truth a shield, the spirit of thankfulness a club, the spirit of complete-mindfulness a bow, and the spirit of liberality an arrow; the spirit of moderation a spear, the spirit of perseverance a gauntlet, and put forth the spirit of destiny as a protection. In this manner it is possible to come to heaven and the sight of the sacred beings.
        Chapter XLIII, 1-4.

THE sage asked the Spirit of Wisdom: Which is that good work which is greater than all good works?

The Spirit of Wisdom answered thus: To be grateful in the world, and to wish happiness to every one. This is greater and better than every good work, and no commotion whatever is necessary for its performance.[24]

Chapter LXIII, 1-6.

[24] After the translation by E. W. West.

THE CONFUCIAN CANON

BEING SELECTIONS FROM THE SHU-KING, THE SHI-KING, THE YI-KING, THE LI-CHI, THE HSIAO KING, THE ANALECTS OF CONFUCIUS, THE DOCTRINE OF THE MEAN, THE GREAT LEARNING, AND THE WRITINGS OF MENCIUS

I am a transmitter and not an originator, one who be-lieves in and loves the ancients. . . . Simply a man who in his eager pursuit of knowledge forgets to eat, whose joy in this pursuit is such that he forgets his troubles and does not perceive that old age is coming upon him. I am not one who was born in the possession of knowledge; I am one who is fond of antiquity and earnest in the study of it. Confucius, The Analects, Book VII.

Confucius said: The flowing progress of virtue is more rapid than the transmission of imperial orders by stage and courier.

Since there were living men until now, there never was another Confucius.

Mencius, Kung-Sun Ch'ou, I.

THE CONFUCIAN CANON

Confucius (Latinized form of Kung-fu-tzu, Holy Master Kung), the Teacher of Ten Thousand Ages (551-479 B.C.), established the system of morality which became the basis of Chinese politics, jurisprudence, and education, and has been for almost twenty-five hundred years the dominant influence in the lives of a fourth of the human race.

The following excerpts are from the Classical Books of China, known as the Five King, revised and edited by Confucius; from the Hsiao-King, attributed in part to Confucius; and from the remaining works of the Confucian Canon known as the Four Books, i.e., the Analects, the Great Learning, the Doctrine of the Mean, and the Works of Mencius, all compiled by disciples of the Master, carrying on his doctrine and often recording his very words. None of the Books of the Confucian Canon profess to be inspired, nor do they contain any system of theology or inculcate the worship of any god.

THE SHU-KING

The Shu-King (The Book of Records) deals with the history of China from the twenty-fourth to the seventh century before Christ, and from the twenty-second century down it is contemporaneous with the events which it describes. The speeches of the sovereigns and sages with which it abounds are marked by a comparatively mature knowledge and an advanced ethical culture.

THE Emperor said: Hsieh,[1] the people are still wanting in affection for one another, and do not docilely observe

---

[1] The names in the Chinese Classics are written in a variety of ways. In these selections the Peking pronunciation has been chosen as the standard, and the Wade system of transliteration.

the five precepts [2] of relationship. Be thou the Minister of Instruction, and reverently and with gentleness further the five virtues.

K'wei, I appoint you to be Director of Music, and to teach our sons, so that the straightforward shall yet be mild; the gentle dignified; the strong not tyrannical; the impetuous not arrogant.

Poetry is the expression of feeling; singing is the prolonged utterance of that expression. The notes should accord with the measure; the reed regulates the voice and the eight instruments, and you must harmonize them all. In this way spirits and men are brought into accord.

The Canon of Shun.

Do NOT *fail* to observe the laws and ordinances. Find not your enjoyment in idleness, nor go to excess in pleasure. In your employment of men of worth let none come betwixt you and them.

Put away evil without hesitation. Study that all your purposes may be with the light of reason. Go not against the right to get the praise of the people. Oppose not the people's wishes to follow your own desires.

The virtue of the ruler is seen in his good government, that government in the nourishing of the people. Caution them with gentleness, correct them with the majesty of the law, that your success may not suffer diminution.

The Emperor said to Yu, about to assume the administration: The mind of man is restless, prone to err. Be discriminating, uniform in the pursuit of right, that you may sincerely hold fast to the Mean. Do not listen to unsubstantiated words, do not follow plans about which you have not sought counsel.

Of all who are to be loved, is not the ruler the chief? Of all who are to be feared, are not the people the chief? The multitude being without their sovereign Head, whom

---

[2] Regulating the conduct of (1) parents and children, (2) rulers and subjects, (3) masters and men, (4) husbands and wives, (5) friends and associates.

should they sustain aloft? The sovereign being without subjects, who shall defend the country?

Yi said: Only virtue can compel Heaven;[3] there is no distance to which It does not reach. Pride brings loss, and humility receives increase; this is the way of Heaven.
The Counsels of the Great Yu.

CHUNG-HUI, Minister of the Emperor Tang, said: Show favour to the able and right-principled, and encourage the virtuous; distinguish the loyal, and let the good have free course. Absorb the weak and suppress the head-strong.

Exert yourself, O King, to illustrate the highest virtue, and set up before the people the standard of the Mean. Order your affairs by righteousness; and your heart by propriety; so shall you transmit a grand example to succeeding generations.

He who finds instructors for himself, shall prevail; he who likes to question, becomes enlarged. He who would take care for the end must be attentive to the beginning. To revere and honour the Path prescribed by Heaven is the way ever to preserve Its favour.
The Announcement of Chung-Hui.

I YIN said for the instruction of the young king: Of old the kings earnestly cultivated their virtue, and there were no calamities from heaven. Now your Majesty is entering on the inheritance of his virtue; all depends on how you begin your reign.

To set up love, it is for you to love; to establish respect, it is for you to respect. The commencement is in the family and the state; the consummation in all four seas.

Be but virtuous, in small things as in large, and the myriad regions will rejoice. *The Instructions of I.*

---

[3] The term *Heaven* is used in the Chinese Classics for the Supreme Power ruling the affairs of men with an omnipotent righteousness, and is constantly interchanged in the same sentence with *Ti* and *Shang Ti*, the personal names for God.

WITHOUT the sovereign, the people cannot have the guidance necessary to their lives; without the people, the sovereign can have no sway over the four quarters.

The king did obeisance with his face to his hands and his head on the ground, saying: I, the little child, was without understanding of what was virtuous, and was making myself one of the unworthy.

By my desires I was setting at nought all rules of conduct, and violating by my self-indulgence all rules of propriety. Calamities sent by Heaven may be avoided, but from calamities brought on one's self there is no escape.

I Yin said: The former king was kind to the distressed and suffering, as were they his children, and the people submitted to his commands with sincere delight. O King, regard the example of your illustrious grandfather!

In worshipping your ancestors, think how to prove your filial piety; receiving your ministers, think how to show yourself respectful; in looking at what is distant, try to get clear views; have your ears ever open to lessons of virtue; then shall I acknowledge the excellence of your Majesty with untiring devotion.

Only to the reverent does Heaven show affection. If you would ascend on high, esteem yourself lowly. If you would attain to˙the far-off, take care for your first steps.

Do not slight the occupations of the people nor disregard their difficulties. Do not yield to a feeling of repose on your throne; think of its perils!

When you hear counsel distasteful to your mind, enquire whether it be not right. When you hear advice agreeable to your inclinations, enquire whether it be not contrary to the right.

Let but the One man be greatly good, and the myriad regions through him will be perfected! *The T'ai chia.*

Now, O young King, you who are newly entering on your great appointment, you should be seeking to make new your virtue. At last, as at first, have this as your one object, so shall you make a daily renovation.

Let the officers whom you employ be men of virtue and ability, and the ministers about you be true men. The minister, in relation to his sovereign, has to promote his virtue, and in relation to the people, he has to promote their good.

There is no invariable model of virtue; a supreme regard for what is good gives the model of it. There is no invariable characteristic of the good; it is found where there is conformity to the uniform consciousness.

The sovereign without subjects has none whom he can employ; the people without the sovereign have none whom they can serve. Do not think yourself so large as to deem others small. If the subjects do not find opportunity to develop their ability, the people's lord will be without the proper aids to complete his merit.

The Common Possession of Virtue.

THE Emperor P'an-Keng said: Oh, ye chiefs of regions, ye heads of departments, all ye hundreds of officers, would that ye had sympathy with my people! Do ye think reverently of my multitudes!

I will not employ those who love wealth, but will use and revere those who are vigourously, yet reverently, labouring for the lives and increase of the people, nourishing them and planning for their security.

Seek not to accumulate wealth and treasure, but in fostering the life of the people find your merit. For ever cherish this one purpose in your hearts. *The P'an-Keng.*

THE King made Yueh his prime minister, keeping him at his side. He charged him, saying: Morning and evening present your instructions to aid my virtue.

Suppose me a weapon of steel, I will use you for a whetstone. Suppose me crossing a great stream, I will use you for a boat. Suppose me in a year of drought, I will

use you as a copious rain. Open your mind and enrich
my heart. Be you like medicine which must distress in
order to cure.

Do you and your companions all cherish the same mind
to assist your sovereign, that I may tread in the steps
of my high ancestor and give repose to the multitudes of
this my people.

Yueh replied to the King, saying: Wood by the use of
the line is made straight, and the sovereign who follows
reproof is made sage; who would dare not to act in com-
pliance with this excellent charge of your Majesty?

Yueh, having received his charge, presented himself before the King, and said: It is Heaven which is all-intelli-
gent and observing; let the King take It as his pattern.
Indulging the consciousness of being good, one loses his
goodness; esteeming oneself able, one is bereft of merit.

For all affairs let there be adequate preparation, and
you will not be confounded. Do not be ashamed of your
mistakes and go on to make them crimes. Let the mind
rest in its proper objects, and the affairs of your government will be pure.

The King said: Excellent! Oh Yueh, if you were not so
good in counsel, I should not have heard anything to put
into action.

Yueh did obeisance with his head to the ground, and
said: It is not the knowing that is difficult, but the doing.
The Charge to Yueh.

GREAT Heaven has no predilections: It allies Itself to the
virtuous. The people's hearts have no unchanging attachment; they cherish only the kind.

Seek to be in harmony with your neighbors. Live in amity
with your brethren. Tranquillize and help the lower
people. Do not, affecting illumination, throw old statutes
into confusion.

Even the wise through not thinking may effect a folly;
and the foolish by reflecting become wise.
The Numerous Regions.

THE King said to Chun-chen: Be reverent! Use not your power to exercise oppression; nor the laws to practise extortion. Be gentle, but with strictness of rule. Promote harmony by the display of easy forbearance.

Seek the due middle course. Those who are disobedient to your government and uninfluenced by your instructions, you will punish, remembering that the end of punishment is to make an end of punishing.

Cherish not anger against the obstinate, and dislike. Seek not for perfection in any individual. Have patience, and you will be successful. Advance the good, to induce those who may not be so to follow their example. Do you but reverently observe the statutes, and the people will be found in the way of virtue.   *The Chun-Chen.*

THE King said: Ah, you who direct the government and preside over criminal cases through all the land, are you not constituted the shepherds of Heaven? Reverently apportion the five punishments. It is yours to give to the people repose.

In settling the cases these evils are to guard against; being warped by the influence of power, or private grudge or female solicitation; or by bribes or applications.

In everything stand in awe of the dread majesty of Heaven. With compassion and reverence settle the cases. I think with reverence of the subject of punishment, for its end is to promote virtue.

Now Heaven, wishing to help the people, has made us Its representatives here below. The right ordering of the people depends on the impartial hearing of the pleas on both sides of a case; do not seek for private advantage by means of those pleas; you should ever stand in awe of the punishment of Heaven.

Marquis of Lu on Punishments.

I HAVE deeply thought and concluded: Let me have but one resolute minister dispassionately faithful, without other ability, but exceedingly upright and possessed of generosity; regarding the talents of others as were they his own; who seeing men of surpassing wisdom could love them in his heart more than his mouth might express; such a minister would be able to preserve my descendants and people, and would indeed be a giver of benefits. The decline and fall of a state may arise from a single man. The glory and tranquillity of a state may also arise from the goodness of one man.[4]

The Speech of Ch'in.

The Shi-King

Of the Shi-King (The Book of Odes, 1766-586 B.C.) Confucius said: It is by the Odes that the mind is aroused, and from Music that the finish is received. It is generally believed that the Master revised the collection of ballads which already existed in the archives of the sovereign State of Chow, and, omitting those he considered unworthy, formed the extant edition of three hundred and five pieces.

Let me be reverent! Let me be reverent! Let me not say that Heaven is high aloft above me. It ascends and descends about our doings; It daily inspects us wherever we are. *Sacrificial Odes of Chou, the Ching Chih.*

Great Heaven is intelligent and is with you in all your goings. Great Heaven is clear-seeing and is with you in all your wanderings. *The Major Odes, The Pan.*

Be cautious of what you say; be reverentially careful of your outward behaviour; in all things mild and correct. A flaw in a mace of white jade may be ground away; but for a flaw in speech nothing can be done.

Do not speak lightly; words are not to be cast away. Every word finds its answer; every good deed its recompense.

[4] The above selections from the Shu-King are after the translations by James Legge and Walter Old.

In friendly intercourse with the finest men, you make your countenance harmonious and mild, anxious to do nothing wrong. In your chamber you should be equally free from shame before the light shining in. Do not say, This place is not public, none can see me here. The approaches of spiritual beings cannot be foretold, but all the more they should not be disregarded.

The Major Odes, the Yi.

THE YI-KING

No portion of the Yi-King (The Book of Changes) is older than 1237 B.C., the time of King Wen, he with his famous son the Duke of Chou being the accepted authors. The Appendices, from which these selections are chiefly taken, are six or seven centuries later and frequently quote Confucius' words.

THOSE who multiply good deeds will have joys to overflowing. *The Moaning Winds, Hexigram VII.*

THE Master said: Words and actions are the hinge and spring of the superior man.[5] The movement of that hinge and spring determines glory or disgrace. His words and actions move heaven and earth; may he be careless in regard to them? *Appendix III, Section I, Chapter VIII.*

THE influence of the world would work no change in him; he would do nothing to secure mere fame. He can live withdrawn from the world without regret, suffer reproach without dismay. Rejoicing in opportunity, he carries his principles into action; sorrowing for lack thereof, he holds them in reserve. Nor is he to be torn from his root.

[5] *Chun tzu,* the Chinese term translated as the *perfect,* the *princely,* or the *superior man,* is defined by a Chinese scholar as follows: One who develops in mind, but keeps the heart of childhood; who never feels himself perfect, but tries to be as perfect as possible; who never thinks himself superior to others, but looks to others for something superior to enlighten himself.

He is sincere in his most trivial words, earnest in his every act. He advances in virtue through his leal-heartedness and faith. He holds a high position without pride, a low position without embarrassment.

The great man is in harmony, in his attributes, with heaven and earth; in his brightness, with the sun and moon; in his orderly procedure, with the four seasons; in his relation to what is fortunate or calamitous, with the spiritual operations of Providence. He may precede Heaven, but It will not act in opposition to him; he may follow Heaven, but he will act not otherwise than It.

Appendix IV, Section I, ii. vi.

The Li Chi

The Li Chi (Collection of Treatises on the Rules of Propriety or Ceremonial Usages) goes back in its present form only to 206 B.C., though similar collections existed also in Confucius' time.

THE parrot can speak, yet is nothing more than a bird; the ape can speak, yet is nothing more than a beast. A man who observes no rules of propriety, is not his heart that of a beast? Therefore when the sages arose, they framed the rules of propriety to teach men to make a distinction between themselves and brutes.

Chu Li, Sect. I, Part I.

WHEN the Great Way is followed, the world belongs to all. Only the ablest and wisest are chosen to govern, that harmony may be promoted among men.

Men will love not only their own parents and hold their own children dear, but they will see that all the old are comforted, the able-bodied employed, the young educated, the invalid, orphan and bereft cared for, man given his occupation, woman her home.

Resources will not be left unutilized in the earth, nor worked for personal gain. Capacity will not go undeveloped, nor will it be exerted for one's own advantage merely.

This done, without government intervention, there will be no thefts nor insurrections, no need to close the door at night. This we call the Great Coalition.
The Li Yun, Sect. I.

PROPRIETY and righteousness are the great elements of a man's character!; by means of them his speech becomes the expression of truth, and his intercourse with others the promotion of harmony.

They are like the binding together of the muscles and bones in strengthening the body. They supply the channels by which we can apprehend the ways of Heaven and act as the feelings of men require.

Therefore the sage kings fashioned the lever of righteousness and ceremonial usages to regulate the feelings of men. Those feelings were the field, they fashioned the rules of ceremony to plough it. They set forth the principles of righteousness with which to plant it. They instituted the lessons of the school to weed it. They made love the fundamental subject by which to gather all its fruits, and used music to give repose.

Thus rules of ceremony are the embodied expression of what is right. Humanity is the root of right. The possessor of it is honoured. *The Li Yun, Sect. IV.*

THE rules of propriety serve as instruments to form men's character. They remove from a man all perversity, and increase what is beautiful in his nature. They are to him what their outer coating is to bamboos, what its heart is to a pine or cyprus.

A true heart and good faith are their radical element without which they could not have been established; without their outward and elegant form, they could not have been put into practice. *The Li Ch'i, Sect. I.*

ALWAYS and in everything let there be reverence; with the deportment grave as when one is thinking deeply, with speech composed and definite. This will make the people tranquil.

Pride should not be allowed to grow; the desires should not be indulged; the will should not be gratified to the full, nor pleasure be carried to excess. When you find wealth within your reach, do not get it by improper means. Do not seek for victory in small contentions.

One should not seek to please in an improper way, nor be lavish of words, nor encroach on or despise others, nor be fond of familiarity. Propriety is seen in humbling one's self and giving honour to others.

Chu Li, Sect. I, Part I.

FOR all sons it is the rule, in winter to warm the bed for their parents, and to cool it in summer; in the evening to adjust everything for their repose, and to enquire about their health in the morning.

When two men are sitting or standing together, do not join them as a third.   *Chu Li, Sect. I, Part II.*

THE rites of mourning are the extreme expression of grief and sorrow. Calling the soul back is the way love receives its consummation; it has in it the mind expressed in prayer.

That the bones and the flesh should return to the earth is what is appointed. But the soul in its energy can go everywhere; it can go everywhere!

The T'an Kung, Sect. II, Parts I & III.

THE filial piety taught by the ancient kings required that the eyes of the son should not forget the looks of his parents, nor his ears their voices; and that he should retain the memory of their aims, and wishes.

As he gave full play to his love, they seemed to live again; and to his reverence, they seemed to stand before him. So seeming to live and stand, so unforgotten by him, how could his sacrifices be without the accompaniment of reverence? *Chi I, Sect. I.*

SACRIFICE is not a thing that comes to a man from without; it issues from within, and has its birth in his heart. When the heart is deeply moved, expression is given to it by ceremonies. *Chi T'ung, I.*

By the united action of heaven and earth all things spring up. Thus the ceremony of marriage is the beginning of a line that shall last for a myriad ages.

There must be a sincerity in the marriage presents; and all communications to the woman must be good. She should be admonished to be upright and sincere. Faithfulness is requisite in all service to others, and faithfulness is the virtue of the wife. Once mated with her husband, all her life she will not change, and when her husband dies, she will not marry again.

The Chiao Te Seng, Sect. III.

THE kings of Yin made their solemn proclamations, yet the people began to rebel; those of Chou made their covenants, and the people distrusted them. If there be not the heart of righteousness, self-consecration, good faith, and guilelessness, though a leader try to knit the people firmly to him, will not all bonds between them be dissolved? *The T'an Kung, Sect. II, Part III.*

WHEN the ruler of the people loves them as his sons, they feel to him as to a parent; when he binds them to him by good faith, they do not turn away; when he presides over them with courtesy, their hearts are docile to him.

The Master said: To the people the ruler is as their heart; to the ruler the people are as his body. When the heart is composed, the body is at ease; when the heart is reverent, the body is respectful; when the heart loves anything, the body is sure to rest in it.

So, when the ruler loves anything, the people too desire it. The body is the complement of the heart; a wound in it makes the heart suffer also. So the ruler is preserved by the people, and perishes also through the people.

Szu I, 3 & 17.

In passing by the side of Mount T'ai, Confucius came on a woman who was wailing bitterly by a grave. The Master bowed forward to the cross-bar,[6] and hastened to her: Your wailing, said he, is altogether like that of one who has suffered sorrow upon sorrow.

She replied: It is so. My husband's father was killed here by a tiger. My husband was also killed, and now my son has died in the same way. The Master said: Why do you not leave the place? The answer was: There is no oppressive government here. The Master then said to his disciples: Remember this, my little children. Oppressive government is more terrible than tigers.

The T'an Kung, Sect. II, Part III.

The Master said: The superior man is careful. His generous largeness cannot be hid. His courtesy keeps shame at a distance.

Humanity is the right hand; following the straight path is the left. Those whose humanity is large, while their righteousness is slight, are loved but not honoured.

Those whose righteousness is great while their humanity is slight, are honoured but not loved.

The superior man does not assert the honour due to his person. He is not ambitious of position, and is very moderate in his desires. He gives place willingly to men of ability and virtue.

Dissatisfaction and calamity come to him whose lip-kindness is not followed by the corresponding deeds.

---

[6] It was the prescribed mark of reverence to a person in mourning to bow forward to the cross-bar of the vehicle in which one was riding.

Therefore the superior man will rather incur the resentment arising from his refusal than the charge of not fulfilling his promises. *Piao Chi, 5-49.*

DUKE AI of Lu said to Confucius: Allow me to ask what is the conduct of the scholar.

Confucius replied: The scholar does not consider gold and jade as precious treasures, but leal-heartedness and good faith; he does not desire lands and territory, but holds the establishment of righteousness as his domain; he does not desire great accumulation of wealth, but looks on many accomplishments as his riches. He will have no fellowship with what is not right.

Though a multitude attempt to drive him from his ground, and his way be stopped by force of arms, he will look death in the face without changing the principles which he maintains; any rumors against him he does not pursue to their source; he may be killed, but he cannot be disgraced.

The scholar has his associations with men of the present day, but the men of old are the subjects of his study. Following their example in the present time, he will become a pattern for future ages.

If his own age does not understand and encourage him, or calumniators and flatterers band together to endanger him, his person may be placed in peril, but his aim cannot be taken from him. He will still pursue it, and never forget the afflictions of the people; such is the anxiety which he cherishes.

The scholar learns extensively, but his researches never end; he does what he does with all his might, but is weary never. He estimates men's merits, and takes into consideration all their services, selecting those of virtue and ability to put forward, without expecting recompense from them; if benefit results to the state, he does not seek riches or honour for himself.

The scholar keeps his person free from stain, and continually bathes and refreshes his virtue; he does not hastily agree with those who think like himself, nor condemn those who think differently; so does he stand alone and take his own solitary course.

The scholar values a generous enlargement of mind, while bold and resolute in his intercourse with others; he acquaints himself with elegant accomplishments, and thus smoothes and polishes all his corners and angles; though the offer were made to share a state with him, it would be no more to him than the small weights of a balance.

Gentleness and goodness are the roots of humanity; respect and attention the ground on which it stands; generosity and large-mindedness are the manifestation of it; humility and courtesy are the ability of it; the rules of ceremony are the demonstration of it; singing and music are the harmony of it; sharing and distribution are the giving of it. The scholar possesses all these qualities in union.   *Ju Hsing, 2-18.*

JADE uncut will not form a vessel for use; and if men do not learn, they do not know the Way.

A superior man in his teaching leads and does not drag, thus producing harmony; he strengthens and does not discourage, making attainment easy; he opens the way, but does not conduct to the end, making the learner thoughtful. Then may he be pronounced a skilful teacher.

The master who skilfully waits to be questioned may be compared to a bell when sounded. Struck with a small hammer, it gives a small sound. Struck with a great hammer, it gives a great sound. But let it be struck leisurely and properly, and it gives out all the sound of which it is capable.   *Hsio Chi, 2-18.*

MUSIC has its origin in Heaven. It is harmony that is chiefly sought in it; it therein follows Heaven.

When we think of ceremonies and music, how they reach to the height of heaven and embrace the earth; how there is in them communication with the spirit-like processes of nature, we must pronounce their height the highest, their reach the farthest, their depth the most profound, and their breadth the greatest.

Virtue is the strong stem of man's nature, and music is the blossoming of virtue. In it we have the expression of feelings that do not admit of change. Music embraces what all share equally. To go to the very root of our feelings is its province.

Ceremonies and music resemble the nature of Heaven and Earth, penetrate to the virtues of the spiritual Intelligences, bring down the spirits from above, and raise up those whose seat is below. They give a sort of substantial embodiment of what is most subtle as well as material.

Therefore when the Great Man uses his ceremonies and music, Heaven and Earth will in response to him display their brilliant influences. They will act in happy union, and the energies of nature, now expanding, now contracting, will proceed harmoniously. The genial airs from above and the responsive action below will overspread and nourish all things.

When one has mastered completely the principles of music, the natural, gentle, and honest heart is easily developed, and with this development comes joy. This joy merges in a feeling of repose. The man in this constant repose becomes Heaven-like, his action spirit-like. So is it when by mastering music one regulates his mind and heart.

Therefore in the ancestral temple, rulers and ministers, high and low, listen together to music, and all is harmony and reverence; at the district and village meetings of the heads of clans, old and young listen together to it, and all is harmony and deference. Within the gate of the family, fathers and sons, brothers and cousins, listen together, and all is harmony and affection.

In this way, fathers and sons, rulers and subjects are united in harmony, and the people of the myriad states are associated in love. Such was the method of the ancient kings when they framed their music.

Yao Chi, Sect. I, II, III.

The Hsiao King

The Hsiao King (The Book of Filial Piety), a favorite classic of the emperors of China, contains memoranda of conversations between Confucius and his disciple Sen (Tzu-yu), and can be traced back to about 400 B.C.

Once when Confucius was unoccupied, and his disciple Sen was sitting in attendance on him, the Master said: Sen, the ancient kings had a perfect virtue and all-embracing rule of conduct through which they were in accord with all under heaven. By its practice the people were brought to live in peace and harmony, and there was no ill-will between superiors and inferiors. Do you know what it was?

Sen rose from his mat, and said: How should I be able to know this?

The Master said: Filial piety is the root of all virtue out of which grows all moral teaching. Sit down, and I will explain the subject to you.

It commences with the service of the parents; it proceeds to the service of the ruler; it is completed by the establishment of the character. He who loves his parents will dare not to be hated by any man, nor will he who reveres his parents risk being contemned by any.

Filial piety is the first law of Heaven, the righteousness of earth, and the practical duty of man.

Sen said: I would ask whether in the virtue of the sages there was not something greater than filial piety.

The Master replied: Of all natures produced by Heaven and Earth, man is the noblest. Of all actions of man none is greater than filial piety.

Now the feeling of affection arises at the parents' knees, and as the duty of nourishing one's parents is exercised, the affection daily merges in a feeling of awe. From awe the sages proceeded to teach reverence, and from affection, love.

The relation and duties between father and son contain in them the principle of righteousness between ruler and subject. The son derives his life from his parents, and no greater gift could possibly be transmitted; hence he who does not love his parents is a rebel against virtue.

In his general conduct to his parents the filial son manifests the utmost reverence; in his nourishing of them, he tries to give the utmost pleasure; when they are ill, he feels the greatest anxiety; mourning for them dead he shows every demonstration of grief; sacrificing to them, displays the utmost solemnity.

He who thus serves his parents, in a high situation will be free from pride; in a low situation, from insubordination, and among his equals he will not be quarrelsome.[7]

The Analects

The Analects or Sayings of Confucius (Lun Yu) were transmitted orally at first, taking the form in which we have them some two generations after the Master's death.

THE Master said: Fine words and an insinuating mien rarely go with true virtue.

Make faithfulness and sincerity your grand object. Have no friends not equal to yourself. If you have done wrong, be not ashamed to make amends.

I will not be grieved that men do not know me; rather will I grieve that I do not know men.

Hsio Erh, III, VIII, XV.

A VIRTUOUS ruler is like the Pole-star, steadfast whilst all the other stars turn round it.

The great man is catholic-minded and no partisan.

[7] The above selections from the Shi-King, Yi-King, Li Chi and Hsiao King are after the rendering by James Legge.

Learning without thought is labour lost; thought without learning, perilous.

Shall I teach you what true knowledge is? When you know, to know that you know; and when you do not know, to own that you do not know, this is true knowledge.   *Wei Cheng, I, XIV, XV, XVII.*

A MAN without charity in his heart, what has he to do with ceremonies? A man without charity in his heart, what has he to do with music?

He who has sinned against Heaven has none to whom he may pray.   *Pa Yih, III, XIII.*

HAVING found the Truth in the morning, what matters it if one come to die that night?

I am not concerned that I have no place; I am concerned how to fit myself for one. I am not concerned that I am not known; I seek to be worthy to be known.

Addressing his disciple Tseng Sen, the Master said: Sen, a single principle runs through all my teaching. When the Master had gone out, the disciples asked: What principle does he mean? Tseng said: Our Master's teaching is simply this: Loyalty to one's self and charity to one's neighbor.

When you meet a man of worth think how you may equal him; when you see a man of contrary character, examine your own heart. *Li Jen, VIII, XIV, XV, XVII.*

YAN YUAN and Tzu-Lu being by his side, the Master said: Come, tell me, each of you, the wish of your hearts.

Tzu-Lu said: I should like, having chariots and horses, and light fur dresses, to share them with my friends; nor should I mind if they were worn out in this way.

Yan Yuan said: My wish is to make no parade of goodness and no display of toilsome service rendered.

Tzu-Lu then said: I should like, sir, to hear what your heart is set upon.

The Master said: To comfort the aged, to be faithful to friends, to love and cherish the young.

Kung-Yeh Chang, XXV.

THE life of a man is his rectitude; life without it may you have the good fortune to avoid!

They who know the truth are not equal to those who love it, nor they who love it to those who rejoice therein.

The man of virtue makes the difficulty to be overcome his first concern, success a subsequent consideration.

The man of knowledge finds pleasure in the sea, the man of virtue in the mountains. For the man of knowledge is restless, the man of virtue calm.

Perfect is the virtue which adheres to a constant mean. It has long been rare among men.

Yung Yeh, XVII, XVIII, XX, XXI, XXVII.

COARSE rice for food, water to drink, my bended arm for a pillow, with only these I can find happiness. Riches and honour obtained by unrighteousness are to me as a passing cloud.

When I walk along with two others, they may serve as my teachers. I will select their good qualities and follow them, their bad qualities and avoid them.

Is virtue then a thing so remote? I have only to wish for virtue, and lo, it is at hand!

In letters I am perhaps equal to other men, but the character of the superior man, carrying out in his conduct that which he professes, I have not yet attained to.

The Master being grievously ill, Tzu-Lu asked leave to pray for him. Is there precedent for this? the Master asked. Tzu-Lu replied: There is. In the Eulogies it is written: Pray to the spirits of heaven and earth. The Master said: My prayers began long since.[8]

Shuh Erh, XV, XXI, XXIX, XXXII, XXXIV.

[8] Compare Socrates' answer to Hermogenes, p. 272.

WITHOUT due self-restraint courtesy becomes laborious bustle, carefulness timidity, valour violence, straightforwardness merely rude.

Learn as if you could not reach your object and feared also to lose it.   *T'ai-Pai, II, XVII.*

I HAVE not seen one who loves virtue as he loves beauty.

Though in making a mound I stop short when but one basketful more would finish my work, I have failed. But if in levelling it to the ground I advance my work only one basketful at a time, the fact remains, I advance.

A great army may be robbed of its leader, but nothing can rob one poor man of his will.

It is only when the year grows cold that we know the pine and cyprus to be evergreen.[9]
                    Tzu Han, XVII., XVIII, XXV, XXVII.

TZU-LU asked about serving the spirits of the dead. The Master replied: While you are not able to serve men, how can you serve their spirits? Tzu-lu went on to enquire about death. The Master said: Before you know what life is, how can you know about death?   *Hsian Tsin, XI.*

CHUNG KUNG asked about man's proper regard for man. The Master said: When you go forth from your door, behave to all as though you were meeting some distinguished guest. When employing the people, be as though you were taking part in a great religious function. What you would not wish done to yourself, do not unto others.

Ssu-ma Niu asked for a definition of the perfect man. The Master said: The perfect man knows neither grief nor fear. If on searching his heart he find no guilt, why should he grieve? What should he fear?

Tzu-chang asked what constituted clearness of vision. The Master said: He whose mind is proof against the slow-soaking poison of slander and the sharp stings of

[9] Men are best known in times of adversity.

calumny, may be called clear-sighted and far-seeing as well.

The noble-minded man makes the most of others' good qualities, not the worst of their bad ones.

Chi K'ang Tzu questioned Confucius on a point of government, saying: What think you of the cutting off of the lawless for the good of those who keep the law? Confucius replied: Sir, in the administration of government why resort to the death penalty? Show a desire to be good, and your people will be good. The virtue of the ruler is like unto the wind; that of the people, like unto grass. The grass must bend when the wind blows across it.

Tzu-chang asked: What must a man do in order to be held distinguished? The Master said: What mean you by distinguished? Tzu-chang replied: I mean one whose fame fills both his private circle and the State at large. The Master said: That is notoriety, not distinction. The man of true distinction is simple and honest, a lover of justice and duty. He weighs men's words and observes the expression of their faces. He is anxious to put himself below others. Such a one is truly distinguished.

Fan ch'e rambling with the Master under the trees about the rain-altars, said: I would ask how to raise the standard of virtue, to reform dissolute habits, and to discover illusions. The Master said: Truly a good question! If doing what is to be done be made the first concern and success secondary, is not this to raise the standard of virtue? And to attack the evil in one's self rather than in others, is not this to reform dissolute habits? As to illusions, is not one morning's fit of anger, causing a man to disregard his own life and involve those near and dear to him,—is not this an illusion?

Fan ch'e asked about benevolence. The Master said: It is to love all men. He asked about knowledge. The Master said: It is to know all men.

Yan Yuan, II, VI, XVI, XIX, XXII.

THE Master said: The way of the superior man is three-fold. Virtuous, he is free from anxiety; wise, he is free from perplexity; bold, he is free from fear.

He whose care extends not far ahead will find trouble near at hand.

He who requires much from himself and little from others, will banish complaints.

Tzu-kung asked, saying: Is there any one maxim which may serve as a rule of practice for the whole of one's life? The Master replied: Is not the maxim of charity such? Do not unto others what you would not they should do unto you.

The real fault is to have faults and not to try to amend them.

The superior man is correctly firm and not firm merely. *Wei Ling Kung, XI, XIV, XXIII, XXIX, XXXVI.*

TZU-CHANG asked Confucius about perfect virtue. Confucius said: Gravity, generosity, sincerity, earnestness and kindness: if you are grave, you will not be treated with disrespect; if you are generous, you will win all; if you are sincere, people will trust you; if you are earnest, you will accomplish much; if you are kind, you will be able to employ the service of others. *Yang Ho, VI.*

THE Master was mild, yet dignified; majestic, yet not fierce; respectful, yet easy. *Shuh Erh, XXXVII.*

THERE were four things from which he was entirely free. He had no foregone conclusions, no arbitrary predeterminations, no obstinacy, and no egoism. *Tzu Han, IV.*

TSENG TZU said: I daily examine myself on three points: Whether in working for others, I may not have been faithful; whether in my intercourse with friends, I may not have been true; and whether after teaching, I have practised what I preached. *Hsio Erh, IV.*

Chi Tzu-cheng said: The higher type of man is possessed of solid qualities and that is all. What has he to do with the ornamental? Tzu-kung replied: I am sorry, Sir, to hear such words from you; for a four-horse chariot cannot overtake the spoken word. The value of the ornament and the value of the substance are closely connected. Stripped of hair, the hide of the tiger or leopard is very like that of a dog or sheep.   *Yan Yuan, VIII.*

Tzu-chang said: The trained official, when he sees danger threatening, is prepared to sacrifice his life. When the opportunity of gain is presented to him, he thinks of righteousness.

Tzu-kung said: For one word a man is often deemed to be wise, and for one word foolish. We ought to be careful indeed what we say! [10]   *Tzu-chang, I, XXV.*

The Doctrine of the Mean

The Chung Yung (the State of Equilibrium and Harmony, or, as it is generally known, The Doctrine of the Mean), while included among the treatises of the Li Chi, is usually classed with the Four Books. It is ascribed to Szu-Szu, the grandson of Confucius, and must have been written between 450 and 400 B.C.

There is nothing more visible than what is secret, and nothing more manifest than what is minute. Therefore the moral man is watchful over himself when alone, and internally examines his heart, that there may be nothing wrong there, and no occasion for dissatisfaction with himself.

When there are no stirrings of pleasure, anger, sorrow or joy, we call it the State of Equilibrium. When those feelings have been developed, in due measure and degree, we call it the State of Harmony.

[10] The above selections from the Analects are based upon James Legge's and Lionel Giles' translations, the latter by permission, from: *Sayings of Confucius* (Wisdom of the East Series), New York, E. P. Dutton & Company.

Let the State of Equilibrium and Harmony exist in perfection, and a happy order will prevail throughout heaven and earth, and all things will flourish.

Confucius said: The superior man illustrates this State, but rare have they long been who could attain to it!

To search for what is mysterious and practise miracles in order to be mentioned with honour in future ages, this is what I do not do.

The superior man who follows the Doctrine of the Mean, may be all unknown and unregarded by the world, but he feels no regret.

The Path is not far distant. When a man practises fidelity to himself and to others, he is not far from it. What you do not wish others to do unto you, do not unto them.

Is it not just perfect sincerity which marks the perfect man? The perfect man can find himself in no position in which he is not himself. He rectifies himself, and seeks for nothing from others. He does not murmur against Heaven; he does not rail against man, but is quiet and calm, awaiting the appointments of God.

In archery we have something like the way of the superior man. When the archer misses the center of the target, he turns round and seeks for the cause of his failure in himself.

How abundant and rich is the power of the Spiritual Beings! We look for them, but do not see them; we listen for, but do not hear them; yet they enter into all things, and nothing is without them. Like the rush of mighty waters, their presence is felt sometimes above us, sometimes around.

Heaven is bountiful to things according to their qualities. The tree that is flourishing It nourishes, that which is ready to fall, It overthrows.

The sage studies extensively what is good, inquires critically into it, ponders it carefully; clearly discriminates and earnestly practises it.

While there is anything he has not studied, or in what he has studied there is aught he cannot understand, he will not intermit his labour. While there is anything he has not tried to sift, or in his sifting which is not clear, he will not intermit his labour. While there is anything which he has not practised, or any want of vigour in his practice, he will not intermit his labour.

If another succeed by one effort, he will use a hundred efforts; if another succeed by ten, he will use a thousand. Such being his attributes, without any manifestation, he is displayed; without movement, he affects changes; without exertion, he completes.

Therefore the actions of the superior man are the law for ages and his words the pattern for all under heaven. Those who are far from him look longingly for him, and those who are near are never weary of him.

He may be compared to heaven and earth in their supporting and containing, their overshadowing and curtaining all things. He may be compared to the four seasons in their alternating progress, and to the sun and moon in their successive shining.

All-embracing is he, vast like Heaven. Deep and active as a living spring of water. He shows himself, and all revere him; he speaks, and they believe; he acts, and they are pleased.

Wherever ships and carriages reach; wherever the strength of man can penetrate; wherever the heavens overshadow and the earth sustains; wherever the sun and moon do shine; wherever frosts and dews do fall, all who have blood and breath unfeignedly love and honour him.[11]

Wherein the perfect man cannot be equalled is simply this; his work which others cannot see. Therefore, even when he does not act, he has the feeling of reverence; and though he does not speak, the feeling of truthfulness.

[11] It is thought that these last three verses are his grandson's eloquent eulogium of Confucius.

The Great Learning

The Great Learning (Ta Hsio), one of the treatises included in the Li Chi, is more often classed as one of the Four Books. Its author is said to be Confucius' disciple Tseng.

THE object of the Great Learning is to set forth illustrious virtue, to renovate the people, and to rest in the highest excellence.

The men of old who wished to inculcate illustrious virtue throughout the kingdom ordered well their states. Wishing to order well their states, they first regulated their families. Wishing to regulate their families, they first rectified their own hearts. Wishing to rectify their own hearts, they first sought to be sincere in their thoughts. Wishing to be sincere in their thoughts, they extended to the utmost their knowledge.

From the loving example of one family, the whole state may become loving, and from its courtesies, courteous; while from the ambition and perverseness of one man, the whole state may be thrown into rebellious disorder.

Therefore the ruler must have in himself the qualities which then he may require in others. What a man dislikes in his superiors let him not display in his treatment of inferiors; and what he dislikes in his inferiors, let him not display in his service of superiors.

Thus the ruler has a principle with which, as with a measuring square, to regulate his course. Hence to accumulate wealth is to scatter the people, and to distribute wealth is to cause them to adhere.

The Book of Mencius
372-289 B.C.

Mencius (Latinized form of Meng-tzu), the disciple of Confucius, exceeded him in his fearless denunciation of the evils of his day, like the prophets of Israel employ-

*ing now persuasion, now reproof or biting sarcasm
against heresy and oppression.*

MENCIUS went to see King Huei of Liang. The king said:
Venerable Sir, since you have not counted it far to come
here, a distance of a thousand *li*, may I presume that you
are likewise provided with counsels to profit my kingdom?

Mencius replied: Why must your Majesty say *profit?*
What I am provided with are counsels to benevolence
and righteousness; these are my only topics.

If your Majesty say: What shall be done to profit my
kingdom? The great officers will say: What shall be done
to profit our families? And the inferior officers and the
common people will say: What shall be done to profit
our persons? Superiors and inferiors will try to snatch
this profit the one from the other, and the kingdom will
be endangered.

Let your Majesty also say: Benevolence and righteousness, these shall be my only themes. Why must you say
profit?

King Huei said: I wish quietly to receive your instructions.

Mencius replied: Is there any difference between killing
a man with a stick and with a sword? The king said:
There is no difference. Is there any difference between
doing it with a sword and with a style of government?
There is no difference.

Mencius then said: In your kitchen there is fat meat; in
your stables are fat horses. But your people have
the look of hunger, and on the wilds are those who have
died of famine. This is to lead on beasts to devour
men.

When a prince, the parent of his people, so administers
his government as to lead on beasts to devour his people,
what becomes of that parental relation?

King Huei Liang, I, Chapters I and IV.

Not one of the princes is able to exceed the others. This is from no other reason but that they love to make ministers of those whom they teach, and love not to make ministers of tnose by whom they might be taught.
Kung-Sun Ch'ow, II, Chapter II.

Benevolence is the most honourable dignity conferred by Heaven, and the quiet home in which a man should dwell; and righteousness is his straight path.

Alas for them who leave the tranquil dwelling empty and do not abide therein; who abandon the right path and pursue it not!

To dwell in love, the wide house of the world; to stand in propriety, the correct seat of the world; and to walk in righteousness, the great path of the world; when he obtains his office to practise his principles for the good of the people, and when his desire for office is disappointed to practise them alone; to be above the power of riches and honours to make dissipated, of poverty and mean conditions to make swerve from the right, of might and force to bend; these are the traits of the noble man.
Kung-Sun Chow, Li Low & T'eng Wen Kung.

The path of duty lies in what is near, men seek it in the remote. The work of duty lies in what is easy, and men seek it in what is difficult. If every man would love his parents and duly respect his elders, the whole empire would enjoy tranquillity. *Li Low, I, Chapter XI.*

Wan Chang asked Mencius, saying: I would ask, what are the principles of friendship?

Mencius replied: Friendship should be without any presumption on the ground of superior age, or station, or circumstance. Friendship with a man is friendship with his virtue; it does not admit of assumptions of authority.
Wan Chang, II, Chapter III.

Kao-tzu said: Man's nature is like water whirling round in a corner. Open a passage for it to the east, it flows to the east; open a passage to the west, it flows to the west. Man's nature is indifferent to good and evil, as water is indifferent to the east and west.

Mencius replied: Water indeed will flow indifferently to the east or west, but will it flow indifferently up or down? The tendency of man's nature to good is like the tendency of water to flow downwards. There are none but have this tendency to good, just as all water flows downwards.

The trees of the New Mountain were once beautiful. Being situated, however, in the borders of a large state, they were hewn down with axes and billhooks, and could they retain their beauty?

Still, through the activity of the vegetative life day and night, and the nourishing influence of the rain and dew, they were not without buds and sprouts; but then came the cattle and goats and browsed upon them.

To these things is owing the bare and stripped appearance of the mountain, which when people see they think it was never finely wooded. But is this the nature of the mountain?

And so also of what properly belongs to man; shall it be said that the mind of any man was without benevolence and righteousness? The way in which a man loses his proper goodness of mind is like the way in which trees are denuded by axes and billhooks. Hewn down day after day, can the mind retain its beauty?

But there is a development of its life day and night, and in the calm air of the morning, just between night and day, the mind feels in a degree the desires and aversions proper to mankind; but the feeling is not strong, and it is fettered and destroyed by the chances of the day.

Those who follow that part of themselves which is great are great; those which follow that part which is little are little men.

The senses of hearing and seeing cannot reason and are obscured by external things. When one thing comes into contact with another it leads it away. To the mind alone belongs the function of thought. By thought it perceives the truth: by neglecting to think, it fails therein.

These, the senses and the mind, are what Heaven has given to us. Let a man stand fast in his nobler part, and the inferior part will not be able to take it from him. It is simply this which makes the great man.

Kao Tzu, I, Chapters II., VIII., XV.

I LIKE fish and I also like bear's paws. If I cannot have the two together, I will let the fish go and take the bear's paws.

I like life and I also like righteousness; if I cannot keep the two together, I will let life go and choose righteousness.

I like life indeed, but there is that which I like more than life, and therefore I will not seek to preserve it by improper means. I dislike death indeed, but there is that which I dislike more than death, hence there are occasions of danger I will not avoid.

Kao Tzu, I, Chapter X.

SHUN rose from among the channeled fields; Foo Yue was called to office from the midst of his building frames; Kaou-kih from his fish and salt; Kwan E-woo from the hands of his gaoler; and Pih-le from the market place.

Thus, when Heaven is about to confer high office on man, it first exercises his mind with suffering, his sinews and bones with toil. It exposes his body to hunger, and subjects him to extreme poverty. It confounds his undertakings. By all these means it stimulates his mind, hardens his nature, and supplies his incompetencies.

Kao Tzu, II, Chapter XV.

THE great man is he who does not lose his child's heart.

Li Lou, II, Chapter XII.

THERE are three things in which he delights, and to be ruler over the empire is not one of them.

That his father and mother are both alive, and that the condition of his brothers affords no cause for anxiety, is one delight.

That, when looking up, he has no occasion for shame before Heaven, and below, no occasion to blush before men; this is the second delight.

That he can get from the whole empire the most talented individuals, and teach and nourish them, this is the third delight.

Tsin Hsin, I, Chapter XX.

THE disease of men is this: that they neglect their own fields and go weed the fields of others; and what they require from others is great, while what they lay upon themselves is light.[12]

Tsin Hsin, II, Chapter XXXII.

[12] The above selections from the Doctrine of the Mean, the Great Learning and the Works of Mencius are after the translation by James Legge.

THE BOOK OF LAO TZU

BEING SELECTIONS FROM HIS TAO TEH KING AND THE WRITINGS
OF HIS FOLLOWER CHUANG TZU

I know how birds can fly, fishes swim,
and animals run. But the runner may be
snared, the swimmer hooked, and the flyer
shot by arrow. But there is the dragon:—
I cannot tell how he mounteth on the wind
through the clouds, and riseth to heaven.
Today I have seen Lao-Tzu, and can only
compare him to the dragon.

Confucius.

After a long time, seeing the decay of
the dynasty, Lao-tzu left Chou and went
away to the barrier-gate leading out of
the kingdom on the north-west. The ward-
en of the gate said to him: Thou art about
to withdraw thyself from sight. First com-
pose for me a book. On this, Lao-tzu wrote
a book setting forth his views on the Tao
and its attributes. He then went away,
and it is not known where he died.

Ssu-ma Chian, Ist cent. B.C.

THE BOOK OF LAO TZU

Lao-Tzu, the Old Philosopher (604 B.C.—517 ?), though not the founder, was yet the greatest exponent of Taoism, one of the Three Religions of China; and he was undoubtedly the first man to preach the gospel of peace. He was more of a metaphysician, less of a moralist than Confucius, whom he preceded by some fifty years. The Tao Teh King (Classic of Tao and Virtue), the only record of his views, was recognized as a canon about 156 B.C.

THE TAO TEH KING

THE Tao [1] which can be expressed in words is not the eternal Tao; the name which can be uttered is not its eternal name. Without a name it is the origin of heaven and earth: having a name, it is the Mother of all things. Always without desire we must be found if we would sound its profound mystery; clogged by earthly passion we see but its outer fringe. *Ch. 1.*

How deep and unfathomable it is! How pure and still, as if it would be ever so! *Ch. 4.*

WE look at it, and we do not see it; we listen to it, and we do not hear it; we try to grasp, but cannot hold it. We may call it the form of the formless, the semblance of the invisible, the fleeting and indeterminable.

Would we go to meet it, we cannot see its face; would we go behind it, we cannot see its back. *Ch. 14.*

---

[1] Tao (literally, *road*), has been variously translated as the Way, or Reason, or Logos: as the Nirvana of Taoism, or as an abstract cause, or the initial principle of life and order to which worshipers could assign the attributes of immateriality, eternity, immensity, invisibility. The translation of St. John's Gospel into Chinese begins: In the beginning was the Tao, and the Tao was with God, and the Tao was God.

THERE is something, chaotic yet complete, which existed before heaven and earth. Oh, how still it is, formless, standing alone and suffering no change, reaching every·where, exhausted never! It may be regarded as the Mother of the Universe.

Its name I know not. To designate it, I call it Tao. Essaying to describe it, I call it Great. Great, it passeth on; passing on, it becometh remote; having become remote, it doth return.

Man taketh his law from the Earth; Earth taketh its law from Heaven; Heaven taketh its law from Tao, and Tao its law from itself. *Ch. 25.*

THOUGH in its primordial simplicity the Tao may be small, the whole world dareth not to deal with one embodying it as a minister. Could kings and feudal princes hold and keep it, all creation would spontaneously offer homage. Heaven and Earth [2] would unite in sending down sweet dew, and the people would be righteous of their own accord.

The relation of Tao to all the world is like that of the great rivers and seas to the streams from the valleys. *Ch. 32.*

ALL-PERVADING is the great Tao! It is on the left hand and on the right. *Ch. 34.*

To him who doth hold the mighty form of Tao the whole world will repair. They come and receive no hurt, but find rest, peace and tranquillity. *Ch. 35.*

TAO produceth all things; its virtue nourisheth them; its nature giveth them form; its force doth perfect them.

Thus it is that Tao, engendering all things, doth nourish, develop, and foster them; ripen them, tend and protect them.

[2] Heaven and Earth, a sort of binomial power acting in harmony with Tao, covering, protecting, nurturing all things.

PRODUCTION without possession, action without aggression, development without domination, this is its mysterious operation.   *Ch. 51.*

THE Great Way is very level and smooth; but people love the byways.   *Ch. 53.*

WHY was it men of old esteemed Tao so much? Was it not because it may be had for the seeking and can remit the sins of the guilty?   *Ch. 62.*

IT is the way of Tao to consider the small as great, the few as many; and to recompense injury with kindness.
                                                        Ch. 63.

CLAY is fashioned into vessels; it is on their empty hollowness that their use depends. Doors and windows are cut out to make a dwelling, and on the empty space within its use depends.
Thus while the existence of things may be good, it is the non-existent in them which makes them serviceable.
                                                        Ch. 11.

WHO is there can make muddy water clear? Yet let it but be still, and it will gradually become clear. Who can secure the state of repose? Yet let but time go on, and the state of repose will gradually arise.   *Ch. 15.*

HE who knoweth to shut useth no bolts, yet thou canst not open. He who knoweth to bind useth no cords, yet thou canst not undo.   *Ch. 27.*

IF any would procure the kingdom for himself by his own action, he will not succeed. The kingdom is a spirit-like thing, and cannot be got by active doing. He who would so win it, doth destroy it; he who would hold it in his grasp doth lose it.   *Ch. 29.*

Tao is eternally inactive, yet leaveth nothing undone. If kings and princes could but hold it fast, all things would be transformed. *Ch. 37.*

The softest things in the world do overcome the hardest; that which hath no substance entereth where there is no crevice.

Few there are in the world who attain to the teaching without words, and the advantage arising from non-action. *Ch. 43.*

Without going outside the door, one may know the whole world; without looking out of the window, one may see the Way of Heaven. *Ch. 47.*

It is the way of Heaven not to strive, yet it can overcome; not to speak, yet it obtaineth response; it calleth not, yet men come of themselves; it is slow to move, yet effecteth its designs.

Heaven's net is vast; though its meshes are wide, it doth let nothing through. *Ch. 73.*

There is nothing in the world more soft and weak than water, yet for attacking what is hard and strong nothing can surpass, nay equal it. *Ch. 78.*

Wherever a host hath been stationed, briars and thorns do spring up. In the track of great armies there follow lean years. *Ch. 30.*

Arms, however beautiful, are instruments of evil omen, hateful to all creatures. They who have the Tao will have none of them. Calm and repose are what they cherish; not victory by force of arms. *Ch. 31.*

When Tao doth prevail upon earth, horses are used to work the fields; when Tao doth not prevail, war-horses breed in the border-lands. *Ch. 46.*

WHEN opposing warriors join in battle, he who hath pity
doth conquer.   *Ch. 69.*

THE sage holdeth in his embrace humility and doth manifest it to all under heaven. He is free from self-display,
therefore he doth shine; from self-assertion, therefore
he is distinguished; from self-exaltation, therefore he
riseth superior to all. Inasmuch as he doth not strive,
none may strive with him.   *Ch. 22.*

THE perception of what is small is the secret of clear-
sightedness; the guarding of what is soft and tender is
the secret of strength.   *Ch. 52.*

THE tree which filleth the arms grew from the tiniest
sprout; the tower of nine storeys rose from a little mound
of earth; the journey of a thousand miles began with a
single step.   *Ch. 64.*

THE reason why rivers and seas receive the homage of a
hundred mountain streams is that they keep below them.
Thus they are able to reign over all the mountain
streams.

So the sage, wishing to be above men, putteth himself
below them; wishing to be before them, he putteth himself behind them.

Thus, though his place be above men, they do not feel his
weight; though his place be before them, they do not
count it an injury.   *Ch. 66.*

I HAVE three precious things which I prize and hold fast.
The first is gentleness; the second frugality; the third
humility.

Be gentle, and thou canst be bold; frugal, and thou canst
be liberal; put not thyself before others, and thou mayest
become a vessel of the highest honour.

Gentleness bringeth victory. Those whom Heaven would
save, it fenceth round with gentleness.   *Ch. 67.*

He who knoweth others is clever, but he who knoweth himself is enlightened. He who overcometh others is strong; he who conquereth himself is mighty. He is rich who knoweth when he hath enough. *Ch. 33.*

The great man abideth by what is solid, and escheweth what is flimsy; dwelleth with the fruit and not the flower. *Ch. 38.*

The sage doth not hoard for himself. The more he expendeth for others, the more he doth possess; the more he giveth to others, the more he hath himself. *Ch. 81.*

Where palaces are splendid, fields will be waste, granaries empty. The wearing of gay embroidered robes, fastidiousness in food and drink, too great abundance of property and wealth, such is flaunting robbery. *Ch. 53.*

Be square without being angular. Be honest, without being mean. *Ch. 58.*

Sincere words are not fine; fine words are not sincere. *Ch. 81.*

To the good I would be good; to those who are not good I would also be good in order to make them so.

With the faithful I would keep faith; with the unfaithful I would also keep faith, in order that they may become faithful.[4] *Ch. 49.*

Selections from the Writings of Chuang-Tzu, a follower of Lao-tzu, who lived in the third or fourth century before Christ.

The Perfect man hath no thought of self; the Spirit-like man no thought of merit; the Sagely-minded man no thought of fame.

[4] The above selections from the Tao Teh King have been compiled from the renderings by James Legge and Lionel Giles, the latter by permission, from: *Sayings of Lao Tzu* (Wisdom of the East Series) New York, E. P. Dutton & Company.

The name is but the guest of the reality;—shall I be playing the part of the guest? *I, i, 1.*

THE Perfect man is Spirit-like. Great lakes might boil about him, he would not feel their heat; the Ho and the Han might be frozen up, he would not feel the cold; the hurrying thunderbolts might split the mountains, the wind shake the ocean, he would not be afraid.

Being such, he mounteth the clouds, he rideth the sun and moon, he rambleth at ease beyond the four seas. Death nor life worketh change in him, much less the thought of gain or injury.

How do I know that the love of life is not a delusion? That the fear of death is not like losing one's way, and not knowing that one is really going home?

Those who dream of the pleasures of drinking may in the morning wail and weep; those who dream of wailing and weeping may in the morning go out to hunt.

While they dreamt they knew not that it was a dream; but they knew it when they awoke. And there is the great awaking, after which we shall know that this life was a great dream.

Let us make our appeal to the Infinite, and take up our position there. *II, i, 2.*

THE ancients described death as the loosening of the cord on which God suspended the life. What we can point to are the faggots that have been consumed; but the fire is transmitted elsewhere, and we do not know that it is over and ended.[5] *III, i, 3.*

How do we know that what we call the Heavenly in us is not the human? And that what we call the human is not the Heavenly? There must be the True man, and then there is the true knowledge.

[5] The *faggots* represent the body, the *fire* the animating spirit. As the faggots are consumed by the fire, so the body perishes at death. But the fire may be transmitted to other faggots.

The True men of old did not dream when they slept, had no anxiety when they awoke, and cared not that their food should please.

The True men of old knew nothing of the love of life or of the hatred of death. Composedly they went and came. Their foreheads beamed simplicity. *VI, i, 6.*

THE man of Tao doth not become distinguished; the greatest virtue is unsuccessful. *XVIII, ii, 10.*

HERE now is a great founder casting his metal. If the metal were to leap up and say: I must be made into a sword like the Mo-yeh,[6] the founder would regard it as incongruous.

When once we understand that heaven and earth are a great melting-pot, and the Creator a great founder, where can we have to go that shall not be right to us? We are born as from a quiet sleep, and we die to a calm awaking.

If Meng-sun is to be transformed into something else, he will simply await the transformation which he knoweth not yet. Death is to him like the issuing from one's dwelling at dawn. *VI, i, 6.*

BE scrupulous yet gentle, like the tutelary spirit of the land. Be large-minded like space. Hold all things in your love, specially favouring and supporting none.[7]

XVII, ii, 10.

[6] The name of a famous sword made for the king of Wu.

[7] The above selections from the Writings of Chuang-tzu are based on the rendering by James Legge.

THE BOOK OF BUDDHA

BEING SELECTIONS FROM THE ANCIENT BUDDHIST CANON

God in the form of mercy.
Inscription on a statue of the
Buddha at the Jamalgiri at Gaya.

Now regarding the venerable Gotama, such is the
high reputation noised abroad: That the Blessed
One is a saint, a fully awakened one, abound-
ing in wisdom and goodness, happy with knowledge
of the worlds, unsurpassed as a guide to mortals
willing to be led, a teacher of gods and men, a
Buddha. He, by Himself, doth thoroughly know and
see, as it were, face to face this universe,—
the worlds above of the gods and the world below
with its princes and its peoples,—and having
known it, He maketh His knowledge known to others.
The truth, lovely in its origin, lovely in its
progress, lovely in its consummation, doth He pro-
claim, both in the spirit and in the letter; the
higher life doth He make known in all its fullness
and in all its purity.
Ambattha Sutta, Dialogues of the Buddha.

Buddha is the joy of the whole world; the helper
of the helpless; a mine of mercy; universal friend;
nearest relative; stronger than the strongest; more
merciful than the most merciful; more beautiful
than the most beautiful.
Statement of Singhalese Buddhists.

Si fuisset Christianus, fuisset apud Deum maximus.
Marco Polo.

THE BOOK OF BUDDHA

Prince Siddhattha Gotama, the Buddha, the Enlightened, (Sanskrit budh, to wake), lived in India from about 556 to 477 B.C., and was the father of the Buddhist faith which after a lapse of over twenty-four hundred years numbers as its adherents about one-twelfth of the human race. Unlike Mohammedism and Christianity, it has never resorted to the sword and persecutions, but has been uniformly peaceful in its progress. Buddha taught that all existence is transitory and full of sorrow, but that man can accomplish his own salvation from both existence and sorrow by embracing the noble Eightfold Path of right thinking and acting. The following account of his life is formed of excerpts from the ancient Buddhist Canon dating from about the 3rd century B. C.

I

THE BIRTH OF THE BODISAT [1]

AT that time, it is said, the Midsummer Festival was proclaimed in the city of Kapilavastu, and the people were enjoying the feast. And Queen Maha-Maya took part in the festivities for the six days previous to the day of full moon.

And the day of full moon she rose early and bathed in perfumed water: and she dispensed four hundred thousand pieces of money in great largesse, and vowing to observe the Eight Commandments, she entered her chamber, and lying on the royal couch she fell asleep and dreamt.

[1] One who is about to become a Buddha but has not as yet attained Nirvana.

And on the next day the Queen awoke and told her dream to the King. And the King caused sixty-four eminent Brahmans to be summoned and spread seats for them on ground festively prepared with green leaves and dalbergia flowers. And when he had satisfied their every desire, he told them the dream and asked them what would come of it.

The Brahmans said: Be not anxious, O King! A child hath planted itself in the womb of thy Queen. Thou shalt have a son, who, if he continue to live the household life, will become a Universal Monarch; but if he leave the household life and retire from the world, he will become a Buddha and will remove from the world the veils of ignorance and sin.

Now the moment the future Buddha was conceived in the womb of his mother an immeasurable light spread through the ten thousand worlds. The blind recovered their sight as if from desire to behold his glory; the deaf received their hearing; the dumb spake one with another. The crooked became straight; the lame recovered their power to walk; prisoners were loosed from their bonds and chains. All mortals began to speak kindly one with another; in all quarters of the heavens the weather became fair; a mild, cool breeze began to blow, very refreshing to men. Everywhere the earth was covered with lotuses, and celestial music was heard.

From the time the future Buddha was thus conceived, four angels with swords in their hands kept guard to shield from harm the Bodisat and his mother. Pure in thought, having reached the highest aim and the highest honour, happy and unwearied was the mother.

So Queen Maha-Maya cherished the Bodisat in her womb, as it were oil in a vessel, for ten lunar months; and being then far gone with child, and desirous of going home to her own people, she spake to King Suddhodana and said:

O King, I wish to go to Devedaha, to the city of my

people. So be it, said the King. And from Kapilavastu to the city of Devedaha he had the road made plain, and garnished with plaintain-trees; and seating the Queen in a golden palanquin, he sent her away with a great retinue.

Now between the two towns there is a pleasance of sala-trees belonging to the people of both cities, called the Lumbini Grove. At that time, from the roots to the topmost branches, it was a mass of fruits and flowers; and among the blossoms swarms of various-colored bees flew in and out and flocks of birds of different kinds were sweetly caroling.

And the attendants carrying the Queen entered the wood; and then her pains came upon her and she was delivered. At that moment came four pure angels bearing a golden net; and receiving the Future Buddha they placed him before the mother and said: Rejoice, O Queen! A mighty son is born to thee!

The people of both towns took the Bodisat and went to Kapilavastu. On that day too, the choir of angels were astonished and rejoiced, saying: In Kapilavastu, to Suddhodana the King, a son is born, who will become a Buddha! [2]

At that time a hermit Asita [3] saw these angels, and asked them: Why are ye thus rejoicing, glad at heart?

The angels replied: To Suddhodana the King a son is born who will found a kingdom of righteousness. To us it will be given to see his infinite grace and to hear his word. Therefore it is that we are glad!

The hermit quickly came, and entering the King's house, sat down on the seat set apart for him, and said: They say a son is born to thee, O King! Let me see him. The King ordered his son to be brought in.

Now the hermit perceiving that he would most certainly become a Buddha, smiled, saying: This is a wonderful

[2] Comp. Luke II. 9-14.   [3] Comp. Luke II. 25.

child! Then reflecting: It will not be my good fortune to behold this so wonderful child when he hath become a Buddha. Great, indeed, is my loss! he wept.

II

His Renunciation of the World

The Bodisat in due course grew to manhood. And the King had three mansions made, suitable for the three seasons, and he provided him with forty thousand dancing girls. So the Bodisat like a god surrounded by troops of houris lived, as the seasons changed, in each of these mansions in the enjoyment of great majesty. And Yasodhara was his principal queen.

Now one day the Future Buddha, wanting to go to his pleasance, ascended his chariot, resplendent as a mansion in the skies, and went toward the garden. The angels thought: The time for young Siddhattha to attain enlightenment is near; let us show him the Omens! And they made a son of the gods represent a man wasted by age, with decayed teeth and grey hair, bent and broken in body.

Then the Bodisat asked his charioteer: What kind of a man is this whose very hair is not as that of other men? When he heard his servant's answer, he said: Woe upon birth, since through it decay must come to every living being! And with agitated heart he turned back and entered his palace.

Again one day when the Future Buddha, as he went to his pleasance, saw a man who was ill, he made the same inquiry as before; and then, with agitated heart turned back.

Once more, when, as he went to his pleasance, he saw a dead man, he made the same inquiry as before, and then, with agitated heart, turned back and reëntered his palace.

Once again, when he saw one who had abandoned the world, carefully and decently clad, he asked his charioteer: Friend, what kind of a man is that? He answered: That is a mendicant friar. And he described the advantages of renouncing the world. And that day the Future Buddha, cherishing the thought of renouncing the world, went on to his pleasance.

At that time Suddhodana the King, who had heard that the wife of the Bodisat had brought forth a son, sent a message, saying: Make known my joy to my son!

The Future Buddha, hearing this, said: An impediment hath come into being! When the king asked: What did my son say? and heard that saying, he gave command: From henceforth let Rahula (Impediment) be my grandson's name.

But the Bodisat in his splendid chariot rode into the town with great magnificence and exceeding glory and he entered his palace in great splendour and lay on his couch of state. Thereupon women clad in beautiful array, skilful in the dance and song, and lovely as celestial nymphs, brought their instruments of music and ranging themselves in order, danced and sang and played.

But the Bodisat, his heart estranged from sin, took no pleasure in the spectacle and fell asleep. And the women, saying: He for whose sake we were performing is gone to sleep; why should we play any longer? set aside the instruments they held, and lay down to sleep.

The lamps were just burning out when the Bodisat, waking up, saw them with their stage properties laid aside and sleeping, some grinding their teeth, some yawning, some muttering in their sleep, some gaping, and some with their dress in disorder.

To him that magnificent apartment, as splendid as Sakka's heavenly mansion, began to seem like to a charnel-house of loathsome corpses. Life seemed to him like staying in a house devoured with flames. He gave vent to the solemn utterance: It all oppresseth me! It is intolerable! And his mind turned ardently to the state of those who have renounced the world.

Resolving that very day to accomplish the Great Renunciation, he rose from his couch, went to the door and called: Who is there? Channa, who had been sleeping with his head on the threshold, answered: Sir, it is I.

Then said he: I am resolved today to accomplish the Great Renunciation. Saddle a horse for me! Now after the Bodisat had sent Channa on this errand, he thought: I will just look at my son. And he went to the apartments of his wife and opened her chamber door.

A lamp, fed with sweet-burning oil, was burning dimly in the inner chamber. The mother of Rahula was asleep on a bed strewn with jasmine flowers, resting her hand on the head of her son. Stopping with his foot on the threshold the Bodisat thought: If I lift her hand to take my son, she will awake; that will prevent my going away. I will come back to see him when I become a Buddha. And he left the palace.

The Bodisat adopted the outward signs of an Arahat, and dressed himself in the sacred garb of Renunciation. And he enjoined upon Channa to go and assure his parents of his safety. And Channa did homage to the Bodisat reverently and went.

Now the Bodisat thought: I will perform the uttermost penance. And he brought himself to live on one seed of the oil plant, or one grain of rice a day, and even to fast entirely.[4]

By this fasting, however, he waxed thin as a skeleton; the colour of his body, once fair as gold, grew dark. And one day, when walking up and down, plunged in intense meditation, he was overcome by severe pain; and he fainted and fell.

And he recovered consciousness again and stood up. But he perceived that penance was not the way to Wisdom; and begging through the villages and towns, he collected ordinary food and lived upon it.

[4] Comp. Luke IV. 1-13.

III

His Enlightenment

The Lord gracious, beautiful to behold, with senses stilled and mind restrained, as one who hath attained the supreme calm of self-conquest, subdued and guarded.

The Udana.

Early on the full-moon day in the month of May, the Bodisat had seen five dreams; and considering their purport he had drawn the conclusion: Verily this day I shall become a Buddha. And at the end of the night he washed and dressed himself, and he went early and sat at the foot of the Bodhi-tree,[5] lighting it up with his glory.

Then the Bodisat turned his back upon the trunk of the Bodhi-tree, and with his face towards the east, made the firm resolve: My skin and sinews and bones may become arid, and the very blood in my body may dry up; but till I attain to complete insight, this seat I will not leave! And he sat himself down firm and immovable, and not to be dislodged by a hundred thunderbolts.

At that time Mara, the Evil One, thinking: Siddhattha the Prince wanteth to free himself from my dominion, but I will not let him yet get free! went to his hosts, and sounding his war-cry, led them forth to battle.[6]

The angels of the ten thousand worlds continued speaking the praises of the Great Being, but as the army approached and surrounded the Bodhi-tree, not one was able to stay, and they fled each one from the spot, and the Great Being sat there alone.

But Mara said to his host: Friends, there is no other man like Siddhattha, the son of Suddhodana. We cannot give him battle face to face. Let us attack him from behind!

[5] *Ficus religiosa;* meaning here, on the side, tree of enlightenment.
[6] Comp. Luke IV. 1-13.

The Great Being looked around and saw that all the angels had fled. Then beholding the hosts of Mara coming thick upon him, he thought: Against me alone this mighty host is putting forth all its energy and strength. Father nor mother are here, nor brother, nor any other relative.

But I have those Ten Perfections, like old retainers, long cherished at my board. It behooveth me then to make the Ten Perfections my shield and my sword and to strike a blow with them that shall destroy this strong array. So he sat meditating on the Ten Perfections.

Then Mara, saying: Thus will I drive away Siddhattha; caused a whirlwind to blow. And immediately such winds rushed together from the four corners of the earth as could have torn down the peaks of mountains half a league, two leagues, three leagues high. But through the majesty of the goodness of the Great Being, they reached him with their power gone, and even the hem of his robe they were unable to shake.

Then saying: I will overwhelm him with water, Mara caused a mighty rain to fall. And the clouds gathered, overspreading one another by hundreds and by thousands, and poured forth rain; and a great flood, over-topping the trees of the forest, approached the Great Being. But it was not able to wet on his robe even the space where a dew-drop might fall.

Then Mara caused a storm of rocks to fall. And mighty mountain peaks came through the air, spitting forth fire and smoke.

Then saying: By this will I terrify Siddhattha, and drive him away! he brought on a thick darkness. And the darkness became fourfold: but before it reached the Future Buddha, it disappeared as darkness disappeareth before the brightness of the sun.

And the angels stood on the edge of the rocks that encircle the world; and stretching forward in amazement, they watched, saying: Lost, lost is Siddhattha the Prince, the glorious and beautiful!

But the army of Mara fled this way and that, so that not even two were left together. Then the heavenly hosts, when they saw that the army of Mara had fled, cried: The tempter is overcome! Siddhattha the Prince hath prevailed!

It was before the sun had set that the Great Being thus put to flight the army of the Evil One. Then, whilst the Bodhi-tree paid him homage by raining its sprigs red like coral upon his priestly robe, he acquired in the first watch of the night the Knowledge of the Past, in the middle watch of the night the Knowledge of the Present, and in the third watch of the night the Knowledge of the Chain of Causation which leadeth to the origin of evil.

And when the Great Being at dawning of the day attained to complete enlightenment, the ten thousand worlds became glorious as on a festive day. The blind from birth received their sight; the deaf could hear; cripples could use their limbs; captives went free. Thus in surpassing glory and honour did He attain omniscience, and breathe forth the solemn Hymn of Triumph.[7]
Introduction of the Jataka.

Many a House of Life
Hath held me—seeking ever him who wrought
These prisons of the senses, sorrow-fraught;
Sore was my ceaseless strife!

But now,
Thou builder of this Tabernacle—thou!
I know thee! Never shalt thou build again
These walls of pain,
Nor raise the roof-tree of deceits, nor lay
Fresh rafters on the clay;
Broken thy house is, and the ridge-pole split!
Delusion fashioned it!
Safe pass I thence, deliverance to obtain.[8]

[7] Adapted from Rhys Davids' translation.
[8] Edwin Arnold's translation.

IV

THE CHAIN OF CAUSATION

One thing only, the uprooting of sorrow!   *Buddha.*

AT that time the Blessed Buddha, having just attained to the Buddhaship, dwelt at Uruvela, on the bank of the river Neranjara, at the foot of the Bodhi-tree, for seven days together enjoying the bliss of emancipation.

Then the Blessed One fixed His mind upon the Chain of Causation:

> From ignorance springeth karma; [9]
> From karma springeth consciousness;
> From consciousness spring name and form; [10]
> From name and form spring the six organs of
>   sense; [11]
> From the six organs of sense springeth contact;
> From contact springeth sensation;
> From sensation springeth desire;
> From desire springeth attachment;
> From attachment springeth existence;
> From existence springeth birth;
> From birth spring old age and death, grief,
>   lamentation, suffering, dejection and des-
>   pair.

Thus doth all this suffering arise. But by the destruction of ignorance all that which issueth therefrom is also destroyed.

Then the Blessed One pronounced this solemn utterance: When the real nature of things becometh clear to the ardent, meditating Brahman, he standeth dispelling the hosts of Mara like the sun that illumineth the sky.

Mahavagga I. i.

[9] Action and the destiny resulting therefrom.
[10] Individual beings.
[11] The five senses and the mind.

V

Brahma's Request

THEN the Blessed One, at the end of those seven days, arose from that state of meditation and went to the Ajapala banyan tree.

Then in the mind of the Blessed One who was alone and had retired into solitude the following thought arose: I have penetrated this doctrine which is profound, hard to perceive and to understand, which bringeth quietude of heart, which is sublime, unattainable by reasoning, intelligible only by the wise.

But this is a people given to desire, intent upon desire, delighting in desire. To this people, therefore, the law of causality will be a matter hard to understand; this too were a matter hard for them to discern,—the tranquillization of all the activities of worldly life, the renunciation of the common life of the senses, the destruction of desire, quietude of heart, Nirvana.

Now if I proclaim this doctrine, and men are not able to understand my preaching, there would result but weariness and annoyance to me. When the Blessed One pondered this matter, His mind became inclined not to preach the doctrine.

But Brahma-Sahampati,[12] becoming aware of the reflection of the Exalted One, thought: Woe! the world perisheth! Woe! the world is destroyed if the mind of the Tathagata,[13] the holy, supreme Buddha, inclineth not to preach the doctrine!

Then, even as a strong man might stretch his bent arm out, or draw back his outstretched arm, he appeared before the Exalted One. And Brahma-Sahampati raised his joined hands towards the Blessed One and said:

[12] *Brahma* is the chief God of the Hindus, *Sahampati* occurs only in this connection and its exact significance is unknown; it probably means, *Lord Might.*

[13] Variously interpreted as *The Perfect One, he who hath arrived at the goal,* i.e., Nirvana.

May the Blessed One preach the doctrine! May the Perfect One preach the doctrine! There are souls whose eyes are dimmed by hardly any dust; but if they do not hear the doctrine they cannot attain salvation. Do Thou open the door of the Immortal; let them hear the doctrine discovered by the Spotless One!

As standing on a mountain's crest a man might overlook the people far below, even so do Thou, O All-wise One, ascending to the terraced heights of Truth, from grief released, the Seer of all, look down upon the nations sunk in grief, oppressed by birth and decay.

Arise, O Conqueror, Victorious One! Lord of the Caravan! Freed from debt Thyself, wander through the world, sublime and blessed Teacher, and preach the doctrine! There will be people who can understand!

As in a pool of blue or red or white lotuses, some lotus plants do not emerge, but thrive hidden beneath the surface; and other lotus plants rise to the surface; and others again emerge above the water unwetted by it; even so the Exalted One looked over the world with a Buddha's eye and saw souls whose eyes were scarcely dimmed by dust, and souls whose eyes were sorely dimmed by dust, souls sharp and blunt of sense, of good and evil disposition, souls docile, souls perverse.

And when He had thus seen them, He answered Brahma-Sahampati: Wide opened is the door of the Immortal to all who have ears to hear! Let them send forth faith to meet it!

Then Brahma-Sahampati understood: The Blessed One granteth my request that He should preach the doctrine. And he bowed down before the Blessed One, and passed around Him with his right side toward Him;[14] and straightway disappeared.[15]   *Mahavagga I. v.*

[14] A sign of reverence.

[15] Compiled from Davids' and Oldenberg's translation and from Mrs. Davids' translation of Brahma Sutta, Samyutta Nikaya. All the extracts from Mrs. Davids' translations as well as that from F. L. Woodward's (p. 211) are by permission from the volumes for the Pali Text Society, Oxford University Press, London.

VI

THE SERMON AT BENARES

It is in just this way, Ananda, that thou must understand how the whole of this life in religion is concerned with friendship, intimacy, association with whatsoever is lovely and righteous.   *Buddha.*

THE Blessed One was once staying at Benares, at the hermitage called Migadaya. And there He addressed the company of the five Bhikkhus,[16] and said:

There are two extremes, O Bhikkhus, from which he who leadeth the religious life must abstain. What are those two extremes?

One is a life of pleasure, devoted to desire and enjoyment; that is base, ignoble, unspiritual, unworthy, unreal. The other is a life of mortification; it is gloomy, unworthy, unreal.

The Perfect One, O Bhikkhus, avoiding these extremes, hath discovered the middle path, a path which openeth the eyes, and bestoweth understanding, which leadeth to rest, to knowledge, to enlightenment, to Nirvana.[17]

And what, O Bhikkhus, is that middle path discovered by the Perfect One? Verily, it is the noble Eightfold Path: [18]

> Right Belief;
> Right Resolve;
> Right Speech;
> Right Conduct;
> Right Occupation;
> Right Effort;
> Right Mindfulness;
> Right Rapture.

This, O Bhikkhus, is that middle path which openeth the eyes, and bestoweth understanding, which leadeth to rest, to knowledge, to enlightenment, to Nirvana!

[16] Mendicant friars.   [17] Means literally, *the blowing out of the flame.*
[18] "The numerical statement of things was a mnemonic necessity in an undocumented world." Wells.

Now this, O Bhikkhus, is the noble truth concerning suffering: Birth is suffering; decay is suffering; disease is suffering; death is suffering. Presence of objects we hate is suffering; separation from objects we love is suffering; not to obtain what we desire is suffering. In brief, the clinging to the five elements of existence is suffering.

This, O Bhikkhus, is the noble truth concerning the cause of suffering. It is the thirst for being which leads to rebirth, together with lust and desire, which finds gratification here and there; the thirst for pleasure, the thirst for power.

This, O Bhikkhus, is the noble truth concerning the extinction of suffering. Verily, it is the destruction, in which no passion doth remain, of this very thirst: the abandoning, the relinquishing, the deliverance from this thirst, the giving it no room.

Now this, O Bhikkhus, is the noble truth concerning the path which leadeth to the extinction of suffering. Verily, it is this noble Eightfold Path, to wit:

Right Belief;
Right Resolve;
Right Speech;
Right Conduct;
Right Occupation;
Right Effort;
Right Mindfulness;
Right Rapture.

Thus spake the Blessed One, and the company of the five Bhikkhus, glad at heart, rejoiced at His words.

And when the royal chariot wheel of the truth had thus been set rolling onward by the Blessed One, the gods of the earth gave a shout, saying: In Benares, at the hermitage of Migadaya, the supreme wheel of the empire of truth hath been set rolling by the Blessed One,—that wheel which can never be turned back by any god, by Brahma or Mara, or anyone in the universe!

And when they heard the shouts of the gods of the earth, the guardian angels of the four quarters of the globe gave forth a shout, saying: In Benares, at the hermitage of Migadaya, the supreme wheel of the empire of truth hath been set rolling by the Blessed One,—that wheel which never can be turned back by any god, by Brahma or Mara, or anyone in the universe!

And thus, in an instant, the sound went up even to the world of Brahma: and the ten-thousand worlds quaked and trembled and shook violently, and an immeasurable bright light appeared in the universe, beyond even the power of the gods.[19]

Dhamma-cakka-ppavattana-sutta and Mahavagga I. vi.

VII

The Sermon of Benares Explained

And what, O priests, is right belief?

The knowledge of suffering, the knowledge of the cause of suffering, the knowledge of the extinction of suffering, and the knowledge of the path leading to the extinction of suffering, this is right belief.

And what, O priests, is right resolve?

The resolve to renounce sensual pleasure, the resolve to have malice toward none, and the resolve to harm no living creature, this is right resolve.

And what, O priests, is right speech?

To abstain from falsehood, to abstain from backbiting, to abstain from harsh language, to abstain from frivolous talk, this is right speech.

And what, O priests, is right conduct?

To abstain from destroying life, to abstain from taking what is not given, to abstain from immorality, this is right conduct.

And what, O priests, is right occupation?

[19] From the translation by Davids.

Whenever a noble disciple, quitting a wrong occupation, gets his livelihood by a right occupation, this is right occupation.

And what, O priests, is right effort?

Whenever a priest purposeth, heroically endeavoureth, applieth his mind, and exerteth himself that evil and demeritorious qualities not yet arisen may not arise; that evil and demeritorious qualities already arisen may be abandoned; that meritorious qualities not yet arisen may arise; purposeth, heroically endeavoureth, applieth his mind and exerteth himself for the preservation, retention, growth, increase, development and perfection of meritorious qualities already arisen, this is right effort.

And what, O priests, is right mindfulness?

Whenever a priest liveth as respecteth the body, the sensations, the mind, the elements of being, observant, strenuous, conscious, contemplative, and hath rid himself of lust and grief, this is right mindfulness.

And what, O priests, is right rapture?

Whenever a priest, having isolated himself from sensual pleasures, and from demeritorious traits, entereth upon the first trance which is produced by isolation and characterized by joy and happiness; when, through the subsidence of reasoning and reflection and still retaining joy and happiness, he entereth upon the second trance which is an interior tranquillization and intentness of the thoughts, and is produced by concentration; when, through the paling of joy, indifferent, contemplative, conscious, and in the experience of bodily happiness, he entereth upon the third trance; when through the abandonment of happiness, through the abandonment of misery, through the disappearance of all antecedent gladness and grief, he entereth upon the fourth trance, which hath neither misery nor happiness, but is contemplation refined by indifference, this, O priests, is right rapture.[20]

Digha-Nikaya, Sutta 22.

[20] Adapted from Warren's translation.

VIII

The Conversion of Yasa

At that time there was in Benares a noble youth, Yasa by name, the son of a treasurer and delicately nurtured. He had three palaces, one for winter, one for summer, one for the rainy season. In the palace for the rainy season he lived during the four months surrounded by female musicians, and he did not descend from that palace.

Now one day, Yasa, the noble youth, while thus attended, fell asleep; and after him his attendants fell asleep. And an oil lamp was burning through the whole night.

And Yasa awoke and saw his attendants sleeping; one with her lute leaning against her armpit; one with her tabor against her neck, a drum in the arms of one; another with dishevelled hair; and they were muttering in their sleep.

When he saw that, the evils of the life he led manifested themselves to him; his mind became weary. And he gave utterance to this solemn exclamation; Alas! what distress! Alas! what danger!

And Yasa, the noble youth, put on his gilt slippers, and went to the gate of his house, and to the gate of the city. And Yasa went to the deer park Isipatana.

At that time the Blessed One, having arisen in the night, at dawn was walking up and down in the open air. And the Blessed One saw Yasa coming from afar. And when He saw him, He left the place where He was walking, and sat down on a seat laid out for Him.

And Yasa gave utterance near the Blessed One to that solemn exclamation: Alas! what distress! Alas! what danger! And the Blessed One said to Yasa: Here is no distress, Yasa, here is no danger! Come, I will teach thee the Truth.

And Yasa, the noble youth, when he heard that there was no distress and no danger, became glad and joyful: and he put off his slippers, and having approached and respectfully saluted the Blessed One, he sat down near Him.

When Yasa was sitting near Him, the Blessed One preached to him in due course: that is to say, He talked about the merits obtained by almsgiving, about the duties of morality, about heaven, about the evils, the vanity, the sinfulness of desires, and about the blessings of the abandonment of desire.

When the Blessed One saw that the mind of Yasa was prepared, impressible, free from obstacles, elated, believing, then He preached what is the principal doctrine of the Buddhas, namely, Suffering, the Cause of Suffering, the Cessation of Suffering, the Path.

As a clean cloth free from stain taketh the dye, thus Yasa, even while sitting there, obtained the pure and spotless eye of truth, the knowledge, that is, that whatsoever is subject to origination is subject also to destruction.

Now the mother of Yasa, having gone up to his palace, did not see him, and she went to the treasurer and said: My son Yasa hath disappeared!

Then the treasurer sent messengers on horseback to the four quarters of the horizon and he went himself to the deer park Isipatana. And he saw on the ground the marks of the gilt slippers; and when he saw them, he followed them up.

And the treasurer went to the place where the Blessed One was, and, having approached Him, he said: Pray, Lord, hath the Blessed One seen Yasa?

Well, householder, sit down. Perhaps sitting here, thou mayst see Yasa. And the treasurer having respectfully saluted the Blessed One, sat down near Him.

Then the Blessed One preached to him in due course about the merits obtained by almsgiving, about the duties of morality, about heaven, about the evils, the vanity, the sinfulness of desires, and the blessings of the abandonment of desire.

And the treasurer, having seen the Truth, having mastered and penetrated the Truth, having dispelled all doubts, having gained full knowledge, said to the Blessed One: Glorious, Lord! Glorious, Lord! Just as if one should set up what had been overturned, or reveal what had been hidden, or point out the way to one who was lost, or bring a lamp into the darkness, thus hath the Blessed One preached the doctrine.

I take my refuge in the Blessed One, and in the Doctrine, and in the fraternity of the Bhikkhus; may the Blessed One receive me from this day forth while my life doth last as a disciple who hath taken his refuge in Him! This was the first person in the world who became a lay disciple by the formula of the holy triad.

And while instruction was being administered to his father, Yasa contemplated the stage of knowledge which he had seen with his mind and understood; and his mind became free from attachment to the world and was released from sensuality, individuality, delusion and ignorance.

Then the treasurer saw Yasa. On seeing him he said: My son Yasa, thy mother is absorbed in grief and lamentation; restore thy mother to life! Then Yasa looked at the Blessed One.

And the Blessed One said to the treasurer: What thinkest thou then, O householder? That Yasa hath won only an imperfect degree of knowledge and insight into the Truth as thou hast thyself? Or that rather he was contemplating the stage of knowledge which he had seen and understood; and that his mind hath thus become free from attachment to the world and released from sensuality, individuality, delusion and ignorance? Now would it then be possible, O householder, that Yasa should return to the world and enjoy pleasures as he did before, when he lived in his house?

Not so, Lord. It is all gain to Yasa, it is high bliss, Lord,
for Yasa, that his mind hath become free from attachment to the world, and released from sensuality, individuality, delusion and ignorance. Might the Blessed
One consent to take His meal with me today together
with Yasa as His attendant?

The Blessed One gave by silence His consent. Then the
treasurer respectfully saluted the Blessed One, and passing round Him with his right side towards Him, departed
thence.

And soon after the treasurer was gone, Yasa said to the
Blessed One; Lord, let me receive from the Blessed One
the ordinations of relinquishment of the world and admittance to the brotherhood!

Come, O Bhikkhu! said the Blessed One. Well taught is
the doctrine; lead a holy life for the sake of the complete
extinction of suffering!

And in the forenoon the Blessed One, having donned His
robes, took His alms-bowl, and went with Yasa as His
attendant to the house of the treasurer. When He arrived
there, He sat down on a seat laid out for Him.

Then the mother and the former wife of Yasa, having
approached the Blessed One and respectfully saluted
Him, sat down near Him.

Then the Blessed One preached to them in due course.
And having seen the Truth, they spake thus: We take
our refuge in the Blessed One, and in the Doctrine, and
in the fraternity of the Bhikkhus. May the Blessed One
receive us from this day forth while our life doth last as
disciples who have taken their refuge in Him! These
were the first women who became lay-disciples by the
formula of the holy triad.

And the mother and the father and the former wife of
Yasa with their own hands served and offered food, both
hard and soft, to the Blessed One and to Yasa: and when
the Blessed One had finished His meal, and cleansed His
bowl and His hands, they sat down near Him.

Then the Blessed One taught, incited, animated, and gladdened the mother, father and former wife of Yasa with religious discourse, and then He rose from His seat and went away.[21] *Mahavagga I. vii. 1.*

IX

Sending Forth the Disciples

And the Blessed One said to the Bhikkhus: I am delivered, O Bhikkhus, from all fetters, human and divine. Ye, O Bhikkhus, are also delivered from all fetters, human and divine.

Go ye now, O Bhikkhus,[22] and wander out of compassion for the world, for the good, for the gain, and for the welfare of gods and men. Let not two of you go the same way. Preach the doctrine which is glorious in its beginning, glorious in its progress, glorious in its end, in spirit and in letter; proclaim a consummate, perfect, and pure life of holiness.

There are beings whose eyes are dimmed by scarcely any dust; if the doctrine is not preached to them, they cannot reach salvation. They will understand the doctrine. I will go also to Uruvela, to Senaninigama, in order to preach the doctrine.

And Mara, the wicked One, went to the Blessed One and addressed Him thus: Thou art bound by all fetters, human and divine. Thou art bound by strong fetters. Thou shalt not be delivered from me, O Samana![23]

Buddha answered unto him: I am delivered from all fetters, human and divine. I am delivered from the strong fetters. Thou art struck down, O Death!

Mara said: The fetter with which the mind is bound, with that fetter will I bind thee. Thou art not to be delivered from me, O Samana!

[21] Adapted from Davids' and Oldenberg's translations.
[22] Comp. Mat. X. 1 and Luke IX. 1.
[23] An ascetic, one who lives under a vow.

Buddha answered unto him: Whatever forms, sounds, odours, flavours, or contacts there are which please the senses, in me desire for them hath ceased. Thou art struck down, O Death!

Then Mara, the wicked One, understood: The Blessed One knoweth me, the Perfect One knoweth me. And, sad and afflicted, he vanished away.[24]

Mahavagga I. xi. 1-2.

X

THE TALK AT RAJAGAHA

But what man doth, by act or word or thought,
That thing owneth he, taketh hence,
To dog his steps like shadow in pursuit.

Buddha, Samuytta Nikaya.

THE Blessed One was dwelling in Rajagaha, on the hill called Vulture's Peak. And the Blessed One addressed the venerable Ananda, and said: Go now, Ananda, assemble in the Service Hall such of the brethren as live in the neighborhood of Rajagaha.

And he did so; and returned to the Blessed One and informed Him, saying: The company of the brethren, Lord, is assembled; let the Blessed One do as seemeth to Him fit.

And the Blessed One arose, and went to the Service Hall; and when He was seated, He addressed the brethren and said: I will teach you, O mendicants, seven conditions of the welfare of a community. Even so, Lord, said the brethren; and the Blessed One spake as follows:

So long as the brethren shall be full of faith, modest in heart, afraid of sin, full of learning, strong in energy, active in mind, and full of wisdom, so long may the brethren be expected to prosper.

Other seven conditions of welfare will I teach you, O brethren! So long as the brethren shall exercise them-

---

[24] Adapted from Davids' and Oldenberg's translations.

selves in the seven-fold higher wisdom, that is to say, in mental activity, search after truth, energy, joy, peace, earnest contemplation, and equanimity of mind, so long may the brethren be expected not to decline but to prosper.

So long as the brethren shall exercise themselves in the seven-fold perception due to earnest thought, that is to say, the perception of impermanency, of non-individuality, of corruption, of the danger of sin, of sanctification, of purity of heart, of Nirvana, so long may the brethren be expected not to decline, but to prosper.

So long as the brethren shall persevere in kindness of action, speech and thought among the saints, both in public and in private, so long as they shall divide without partiality, and share in common with the upright and holy all such things as they receive in accordance with the just provisions of the order, even to the mere contents of a begging bowl;

So long as the brethren shall live among the saints in the practice, both in public and in private, of those virtues, unbroken, intact, unspotted and unblemished, which are productive of freedom, and praised by the wise; which are untarnished by the desire of future life, or belief in the efficacy of outward rites; and which are conducive to high and holy thoughts; so long may the brethren be expected not to decline, but to prosper.[25]

Maha-parinibbana-sutta I.

XI

THE CONVERSION OF SARIPUTTA AND MOGGALLANA

AT that time Sanjaya, a wandering ascetic, dwelt at Rajagaha with a great retinue of followers and Sariputta and Moggallana led a religious life as his disciples. These had given their word to each other: He who first attaineth to Nirvana shall tell the other.

[25] After Davids' translation.

Now one day in the forenoon the worthy Assaji, having donned his robes and taken his alms-bowl, entered the city of Rajagaha for alms. His walking, turning back, drawing back and stretching out of his arms was decorous; he cast his eyes to the ground and was dignified in his bearing.

Now Sariputta saw the worthy Assaji who went through Rajagaha for alms. Seeing him he thought: Indeed this must be a Bhikkhu who is either now a saint, or who hath entered upon the path that leadeth to sainthood.

And the worthy Assaji, having finished his pilgrimage for alms, went back with the food he had received. Then Sariputta went to Assaji, and having exchanged with'him greetings of friendship and civility, stood respectfully at one side.

And he said to Assaji: Thy countenance, friend, is serene; clear and bright is the colour of thy skin. In whose name, brother, didst thou retire from the world? Who is thy teacher? Whose doctrine dost thou profess?

There is, brother, a great ascetic who hath retired from the world out of the Sakya clan. In His, the Blessed Gotama's name have I retired from the world; this Blessed One is my teacher; and the doctrine of this Blessed One do I profess.

And what is the doctrine, Sir, which thy teacher doth hold and profess?

Brother, I am a novice and have but lately received the ordination; and I have newly adopted this doctrine and this discipline. I can not expound the doctrine to thee at great length, but I can tell thee its substance in brief.

Then Assaji pronounced to Sariputta the following text of the Law: Of all things proceeding from a cause, the Tathagata hath explained the cause; and He hath explained their cessation also; this is the doctrine the mighty Monk doth proclaim.

And when he had heard this exposition of the doctrine, Sariputta obtained the clear and spotless Eye of the

Truth: Whatsoever is subject to origination is subject
to cessation also. And he said: If this be the doctrine,
now hast thou reached Nirvana, the sorrowless state.

Then Sariputta drew near to the place where Moggallana
was. And Moggallana saw Sariputta coming from afar;
seeing him he said: Thy countenance, friend, is serene;
clear and bright is the colour of thy skin. Brother, hast
thou really reached Nirvana?

Yes, brother, I have reached Nirvana. And when Mogal-
lana had heard Sariputta's exposition of the doctrine, he
obtained the clear and spotless Eye of the Truth: Whatsoever is subject to origination is subject to cessation
also.

Then Moggallana said to Sariputta: Let us go, brother,
and join the Blessed One; that He, the Blessed One, may
be our teacher.

Sariputta answered him: It is on our account, brother,
that these two hundred and fifty wandering ascetics live
here; let us first inform them of our intention; then they
may do what they think fit. Then Sariputta and Moggallana went to those wandering ascetics and said:
Friends, we go to join the Blessed One, that He, the
Blessed One, may be our teacher.

If ye, sirs, are about to place yourselves under the spiritual guidance of the mighty Monk, we will all place
ourselves under His guidance. And Sariputta and Moggallana took with them those two hundred and fifty wandering ascetics and went to Veluvana.

And the Blessed One saw Sariputta and Moggallana coming from afar: and He thus addressed the Bhikkhus:
There, O Bhikkhus, come two companions; these will
be a pair of true pupils,—a most distinguished, auspi-
cious pair! [26]

Then Sariputta and Moggallana went to the Blessed One,
and prostrated themselves, inclining their heads to the
feet of the Blessed One, and said: Lord, let us receive

[26] Comp. John I. 47.

from Thee the ordinations of relinquishment of the world and admittance to the brotherhood!

Come, O Bhikkhus! said the Blessed One. Well taught is the doctrine. Lead a holy life for the sake of the complete extinction of suffering!

At that time many distinguished young Magadha noblemen led a religious life under the direction of the Blessed One. The people were annoyed, murmured and became angry, saying: The monk Gotama causeth fathers to beget no sons; the monk Gotama causeth wives to become widows; the monk Gotama causeth families to become extinct!

Now He hath ordained one thousand ascetics, and He hath ordained these two hundred and fifty wandering ascetics who were followers of Sanjaya; and these many distinguished Magadha noblemen are now leading a religious life under the direction of the monk Gotama!

Moreover, when they saw the Bhikkhus, they reviled them, saying: the mighty monk hath come to Rajagaha of the Magadha people, leading with Him all the followers of Sanjaya; who will be the next to be led by Him? These Bhikkhus told this thing to the Blessed One.

This noise, Bhikkhus, will not last long; it will last only seven days. And if they revile you, ye should reply: It is by means of the true doctrine that the Tathagatas lead men. Who will murmur at the wise, who lead men by the power of Truth?[27]   *Mahavagga I. xxiii, xxiv.*

XII

AMBAPALI

THEN the Blessed One proceeded, with a great company of the brethren, to Vesali; and there at Vesali the Blessed One stayed at Ambapali's grove.

Now the courtezan Ambapali heard that the Blessed One had arrived at Vesali, and was staying at her mango

[27] After translations by Davids and Oldenberg and Warren.

grove. And ordering a number of magnificent vehicles to be made ready, she mounted one of them, and proceeded with her train towards her garden.

She went in the vehicle as far as the road was passable for carriages; there she alighted; and she proceeded on foot to the place where the Blessed One was, and took her seat respectfully on one side. And when she was thus seated, the Blessed One instructed, aroused, incited and gladdened her with religious discourse.

Then, instructed, aroused, incited, and gladdened with His words, she addressed the Blessed One and said: May the Blessed One do me the honour of taking His meal, together with the brethren, at my house tomorrow? And the Blessed One gave by silence His consent. Then Ambapáli rose from her seat and bowed down before Him, and keeping Him on her right hand as she passed Him, she departed thence.

Now the Likkhavis [28] of Vesali heard that the Blessed One had arrived at Vesali, and stayed at Ambapali's grove. And ordering a great number of magnificent carriages to be made ready, they mounted them and proceeded with their train to Vesali.

And Ambapali drove up against the young Likkhavis, axle to axle, wheel to wheel, yoke to yoke; and the Likkhavis said to Ambapali the courtezan: How is it, Ambapali, that thou drivest up against us?

My Lords, I have just invited the Blessed One and His brethren for their morrow's meal, said she.

Ambapali, give up this meal to us for a hundred thousand! said they.

My Lords, were ye to offer all Vesali with its subject territory, I would not give up so honourable a feast!

Then the Likkhavis cast up their hands exclaiming: We are outdone by this grower of mangoes! We are out-

[28] Among the self-governing communities of Northern India was that of the Likkhavi nobles living in and around Vesali.

reached by this grower of mangoes! And they went on to Ambapali's grove.

When the Blessed One saw the Likkhavis approaching in the distance, He addressed the brethren and said: O brethren, let those of the brethren who have never seen the Tavatimsa [29] gods, behold this company of the Likkhavis, even as a company of Tavatimsa gods.

And then the Likkhavis alighted and went on foot to the place where the Blessed One was, and took their seats respectfully by His side. And when they were thus seated, the Blessed One instructed, roused, incited and gladdened them with religious discourse.

Then they addressed the Blessed One, and said: May the Blessed One do us the honour of taking His meal, together with the brethren, at our house tomorrow?

O Likkhavis, I have promised to dine tomorrow with Ambapali the courtezan.

Then the Likkhavis rose from their seats and bowed down before the Blessed One, and keeping Him on their right hand as they passed Him, they departed thence.

And at the end of the night Ambapali made ready in her mansion sweet rice and cakes, and announced the time to the Blessed One, saying: The hour, Lord, hath come, and the meal is ready.

And the Blessed One made himself ready early in the morning and took His bowl, and went with the brethren to the place where Ambapali's dwelling-house was: and He seated Himself on the seat laid out for Him. And Ambapali set the sweet rice and cakes before the Order with Buddha at their head, and waited upon them.

And when the Blessed One had finished His meal, the courtezan had a low stool brought, and sat down at His side, and addressed the Blessed One, and said: Lord, I present this mansion to the order of the mendicants, of whom Buddha is the chief.

[29] The principal gods of the Vedic pantheon, thirty-three (*Tavatimsa*) in number.

And the Blessed One accepted the gift; and after instructing, rousing, inciting and gladdening her with religious discourse, He rose and departed thence.[30]

Maha-parinibbana-sutta II.

XIII

The Parable of Buddha the Sower

The Exalted One was once staying on South Hill, at Ekanala, a Brahman village. Now it was time for the ploughing, and Farmer Bharadvaja, the Brahman, had yoked five hundred ploughs. Then the Exalted One, taking robe and bowl, drew near to the ploughing.

Now it was time for Farmer Bharadvaja's distribution of food. And the Exalted One drew near and stood on one side. And Farmer Bharadvaja saw the Exalted One standing there for alms, and said: Now I, O recluse, do plough and sow, and when I have ploughed and sown, I eat. Do thou also plough and sow, and when thou hast ploughed and sown, eat!

But I too, Brahman, plough and sow, and when I have ploughed and sown I eat.

But we see neither Master Gotama's team, nor his plough, nor his ploughshare, nor his goad, nor his oxen!

To him the Blessed One made answer: Faith is the seed I sow; penance the rain that watereth it; wisdom is my yoke and plough; the pole is modesty; mindfulness the tie; thoughtfulness my ploughshare and my goad.

Guarded am I in action and in speech; I weed with truth; in kindliness is my salvation; exertion is my ox that never turneth back but beareth onward to Nirvana where grief is no more. Such is the ploughing ploughed by me; it beareth fruit in immortality; whoso this ploughing hath accomplished from all suffering is set free!

Then the Brahman Bharadvaja, having poured rice-milk into a golden bowl, offered it to the Blessed One and

[30] After Davids' translation.

said: Let the Blessed One eat of the rice-milk! The
venerable Gotama is a ploughman, for He plough-
eth a ploughing that beareth the fruit of immortality.

Brahman Sutta, Samyutta Nikaya; and Sutta Nipata.

XIV

THE PARABLE OF THE ELEPHANT

ON a certain occasion the Blessed One dwelt at Savatthi,
in Jetavana monastery in Anathapindika's pleasance.

Now at that time a large number of Samanas, Brahmans,
and wandering monks of various heretical sects, holding
a variety of views, doubters on many points, having
diverse aspirations, entered Savatthi for alms.

Some of these Samanas and Brahmans held that the
world is eternal, and that this view was true and every
other false. Some said: The world is not eternal.

Some said: The world is finite. Some said: The world is
infinite. Some said: Soul and body are identical. Some
said: Soul and body are not identical.

Some said: The Perfect One doth continue to exist after
death. Some said: The Perfect One doth not continue to
exist after death; each contending that his view was true
and every other false.

These quarrelsome, pugnacious monks wounded one another with their mouth-javelins, declaiming: Such is the
truth, such is not the truth: the truth is not such, such
is the truth!

And a number of Bhikkhus went to the Blessed One and
saluted the Blessed One and said: Just now, Sire, a large
number of Samanas and Brahmans and wandering
monks holding various heresies entered Savatthi for
alms, and they are disputing among themselves saying:
This is the truth, such is not the truth: the truth is not
such: such is the truth!

And Buddha said: These heretical monks, O Bhikkhus,

are blind; they know not what is right, they know not what is wrong, they know not what is true, they know not what is false.

In former times, O Bhikkhus, there was a king in this town of Savatthi. And the king, O Bhikkhus, called a man to him and said: Go thou, and collect all the men born blind in Savatthi and bring them here.

So be it, Lord, said that man; and he went and brought all the men born blind to the King and said: Lord, all the men born blind in Savatthi are present.

Pray, then, bring an elephant before them.

So be it, Lord, said that man; and he brought an elephant before the blind men and said: This, O blind men, is an elephant.

And the King said to the blind men: Do ye know what an elephant is like?

Assuredly, Lord, we now know what an elephant is like. Tell me, O blind men, what an elephant is like.

And those blind men, O Bhikkhus, who had felt the head of the elephant, said: An elephant, Sire, is like a large, round jar. Those who had felts its ears, said: It is like a winnowing basket. Those who had felt its tusks, said: It is like a ploughshare.

Those who had felt its body said: It is like a granary. Those who had felt its feet said: It is like a pillar. Those who had felt its back said: It is like a mortar. Those who had felt its tail said: It is like a pestle. Those who had felt the tuft of its tail said: It is like a broom.

And they all fought among themselves with their fists, declaring: such is an elephant, such is not an elephant, an elephant is not like that, it is like this.

In exactly the same way, O Bhikkhus, do these heretical people, blind and without insight, dispute among themselves, saying: This doctrine is true, every other is false.[31]   *Jaccandha, the Udana.*

[31] Translated by Strong.

XV

What Maketh an Outcast

THEN the Blessed One, having taken His robes and His bowl, entered Savatthi for alms. And the Blessed One going for alms from house to house went to the house of the Brahman [32] Aggikabharadvaja.

The Brahman saw the Blessed One coming at a distance, and seeing Him said: Stay there, O shaveling! O wretched Samana! O outcast!

The Blessed One answered unto the Brahman: Dost thou know, O Brahman, an outcast, or the things that make an outcast?

Whoso is angry and beareth hatred, is wicked and hypocritical, hath embraced wrong views, is deceitful; whoso harmeth living beings, in whom is no compassion for living beings, him let one know as an outcast.

Whoso destroyeth or layeth siege to villages and towns, and is known as an enemy; whoso appropriateth by theft the property of others; whoso having contracted a debt, runneth away when called upon to pay, saying: There is no debt I owe thee! him let one know as an outcast.

Whoso for his own sake or that of others or for the sake of wealth speaketh falsely when called as a witness, whoso being rich supporteth not mother or father when past their youth, whoso exalteth himself and despiseth others, being mean by his pride, whoso is a provoker and avaricious, hath sinful desires, is shameless in sinning,— him let one know as an outcast!

Not by birth doth one become an outcast, not by birth doth one become a Brahman. By deeds doth one become an outcast, by deeds doth one become a Brahman! [33]

Vasalasutta of the Sutta-Nipata.

[32] The highest or sacerdotal caste, looking down on the others.
[33] Translated by Fausböll.

XVI

Patisena

*To pervade the world with kindliness, pity, sympathy,—
that is the way to union with Brahma.*

Buddha in Tevijja Sutta.

When Buddha dwelt at Savatthi there was an old mendicant named Patisena who being by nature cross and dull, could not learn so much as one psalm by heart. Buddha accordingly requested Arahats [34] to instruct him day by day, but after three years he still was unable to remember even one psalm.

Then all the people of the country, knowing his ignorance, began to mock him, on which Buddha, pitying his case, called him to His side and gently repeated these words: He who guardeth his mouth, who restraineth his thoughts, who offendeth not with his body, shall obtain deliverance.

Then Patisena, moved by a sense of the Master's goodness to him, felt his heart opened, and straightway repeated the verse. Buddha then said: Thou now, an old man, canst repeat one verse only, and men know this and will still mock thee. Therefore I will now declare the meaning of the verse to thee, and do thou attentively listen.

Then Buddha declared the causes by destroying which men might obtain deliverance, and the mendicant, realizing the truth thus declared, obtained the condition of an Arahat.

Now at that time there were five hundred nuns dwelling in their convent who despatched one of their number to Buddha to request Him to send a priest to instruct them in the Law; and Buddha desired Patisena to go to them for this pupose.

[34] Literally, *noble teachers*—those of the Order who had attained unto saintship.

On hearing this, the nuns began to make merry, and agreed that on the morrow when he came they would say the verse wrong, and so confuse the old man and put him to shame.

On the morrow when he came, the nuns great and small went forth to salute him, and as they did so, they looked at one another and smiled. Then they offered him food. When he had eaten and washed his hands, they begged him to begin his sermon.

Then the aged mendicant ascended the elevated seat, and sitting down began: Sisters, my talent is small, my learning very little. I know only one verse, but I will repeat that and explain its meaning.

Then the young nuns endeavoured to say the verse backwards, but lo! they could not open their mouths, and filled with shame, they hung their heads in sorrow.

Then Patisena, having repeated the verse, began to explain it, head by head, as Buddha had instructed him. And the nuns, hearing his words, were astonished, and rejoicing to hear such instruction, with one heart received it, and became Arahats.[35]

Narrative accompanying the Chinese Dhammapada.

XVII

THE PARABLE OF THE MOUNTAIN

Now the King of Kosala, Pasenadi, came to see the Exalted One at Savatthi. When he was seated, to him thus spake the Exalted One. Well, Sire, whence comest thou?

I have been zealously busied, Lord, with such matters as occupy kings who are of noble birth and anointed, who yield indulgence to their greed for sensuous pleasures, who have won security for their kingdoms and live as conquerors of a wide area of land.

As to that, what thinkest thou, Sire? Suppose a man loyal and trustworthy came to thee from the east, and

[35] Translated by Beal.

said: May it please thee to know, Sire, I have come from the eastern districts; and I saw there a mountain high as the sky moving along, crushing as it came every living thing. Whatever thou canst do, Sire, that do thou!

And suppose other men came, from west, north, and south, all three loyal and trustworthy, and brought like messages. And thou, Sire, seized with mighty dread, and the destruction of human life so terrible, what is there thou couldst do?

In such a mighty peril, Lord, what could I do save live righteously and justly and work good and meritorious deeds?

I tell thee, Sire, I make known to thee: Old age and death come rolling in upon thee! Since old age and death come rolling in upon thee, Sire, what is there thou canst do?

Since old age and death, Lord, come rolling in upon me, what else can I do save live righteously and justly, and work good and meritorious deeds? [36]

Kosalasutta III. 3, Samyutta Nikaya.

XVIII

Unprofitable Questions

On a certain occasion the Blessed One was dwelling at Savatthi in Jetavana monastery in Anathapindika's pleasance. Then drew near Vaccha the wandering monk and greeted the Blessed One; and having passed the compliments of friendship and civility, he sat down respectfully at one side and spake as follows:

How is it, Gotama? Doth Gotama hold that the world is eternal, and that this view alone is true, and every other false?

Nay, Vaccha.

Doth Gotama hold that the world is not eternal, and that this view alone is true, and every other false?

[36] After the translation by Mrs. Davids.

Nay, Vaccha.

Doth Gotama hold that the world is finite, that soul and body are identical, that the saint existeth after death, that the saint doth not exist after death?

Nay, Vaccha.

What objection doth Gotama perceive to these theories that He hath not adopted any one of them?

Vaccha, the theories that the world is eternal, is not eternal, that the world is finite, that soul and body are identical, that the saint existeth after death, that the saint doth not exist after death,—are a jungle, a wilderness, a writhing, and a fetter, and do not tend to absence of passion, quiescence, supreme wisdom, and Nirvana.

This is the objection I perceive to these theories, that I have not adopted any of them: but this, O Vaccha, doth the Tathagata know,—the nature of form, and how it ariseth and perisheth; the nature of sensation and how it ariseth and perisheth; the nature of perception, the predispositions, consciousness, and how they arise and perish.

Therefore say I that the Tathagata hath attained deliverance and is free from attachment, inasmuch as all imaginings, or agitations or proud thoughts concerning an ego or anything pertaining to an ego have perished, faded away, ceased, and been relinquished.

But, Gotama, where is the priest reborn who hath attained to this deliverance for the mind?

Vaccha, to say he is reborn would not fit the case.

Then, Gotama, he is not reborn?

Vaccha, to say he is not reborn would not fit the case. To say that he is both reborn and not reborn, that he is neither reborn nor not reborn would not fit the case.

Gotama, I am at a loss what to think in this matter, and I have become greatly confused.

Enough, O Vaccha! I will now question thee, and do thou make answer as may seem to thee good. Suppose a fire were to burn in front of thee. Suppose someone were to ask thee: On what doth this fire depend? What wouldst thou answer?

I should answer, Gotama: It is on fuel of grass and wood that this fire dependeth.

But, Vaccha, if the fire in front of thee were to become extinct, if someone were to ask thee: In which direction hath that fire gone—east, west, north, or south? What wouldst thou say?

The question would not suit the case, Gotama. For the fire which depended on fuel of grass and wood, when that fuel hath all gone, and it can get no other, being thus without nutriment, is said to be extinct.

In exactly the same way, Vaccha, all form by which one could predicate the existence of the saint hath been abandoned, uprooted, pulled out of the ground like a palmyra tree, and become non-existent. The saint, O Vaccha, who hath been released from what is styled form, is deep, immeasurable, unfathomable, like the mighty ocean.

To say that he is reborn would not fit the case. To say that he is not reborn would not fit the case. All sensation, all perception, all the predispositions, all consciousness by which one could predicate the existence of the saint have been abandoned, pulled out of the ground like a palmyra tree, and become non-existent.

When the Blessed One had thus spoken, Vaccha, the wandering monk, spake to Him as follows: It is as if, O Gotama, there were a mighty sal-tree and it were to lose its dead branches and twigs and its loose shreds of bark, so that afterwards, free from those branches and twigs, and the loose shreds of bark, it were to stand neat and clean in its strength.

In exactly the same way doth the word of Gotama, free from branches and twigs, and from loose shreds of bark, stand neat and clean in its strength.[37]

Sutta 72, Majjhima-Nikaya.

[37] Adapted from Warren's translation.

XIX

What Constituteth Wisdom

Then the Blessed One spake and said: A householder on hearing the Truth hath faith in the Tathagata, and when he hath acquired that faith, full of modesty and pity, he is compassionate and kind to all creatures that have life.

He passeth his life in purity and honesty of heart. He liveth a life of chastity. He speaketh truth; from the truth he never swerveth. Faithful and trustworthy, he injureth not his fellowman by deceit. Putting away slander, he abstaineth from calumny.

What he heareth here he repeateth not elsewhere to raise a quarrel against the people here: what he heareth elsewhere he repeateth not here to raise a quarrel against the people there.

Thus he liveth as a binder together of those who are divided, an encourager of those who are friends, a peacemaker, a lover of peace, impassioned for peace.

Whatever word is humane, pleasant to the ear, lovely, reaching to the heart, urbane, beloved of the people, such word speaketh he.

And he letteth his mind pervade all the quarters of the world with thoughts of love. And the whole wide world, above, below, around and everywhere, doth he continue to pervade with a heart of love, far-reaching, grown great, and beyond measure.

So of all things which have life, there is not one that he passeth by or leaveth aside, but regardeth them all with mind set free, and deep-felt love. Verily this is the way to a state of union with Brahma.[38]

I & II, Tevigga Sutta, Digha Nikaya.

Then Alavaka addressed the Blessed One in the following words: What in this world is the best property for a

[38] Translation by Davids.

man? What, being well-done, conveyeth happiness? What is indeed the sweetest of sweet things? How lived can life be called the best?

The Blessed One said: Faith is in this world the best property for a man; the Law, well-observed, conveyeth happiness; truth is indeed the sweetest of things; and that life can be called the best which is lived with understanding.

Alavaka said: How doth one cross the stream of existence? How doth one cross the sea? How doth one conquer pain? How is one purified?

The Blessed One said: By faith one crosseth the stream; by zeal the sea; by exertion one conquereth pain; by understanding is one purified.[39]

Alavakasutta, Sutta-Nipata.

WHAT the wise man must do when he hath fixed his mind upon that state of calm, that will I declare: Let him be helpful, direct and upright, soft of speech, not overbearing, without care, not needing much, of quiet mind, not greedy when he seeketh alms.

In joy and peace may all things living dwell! Happy-hearted may they be! What living things there be, endowed with motion or motionless, be they great or small, seen or unseen, near or far, already born or striving to be born, all, all, let them be happy-hearted!

As a mother guardeth her little child, her only child, at the risk of her own life, so let every man cherish towards all living things boundless good will. Good will towards all the world, above and below and around, without enmity, without antagonism.

Whether he stand or go, whether he sit or lie, so long as he may live, let him live in this intent. Verily it is this that is called even in this world the life of a Brahman!

Mettasutta, Sutta-Nipata.

[39] Translation by Fausböll.

XX

The Old Mendicant, the Dwarf Bhaddiya and the Temptation of the Brethren

He that would wait upon me, let him wait upon the sick
brethren.   Buddha in Majjhima Nikaya VIII. 6.

Now there was a country called Gandhara in which was
a very old mendicant afflicted with a most loathsome
disease, which caused him to pollute every spot he occupied. Being in a certain monastery belonging to the place,
no one would come near him or help him in his distress.
Then Buddha came with His followers, and obtaining
warm water and what was needed else, they together
visited the place where the old Bhikkhu lay. And the
World-honoured with His own diamond hand began to
wash the body of the mendicant and attend to his maladies.

Then the earth shook, and the whole place was filled with
a supernatural light, so that the King and his ministers,
and all the heavenly host, flocked to the place, and paid
adoration to Buddha. And they inquired how One so
highly exalted could lower himself to such offices as these.
And Buddha declared the matter thus: The purpose of
the Tathagata in coming into the world is to befriend
these poor and helpless and unprotected ones, to nourish
those in bodily affliction, of whatever religion they be;
to help the impoverished, the orphan and the aged: and
by so doing, and persuading others so to do, all His
former vows are accomplished, and He attaineth the
great goal of all life, as the five rivers when they are lost
in the sea.[40]

Narrative accompanying the Chinese Dhammapada.

Now at that time the dwarf Bhaddiya, following step by
step in the wake of a large number of Bhikkhus, came to
where the Blessed One was.

[40] After the translation by Beal.

And when the Blessed One beheld the dwarf Bhaddiya,
coming in the wake of the Bhikkhus, ill-favoured, lowly
in gait and despised by the majority of the Bhikkhus, He
called them to Him and said: Behold, O Bhikkhus, this
mendicant approaching from afar, ill-favoured, lowly in
gait, and despised by the majority of the Bhikkhus.

Even so, Sire.

This mendicant, O Bhikkhus, is mighty in power, great
in strength: his state of perfection is not easily attained,
for the sake of which scions of noble families abandon
their homes for homelessness and in this very existence,
through the higher knowledge, realize and attain to that
supreme consummation, the holy life.[41]

Cula, the Udana.

THE Exalted One was once staying among the Sakyans,
at Silavati. Now very many of the brethren were living
near the Exalted One in zealous, ardent and strenuous
study.

Then Mara, the Evil One, assuming the shape of a
Brahman, clad in a whole antelope-skin, with matted
hair, aged and bent like the rafters of a roof, and holding
a staff of udumbara wood, drew near to those brethren,
and said to them: Your reverences are young to have left
the world, black-haired lads that ye are, blessed with
the luck of youth, without in your early prime having
had the fun belonging to natural desires. Enjoy, young
men, the pleasures of your kind! Do not, abandoning
the things of this life, run after matters involving time!

Nay, Brahman, we have not abandoned the things of this
life to run after matters involving time. It is matters of
time, Brahman, that we have abandoned, who are running after things of this life.

Yea, Brahman, matters of time are natural desires, hath
the Exalted One said, full of sorrow and despair; that
way lieth abundant disaster. But this doctrine is con-

[41] After the translation by Strong.

cerned with things of this life, and is not a matter of time. It biddeth a man to come and behold, it leadeth him on and away, and should be known by the wise as a personal experience.

When they had thus spoken Mara the Evil One departed with sunken head.[42]

Mara Sutta IV, 3, Samyutta Nikaya.

XXI

NAKULAPITAR

THE Exalted One was once staying among the Bhaggi, at the Crocodile Haunt in Bhesakala Grove. Then the housefather Nakulapitar came to the Exalted One, did Him reverence, and sat down at one side. And he addressed the Exalted One saying: Master I am a broken-down old man, far gone in years; I have reached life's end, I am sick and always ailing.

Moreover, Master, I am one to whom rarely cometh the sight of the Exalted One and the worshipful brethren. Let the Exalted One cheer and comfort me, so that it be a profit and a blessing unto me for many a long day.

True it is, housefather, thy body is weak and cumbered. Wherefore, housefather, thus shouldst thou train thyself: Though my body is sick, my mind shall not be sick! Thus, housefather, must thou train thyself.

Then Nakulapitar welcomed and gladly heard the words of the Exalted One, and rising from his seat he saluted the Exalted One by the right, and departed. And he came to the venerable Sariputta, saluted him and sat down at his side.

As he sat there, the venerable Sariputta said to the housefather Nakulapitar: Did it not occur to thee, housefather, to question the Exalted One thus: Pray how far, Master, is body sick and mind sick?

---

[42] After the translation by Mrs. Davids.

I would travel far indeed, Master, to learn from the lips of the venerable Sariputta the meaning of this saying! The venerable Sariputta spake thus: The untaught multitude, unskilled in the worthy doctrine, regard body as the self, the self as having body. I am the body, say they; body is mine; and are possessed by this idea. And so, when body altereth owing to the unstable and changeful nature of the body, then sorrow and grief, woe, lamentation and despair arise in them.

They regard feeling, activities, consciousness, as the self. I am consciousness, they say; consciousness is mine. And they are so possessed by this idea, when consciousness altereth owing to the unstable and changeful nature of consciousness, then sorrow and grief, woe, lamentation and despair arise in them. That, housefather, is how body is sick and mind is sick too.[43]

Text III. 2, XXII, Samyutta Nikaya.

XXII

SUNITA

Now in the first watch of the night the Exalted One surveyed the world. And He marked the saintliness of Sunita's soul, shining like a lamp within a jar. And when the night paled into dawn, He rose and dressed, and with bowl and robe, followed by His Bhikkhu train, He walked to Rajagaha for alms and sought the street where Sunita was sweeping. Dhammapala's Commentary.

I HAVE come of an humble family, I was poor and needy. Mean task was mine, sweeping the withered flowers from the streets and temples. I was despised of men, lightly esteemed and looked down upon. With submissive mien I bent my head in deference to men.

And then I saw the All-Enlightened come with His train of monks, passing, mighty champion, into Magadha's chief town.

[43] After F. L. Woodward's translation.

And I cast away my baskets and my yoke, and ran to bow myself in reverence before Him. From pity for me He halted, that Highest among men. Low at His feet I bent, and begged the Master's leave to join the Rule and follow Him, of every creature Chief.

Then said He, whose tender mercy watcheth all the world, the Master pitiful and kind: Bhikkhu, come! Thereby to me was ordination given.

Then I abode in forest depths alone, and with unfaltering zeal I wrought the Master's word, even the counsels of the Conqueror.

And as the night wore down at dawn and the sun rose, Indra came and Brahma with their train, yielding to me their homage with clasped hands: Hail unto thee, thou nobly born of men! Hail unto thee, thou highest among men!

Then the Master saw how the host of gods surrounded me, and a smile lit up His face, and He spake these words: By holy zeal and chaste living, by restraint and mastery of self becometh a man a Brahman: this is holiness supreme! *Theragatha.*

XXIII

Vasitthi

Her parents gave her in marriage to a clansman's son of equal rank, and she, bearing one son, lived happily with her husband. But when the child was old enough to run about, he died, and she was worn and maddened with grief. *Dhammapala's Commentary.*

Now here, now there, lightheaded, crazed with grief, mourning my child, I wandered up and down, naked, unheeding, streaming hair unkempt, lodged in scourings of the streets, and where the dead lay still, and by the chariot roads,—so three long years I fared, starving, athirst.

And then at last I saw Him, as He went within that blessed city Mithila: great Tamer of untamed hearts, yea, Him, that very Buddha, Banisher of fear.

Came back my heart to me, my errant mind; forthwith to Him I went low worshipping, and there even at His feet I heard the Norm. For of His great compassion on us all, it was He who taught me, even Gotama.

I heeded all He said and left the world and all its cares behind, and gave myself to follow where He taught, and found at last life in the Path that to salvation leads.

Now all my sorrows are hewn down, cast out, uprooted, brought to utter end, in that I now can grasp and understand the base on which my miseries are built.[44]

Therigatha, 133-138.

XXIV

THE ILLNESS OF THE BUDDHA AND PREDICTION OF HIS DEATH

Now when the Blessed One had entered upon the rainy season, there fell upon Him a dire sickness, and sharp pains came upon Him, even unto death. But the Blessed One, mindful and self-possessed, bore them without complaint.

Then this thought occurred to the Blessed One: It would not be right for me to pass away from existence without addressing the disciples, without taking leave of the Order. Let me now, by a strong effort of the will, bend this sickness down again, and keep hold on life till the allotted time be come!

And the Blessed One by a strong effort of the will, bent that sickness down again, and kept His hold on life till the time He fixed upon should come. And the sickness abated upon Him. When He was rid of the sickness, He went out from the monastery, and sat down behind the monastery on a seat spread out there.

[44] After Mrs. Davids' translation.

And the venerable Ananda went to the Blessed One and said: I have beheld, Lord, how the Blessed One had to suffer. And though at the sight of the sickness of the Blessed One my body became weak as a creeper, and the horizon became dim to me, and my faculties were no longer clear, yet nothwithstanding I took some little comfort from the thought that the Blessed One would not pass from existence until at least He had left instructions as touching the Order.

What then, Ananda, doth the Order expect that from me? Surely, Ananda, should there be anyone who harboureth the thought: It is I who will lead the brotherhood; or, The Order is dependent on me; it is he who should lay down instructions in any matter concerning the Order.

Now the Tathagata, Ananda, thinketh not that it is He who should lead the brotherhood, or that the Order is dependent on Him. Why then, should He leave instructions in any matter concerning the Order?

And now, Ananda, I am grown old and full of years, my journey is drawing to a close, I have reached the sum of my days, I am turning eighty years of age; and just as a worn-out cart can only by much additional care be made to move along, so, methinketh, the body of the Tathagata can be kept going only by much additional care.

It is only when the Tathagata, ceasing to attend to any outward thing, or to experience any sensation, becometh plunged in that devout meditation of the heart which is concerned with no material object, it is only then that the body of the Tathagata is at ease.

Therefore, Ananda, be ye lamps unto yourselves. Be ye a refuge to yourselves. Betake yourselves to no external refuge. Hold fast the truth as a lamp. Hold fast as a refuge to the truth!

On one occasion, Ananda, I was resting under the

Shepherd's Nigrodha tree [45] on the bank of the river Neranjara after having reached the Great Enlightenment.

Then Mara, the evil one, came to the place where I was, and standing beside me addressed me thus: Pass away now, Lord, from existence! Now is the time for the Blessed One to pass away!

And when he had thus spoken, I answered Mara and said: I shall not die, O evil one! until not only the brethren and sisters of the Order, but also the lay-disciples shall have become true hearers, wise and well-versed in the Scriptures, fulfilling all the greater and the lesser duties, walking according to the precepts.

Or until they, having themselves learned the doctrine, shall be able to tell others of it, make it known, establish it, and make it clear; until they shall be able to vanquish and refute vain doctrine, and so to spread the wonder-working truth abroad.

I shall not die until this pure religion of mine shall have become successful, prosperous, wide-spread in all its full extent; till, in a word, it shall have been well proclaimed among men.

And now again today, Ananda, the Evil One addressed me in the same words. And when he had thus spoken, I answered him and said: Make thyself happy, the final extinction of the Tathagata shall take place ere long. In three months from this time the Tathagata will die.

Then the Blessed One proceeded, and Ananda with Him, to the Mahavana; and when He had arrived He said: Go now, Ananda, assemble in the Service Hall such of the brethren as dwell about Vesali.

Even so, Lord, said the venerable Ananda. And when he had assembled in the Service Hall such of the brethren as dwelt about Vesali, he went to the Blessed One and said: Lord, the assembly of the brethren hath met to-

[45] Or Bodhi tree, *ficus religiosa.*

gether. Let the Blessed One do even as seemeth to Him fit.

Then the Blessed One proceeded to the Service Hall, and sat down on the mat spread out for Him. And the Blessed One addressed the brethren and said:

O brethren, to whom I have made known the truths perceived by me, having made yourselves thorough masters thereof, practice and meditate upon them, and, out of pity for the world, spread them abroad, that pure religion may last long and be perpetuated, that it may continue for the happiness of the multitudes, for the good and the gain and the weal of gods and men!

The final extinction of the Tathagata will take place ere long. In three months from this time the Tathagata will depart. Be earnest then, O brethren, holy, full of thought! Be steadfast in resolve! Keep watch upon your hearts! Who wearieth not, but holdeth fast to truth and law shall cross this sea of life, shall make an end of grief! [46]

Maha-parinibbana-sutta II & III, Digha Nikaya.

XXV

ANANDA THE BELOVED DISCIPLE

For five-and-twenty years Ananda waited upon Him of the Ten Powers, bringing Him water, washing His feet, accompanying Him, sweeping His cell. During the day he kept at hand to mark the Master's: "This should be procured, that should be done." And at night, taking a stout staff and lantern, he would go nine times around the fragrant cell, making response if the Master called that he might not succumb to drowsiness.

Theragatha and Dhammapala's Commentary.

Now the Blessed One addressed the venerable Ananda and said: Come, Ananda, let us go to the Sala Grove of the Mallas on the farther side of the river Hiranyavati. Even so, Lord, said the venerable Ananda.

[46] After Davids' translation.

And the Blessed One proceeded with a great company of the brethren to the Sala Grove of the Mallas on the farther side of the river Hiranyavati: and when He was come there he said: Spread over for me, Ananda, I pray thee, the couch with its head to the north between the twin Sala trees. I am weary, Ananda, and would lie down.

Even so, Lord, said the venerable Ananda. And he spread a covering over the couch with its head to the north between the twin Sala trees. And the Blessed One laid Himself down on His right side, and He was mindful and self-possessed.

Now at that time the twin Sala trees were one mass of bloom with flowers out of season; and over the body of the Tathagata these dropped and scattered, out of reverence for the successor of the Buddhas of old. And heavenly Mandarava flowers, too, came falling from the sky. And celestial music sounded out of reverence for the successor of the Buddhas of old.

Then the Blessed One addressed the venerable Ananda, and said: The twin Sala trees are one mass of bloom with flowers out of season; over the body of the Tathagata these drop and scatter out of reverence for the successor of the Buddhas of old. And heavenly Mandarava flowers, too, come falling from the sky, and celestial music soundeth.

Now it is not thus, Ananda, that the Tathagata is rightly honoured, venerated, or revered. But the brother or the sister, the devout man or the devout woman, who continually fulfilleth all the greater and the lesser duties, who is correct in life, walking according to the precepts, it is he who doth rightly honour, venerate, and revere the Tathagata with the worthiest homage.

Ananda said: What are we to do, Lord, with the remains of the Tathagata?

Hinder not yourselves, Ananda, by honouring the remains of the Tathagata. Be earnest, be zealous, intent on your own good! There are wise men, Ananda, among the nobles, among the Brahmans, who are firm believers in the Tathagata; they will do honour to His remains.

Now the venerable Ananda went into the monastery and stood leaning against the lintel of the door, weeping at the thought: Alas! I remain still but a learner, one who hath yet to work out his own perfection: and the Master is about to pass away from me, He who is so kind!

Now the Blessed One called one of the brethren and said: Where then is Ananda?

The venerable Ananda, Lord, hath gone into the monastery, and standeth leaning against the lintel of the door, weeping. And the Blessed One said: Go now and call Ananda in my name, and say: Brother Ananda, the Master calleth for thee.

Even so, Lord, said that brother. And he went to the venerable Ananda and said: Brother Ananda, the Master calleth for thee. And the venerable Ananda went to the Blessed One and bowed down before the Blessed One, and took his seat respectfully on one side.

Then said the Blessed One as he sat there by His side: Enough, Ananda, let not thyself be troubled, do not weep! Have I not already told thee that it is in the very nature of all things most near and dear to us that we must divide ourselves from them, leave them, sever ourselves from them?

Whereas, Ananda, anything whatever born, brought into being, organized, containeth within itself the inherent necessity of dissolution, how can it be possible that such a being should not be dissolved? No such condition can exist!

For a long time, Ananda, thou hast been very near to me by acts and words and thoughts of love, kind and good, never varying, and beyond all measure. Thou hast done well, Ananda! Be earnest in effort, and thou too shalt soon be free from the great evils, from delusion and from ignorance!

XXVI

SUBHADDA

Now at that time a mendicant named Subhadda, not a believer, was dwelling at Kusinara. And Subhadda heard the news: This very day, in the third watch of the night, will the final passing away of the Samana Gotama occur. Then the mendicant Subhadda went to the Sala Grove of the Mallas, and he said to the venerable Ananda: Thus have I heard from fellow mendicants, old and well stricken in years, teachers and disciples: Full seldom do Tathagatas appear in the world, and Arahat Buddhas. Yet today, in the last watch of the night, will the final passing away of the Samana Gotama take place.

Now a feeling of uncertainty hath sprung up in my mind; and this faith have I in the Samana Gotama, that He, me thinketh, is able to present the truth, that I may rid myself of this uncertainty. O Ananda, that even I might be allowed to see the Samana Gotama!

And when he had thus spoken the venerable Ananda said: Enough, friend Subhadda! Trouble not the Tathagata. The Blessed One is weary. And again Subhadda made the same request and received the same reply; and the third time he made the same request in the same words and received the same reply.

Now the Blessed One overheard the venerable Ananda with the mendicant Subhadda. And He called Ananda and said: It is enough, Ananda! Do not keep out Subhadda. Subhadda may be allowed to see the Tathagata. Whatever Subhadda will ask me, he will ask from a desire for knowledge, and not to annoy me, and whatever I may say in answer to his questions, that will he quickly understand.

Then the venerable Ananda said to Subhadda: Enter in, friend Subhadda; for the Blessed One giveth thee leave. Then Subhadda, the mendicant, went in to the Blessed One and saluted him courteously and took his seat on one

side. And when he was thus seated, Subhadda said: The
Brahmans, Gotama, who are heads of companies of disciples, founders of schools of doctrine, esteemed as good
men by the multitudes, to wit, Kassapa, Makkhali, Ajita,
Kaccayana, Sanjaya, have they all, according to their
own assertion, thoroughly understood things? Or have
they not? Or are there some of them who have understood, and some who have not?

Enough, Subhadda! Let this matter rest whether they
have thoroughly understood things, or whether they have
not! The truth will I teach thee. Listen to that, and give
ear attentively, and I will speak. Even so, Lord, said
Subhadda!

And the Blessed One spake: In whatsoever doctrine and
discipline, Subhadda, the noble Eightfold Path is not
found, neither in it is found a man of true saintliness.
And in whatsoever doctrine and discipline the noble
Eightfold Path is found, there is found the man of true
saintliness.

Now in this doctrine and discipline is found the noble
Eightfold Path, and in it alone is the man of true saintliness. And in this one, Subhadda, may the brethren live
the life that is right, that the world be not bereft of
Arahats. In this one may the brethren live the perfect
life, that the world be not bereft of those who have
reached the highest fruit.

And when He had thus spoken, Subhadda said: Most
excellent, Lord, are the words of Thy mouth! Just as if
a man were to set up that which is thrown down, or
reveal that which is hidden, or point out the right road
to him who hath gone astray, or bring a lamp into the
darkness, even so, Lord, hast Thou made known the
truth to me.

And I betake myself to the Blessed One as my refuge, to
the Truth, and to the Order. May the Blessed One accept
me as a disciple and true believer from this day forth as
long as life may dure.

And the Blessed One called Ananda and said: Ananda, receive Subhadda into the Order.

And Subhadda said to Ananda: Great is your gain, friend Ananda, great is your good fortune, that ye all have been sprinkled with the sprinkling of discipleship in this brotherhood at the hands of the Master Himself!

So Subhadda, the mendicant, was received into the higher grade of the Order under the Blessed One; and after his ordination he remained alone and separate, earnest, zealous and resolved.

And ere long he attained to that goal of the higher life for the sake of which men go out from all and every household gain and comfort to become houseless wanderers; yea, that supreme goal did he, by himself, while yet in the visible world recognize and realize and see face to face.

So the venerable Subhadda became another among the Arahats; and he was the last disciple that the Blessed One Himself converted.

XXVII

The Buddha Entereth into Nirvana

Now the blessed One addressed the venerable Ananda, and said: It may be, Ananda, that in some of you the thought may arise: The word of the Master is ended, we have no teacher more! But it is not thus that ye should regard it. The truths and the rules of the Order which I have set forth and laid down for you all, let them, after I am gone, be your Teacher.

Then the Blessed One said: It may be, brethren, that there may be doubt or misgiving in the mind of some brother as to the Buddha, or the Truth, or the Way. Enquire, brethren, freely! Do not have to reproach yourselves afterward with the thought: Our teacher was face to face with us, and we could not bring ourselves to enquire of the Blessed One when we were face to face with Him.

And when He had thus spoken the brethren were silent. And the venerable Ananda said to the Blessed One: How wonderful a thing it is, Lord, and how marvellous! Verily, I believe that in this whole assembly of the brethren there is not one brother who hath any doubt or misgiving as to the Buddha or the Truth or the Way.

Then the Blessed One addressed the brethren and said: Behold now, brethren, I exhort you, saying; Transitory are all earthly things. Work out your salvation with diligence! This was the last word of the Tathagata.

When the Blessed One died there arose at the moment of His passing a mighty earthquake, terrible and awe-inspiring; and the thunders of heaven burst forth.[47]

And of those of the brethren who were not yet free from passions, some stretched out their arms and wept, and some fell headlong on the ground, rolling to and fro in anguish at the thought: Too soon hath the Blessed One died! Too soon hath the Happy One passed away! Too soon hath the Light gone out in the world!

But those of the brethren who were free from passions bore their grief, collected and composed at the thought: Transitory are all component things! How is it possible that they should not be dissolved?

Then the venerable Anuruddha exhorted the brethren, and said: Enough, my brethren! Weep not, neither lament! Hath not the Blessed One declared that it is in the very nature of all things near and dear to us that we must leave them, sever ourselves from them?

Then, brethren, whereas anything whatever born, brought into being, and organized, containeth within itself the inherent necessity of dissolution, how can it be possible that such a being should not be dissolved? No such condition can exist! Even the spirits, brethren, will reproach us.

Now the venerable Anuruddha and the venerable Ananda spent the rest of the night in religious discourse. Then

[47] Comp. Mat. XXVII. 51.

Anuruddha said: Go now, brother Ananda, into Kusinara and tell the Mallas of Kusinara, saying: The Blessed One hath passed away; do, then, whatever seemeth to you fit!

Now at that time the Mallas of Kusinara were assembled in the council hall concerning that very matter. And the venerable Ananda told them, saying: The Blessed One hath passed away; do, then, whatever seemeth to you fit!

And when they heard this saying the Mallas, with their young men and their maidens and their wives, were grieved and sad and afflicted at heart.

And some of them wept, dishevelling their hair, and some stretched forth their arms and wept, and some reeled to and fro in anguish at the thought: Too soon hath the Blessed One died! Too soon hath the Happy One passed away! Too soon hath the Light gone out in the world!

Then the Mallas of Kusinara went to the Sala Grove where the body of the Blessed One lay. There they passed the day in paying homage to the remains of the Blessed One with dancing and hymns and music, with garlands and with perfumes, and in making canopies of their garments and preparing wreaths to hang thereon in decoration.

Then the Mallas of Kusinara wrapped the body of the Blessed One in new cloths. And they built a funeral pile of all kinds of perfumes, and upon it they placed the body of the Blessed One.

And when the body of the Blessed One had been burned, there came down streams of water from the sky and extinguished the funeral pile.

Then the Mallas of Kusinara surrounded the bones of the Blessed One in their council hall with a lattice work of spears, and with a rampart of bows; and there for seven days they paid homage to them with dance and song and music, and with garlands and perfumes.[48]

Chapters XXV, XXVI & XXVII are from Maha-parinibbana-sutta, V & VI, Digha Nikaya.

[48] After Davids' translation.

XXVIII

The Division of the Relics

Thus those Mallas offered religious reverence to the relics, and used the most costly flowers and scents for their supreme act of worship.

Then the kings of the seven countries,[49] having heard that Buddha had passed away, sent messengers to the Mallas asking to share the sacred relics.

Then the Mallas, trusting to their martial renown, conceived a haughty mind: We would rather part with life itself than with the relics of the Buddha! So those messengers returned.

Then the seven kings with an army numerous as the rain clouds, advanced on Kusinara; the people who went from the city, filled with terror, soon returned, and told the Mallas that the soldiers and cavalry of the countries round about were coming, with elephants and chariots, to surround Kusinara. The gardens lying without the town, the fountains, lakes, flower and fruit trees were now destroyed by the advancing host, and all the pleasant resting-places lay in ruins.

The Mallas, mounting on the city towers, beheld these supports of life destroyed; they then prepared their war-like engines to crush the foe without; balistas and catapults and flying torches to hurl against the advancing host.

Then the seven kings entrenched themselves around the city, their wings of battle shining in array as the sun's beams of glory shine; the heavy drums rolling as the thunder. The Mallas, greatly incensed, opening the gates, commanded the fray to begin.

But ere the contest had begun, a certain Brahman whose name was Drona addressed those kings and said: From

---

[49] Magadha, Vesali, Kusinara, Kapilavastu and the other regions that had embraced Buddha's doctrine.

the beginning mutual strife hath produced destruction; how can it result in glory or renown? The clash of swords and bloody onset done, it is certain one must perish. Whilst ye aim to conquer these, both sides will suffer in the fray.

Beware of leaning overmuch on strength of body; nought can compare with strength of right. Use then principles of righteousness, the expedients of good-will and love. Conquer your foe by force, ye increase his enmity; conquer by love, ye reap no after-sorrow. The present strife is but a thirst for blood; this thing cannot be endured! If ye desire to honour Buddha, copy His patience and long-suffering.

And now the kings addressed the Brahman thus: The rules of kings are framed to avoid the use of force when hatred hath arisen from low desires. But for the sake of religion we are about to fight.

Now then, if thou desirest to stay the strife, go, and for us demand within the city that they distribute the relics, and so cause our prayer to be fulfilled. Because thy words are right ones, we hold our anger for a while; even as the great angry snake by power of charms is quieted.

And now the Brahman, entering the city, went to the Mallas and said: Without the city those who are kings among men, their bodies clad in weighty armour wait eagerly, glorious as the sun, bristling with rage as the roused lion! These are united to overthrow the city.

But whilst they wage this religious war, they fear lest they act irreligiously, and so they have sent me here to say what they require.

Because we venerate the great Seer we are come. Ye, noble sirs, know well our mind. Why should there be such sorrowful contention? Ye honour what we honour, we both with equal heart revere the spiritual relics of the Lord. To be miserly in hoarding wealth, this is an unreasonable fault; how much more to grudge religion, of which there is so little knowledge in the world?

So now let there be no contention either way; reason ought to minister for peace; the Lord when dwelling in the world ever employed the force of patience; not to obey His holy teaching and yet to offer gifts to Him is base hypocrisy. To adore the great Merciful One and yet to gender wide destruction, how is this possible?

The Mallas hearing the Brahman's words, with inward shame gazed one at the other. Then they opened out the Master's relics and in eight parts equally divided them. Themselves paid reverence to one part, the other seven they handed to the Brahman.

The seven kings having accepted these, rejoiced, and returned with them to their own countries and erected shrines over them.[50]

Kiouen V, Varga 28, Fo-Sho-Hing-Tsan-King.

XXIX

THE TRANSCRIBING OF THE SUTTA-PITAKA [51]

AND the Arahats numbering five hundred, having for ever lost their Master's presence, reflecting that there was now no ground for certainty, returned to Gridhrakuta Mount, assembling in King Sakra's cavern; and the assembly agreed that the venerable Ananda should recite for the sake of the congregation the sermons of the Tathagata from first to last.

Then Ananda in the great assembly ascending the lion throne, declared in order what the Lord had preached, uttering the words: Thus have I heard. The whole assembly, bathed in tears, were deeply moved as he pronounced the words, Thus have I heard.

As he spake, so was it written down from first to last, the complete Sutta-Pitaka.[50]

2287-2289, Fo-Sho-Hing-Tsan-King.

[50] Translation by Beal.
[51] Literally *Sermon-Basket*, one of the three great divisions of the ancient Buddhist Canon.

THERE are certain subjects for meditation that have been
made known by the Blessed One, by Him of knowledge
and insight, by the Arahat, the Buddha supreme. And
they are these:

The idea of the impermanence of every thing and of
 every being;
The idea of the absence of any abiding principle in them;
The idea of the impurity and danger connected with the
 body;
The idea of getting rid of evil dispositions;
The idea of freedom from passion;
The idea of peace;
The idea of dissatisfaction with the things of the world;
The idea of the ecstatic trance;
The idea of love to all beings;
The idea of pity for all beings;
The idea of sympathy with all beings;
The idea of equanimity in all the changing circumstances
 of life;
The idea of death.   *Milinda Pañha V. 6.*

WHOSOEVER is fit, who desires little and is content, given
to seclusion, alert in zeal, resolute in heart, without guile,
seeking neither material gain nor worldly fame or glory,
full of faith; whosoever being such shall take upon himself the vows with the idea of upholding the faith, he is
deserving of twofold honour. For he is loved and longed
for by both gods and men, dear as rare jasmine flowers
to the man bathed and anointed, as sweet food to the
hungry, as cool, clear, fragrant water to the thirsty, as
the blessed attainment of the fruits of Arahatship to the
seeker after holiness.

Just as a lotus flower of glorious, pure, and high descent
is glossy, sweet-smelling, longed-for, loved, untarnished
by the mud, graced with tiny petals and filaments and
pericarps, the resort of many bees, a child of the clear,
cold stream, just so is the disciple of the Noble Ones.

His heart is full of affectionate and tender love, evil is
cast out from within him, pride and self-righteousness;
stable, strong and undeviating is his faith, he enters into
the enjoyment of the heart's refreshment, the highly
desirable peace of the ecstasies of contemplation, he ex-
hales the most excellent and sweet savour of righteousness of life; near is he and dear to men and gods alike,
gods and men delight to honour him; rich is he in the best
of wealth, the wealth that is the fruit of the Path; unalterable in character, excellent in conduct, he has passed
beyond all perplexity, his mind is set upon complete
emancipation, he has seen the truth, the sure and steadfast place of refuge from all fear has he gained.[52]

Milinda Pañha VI. 18, 25.

THE noble and superlative law of Buddha ought to receive the adoration of the world.

Gone to Amrita,[53] that undying place, those who believe
shall follow Him there; therefore let men and angels all,
without exception, worship and adore the great, loving
and compassionate One, who mastered thoroughly the
highest truth in order to deliver all that liveth. Who
hearing of Him doth not yearn with love?

The pains of birth, old age, disease and death; the endless sorrows of the world, the countless miseries of the
hereafter, He hath removed all these accumulated sorrows; say, who would not revere Him? He having shown
the way to all the world, who would not reverence and
adore him?

To sing the praises of the lordly Monk, and declare His
acts from first to last, without self-seeking or self-honour,
without desire for personal renown, but to benefit the
world, hath been my aim.[54]

2303ff., Fo-Sho-Hing-Tsan-King.[55]

[52] This and the above translated by Davids.
[53] Immortality.　　　　　　　　　[54] Translated by Beal.
[55] The Fo-Sho-Hing-Tsan-King and the Milinda Pañha, or Questions of
King Milinda (Menander) from which the closing selections are taken are
not included in the Buddhist Canon; however the latter at least is regarded
as an authority which may be implicitly followed.

As men who see the ocean rollers break
Infer the greatness of the world-embracing sea,
So may they judge of Him whose teachings take
Throughout the listening earth their course of victory.

And when the earth rejoiceth fresh and green,
"The gracious rain" they cry, "hath come at last;"
So judge they when the hearts of weary men
Rejoice, "His gracious words into their lives have
     passed."

As men who scent a fragrance in the air
Know the great forest trees hard-by are flowering,
So, of this perfume sweet of holiness, may they infer,
"Here surely lived a Buddha great, high-towering."[50]
              Milinda Pañha, V, 346; 2, 6 & 8.

[50] After a rendering by K. J. Saunders in *The Heart of Buddhism,* the Association Press.

SELECTIONS FROM THE DHAMMAPADA

*The Dhammapada (The Path of Religion) was accepted
at the Council of Asoka in 240 B.C. as a collection of the
sayings of Gotama; and there is no doubt that it breathes
the very spirit of the Buddha; yet it was not put into
writing till some generations had passed, and probably
contains accretions of a later date from popular proverbs
of India and early hymns by monks.*

MIND is it that doth give to things their quality, their
foundation and their being; whoso doth speak or act with
evil mind, him doth sorrow dog, as followeth the wheel
the beast of burden's foot.

Mind is it that doth give to things their quality, their
foundation and their being; whoso doth speak or act
with a pure mind, him happiness doth follow as a faithful
shadow.

This trembling, wavering mind, so hard to guard and
guide, the wise man maketh straight as a fletcher doth
his shaft.

Whoso doth control this incorporeal cave-dweller, this
far-wandering, solitary mind, shall escape the bonds of
death.

Knowing thy body fragile as a potter's vessel, stablish
thy mind like a fortress; smite Mara with the sword of
wisdom, and guard thy conquest without dalliance!

Esteeming this body as a bubble, regarding it as a mir-
age, break the flower-shafts of Mara, and press on to the
bourne where the monarch Death shall gaze on thee no
more!

Engineers control the water; fletchers straighten the
shaft; carpenters fashion their wood; sages control and
fashion themselves.

Self is the lord of self, who else could be the lord? With
self well-subdued, findeth a man a master such as few can
find.

By self is evil done, by self is one disgraced. By self is evil left undone, by self alone can one be purified.

Wert thou to conquer in battle a thousand times thousand men, he who conquereth self were the greater conqueror.

Better were it to conquer self than all the world beside; not even a god, not Mara with Brahma, can change into defeat thy victory o'er thyself.

By hating hatred doth not cease at any time; by love doth hatred cease; this is the ancient law.

Overcome anger by love; overcome evil with good; meanness with a gift, and a liar with the truth!

Zeal to Nirvana is the path. Sloth is the way to death. The zealous never die. The slothful are already dead.

The scent of flowers is not borne against the wind, though it were sandal, rose-bay or jessamine; but the fragrance of the holy is borne against the wind; the righteous do pervade all space.

More excellent than the scent of sandal and rose-bay, of lily and of jessamine, is the fragrance of good deeds.

As standeth a massive rock unshaken by the wind, so stand the wise unmoved by praise or blame.

Few among men are they who reach the farther shore; the rest, a mighty multitude, run hither and thither along the bank.

Better than a thousand empty words is one pregnant word that bringeth the hearer peace.

Better than sovereignty over earth, better than birth into heaven, than lordship over all the worlds, is the reward of entering the stream of holiness.

Better one day of insight into the deathless state, than a hundred years of blindness to this immortality.

As a noble steed stung by the lash, be ye spirited and swift!

Who have not purely lived, nor stored up treasure in their youth, these perish ruefully like old herons by a lake wherein there are no fish.

Obey the eternal law of the heavens; who keepeth this law liveth happily in this world and the next.

In bliss then let us live, possessing naught; on happiness we shall feed, like the bright gods.

When after voyaging long afar, one returneth safely home, kinsfolk and friends receive him gladly; even so do his good deeds welcome the righteous man when he leaveth this world for the next.

Far off are seen the holy ones like mountains bright with snow; the unholy pass as arrows shot by night.

THE BRAHMAN

Him I call indeed a Brahman who offendeth not by body, word or thought.

A man becometh not a Brahman by his platted hair nor by his birth; in whom is truth and righteousness, he is blessed, he a Brahman.

What use to thee thy platted hair, O fool? Thy raiment of goat-skins? Within thee there is ravening, while the outside thou makest clean!

Him I call indeed a Brahman who hath loosed his shackles, trembleth not, is unfettered, free; who hath burst the bar and is awakened.

Him I call indeed a Brahman who, abstaining from offense, endureth yet reproach and bonds and stripes; patience his power, strength his shield.

Him I call indeed a Brahman who with the intolerant tolerant is, among the passionate passion-free.

Him I call indeed a Brahman from whom hate and anger, pride and envy have dropt like a mustard-seed from a needle's point.

Him I call indeed a Brahman who like the moon reflecteth light, pure, serene, and undisturbed.

Him I call indeed a Brahman who hath traversed this miry road, this vain, impassable world, and crossed over to the farther shore, enrapt and guileless, free from doubts, free from attachment and desire.

Him I call indeed a Brahman who, loosed from bondage to mankind, risen above bondage to the gods, is free from all and every bondage, the conqueror who hath won the worlds! [57]

[57] Compiled from the translations of Max Müller, Kenneth Saunders and W. D. C. Wagiswara, and Albert Edmunds.

THE EDICTS OF ASOKA, KING OF INDIA

BEING SELECTIONS FROM HIS ROCK
AND PILLAR EDICTS

Receiving from heaven a righteous disposition, he ruled equally over the world.

Fo-Sho-Hing-Tsan-King.

THE EDICTS OF ASOKA, KING OF INDIA

Asoka-Vardhana, the first Buddhist to emerge from the regions of myth into authentic history, succeeded his father in the government of India about 274 B.C. With St. Paul and Constantine he is of that small group of men who have raised to dominant positions religions founded by others. Becoming a monk, he established so many monasteries that his kingdom received the name Vihara (LAND OF MONASTERIES). *He made Buddhism the state religion and did more for its propagation in foreign parts than any who preceded or came after him. In a sense we can know him better than any other ancient monarch because he speaks to us in his own words committed to the faithful keeping of the rocks. These rocks are found in thirteen distinct localities in remote provinces of the empire, and the messages engraved thereon, dating from 258-257 B.C. are the earliest known inscriptions in India.*

MINOR ROCK EDICT I

LET great and small exert themselves! This purpose must be written on the rocks as opportunity offereth. And measures must be taken to have it engraved upon stone pillars wherever in my dominions there are stone pillars.

ROCK EDICT XIII

KALINGA was conquered by His Sacred and Gracious Majesty the King when he had been consecrated eight years. One hundred and fifty thousand were carried away captive thence, one hundred thousand were there slain, and many times that number perished.

Directly after the annexation of Kalinga began his Majesty's love of the Law of Piety, his zealous protec-

tion of that Law, and his inculcation of that Law. Thence
ariseth His Majesty's remorse for the conquest of Kalinga, because the conquest of a country involveth the
slaughter, death, and carrying away captive of a people.
That is to His Majesty a matter of profound sorrow and
remorse.

In such a country dwell householders, Brahmans or
ascetics, men of various denominations. To such a people
in such a country befalleth violence or slaughter or separation from their loved ones. Or misfortune befalleth
the friends, comrades, and relatives of those who are
themselves protected, while their affection is undimin-
ished. Thus for them too this is a mode of violence. And
the share of this that falleth on all men is a matter of
profound regret to His Majesty.

Thus of all the people slain, done to death, or carried
away captive in Kalinga, if the hundredth or the thou-
sandth part were now to suffer the same fate, it would
be a matter of great sorrow to His Sacred Majesty.
Moreover, should any do him wrong, that too must be
borne by His Majesty if it can possibly be borne. For His
Majesty desireth that all animate things should have
security and self-control, peace of mind and joyousness.

This is the chiefest conquest, thinketh His Majesty, the
conquest by the Law of Piety; and this hath been won
by His Majesty both in his own dominions and in all the
neighboring realms as far as six hundred leagues; everywhere men follow the instruction of His Majesty in the
Law of Piety. Even where his envoys do not penetrate,
there too men, hearing His Majesty's ordinance based on
the Law of Piety, practise that Law.

And the conquest thereby won is a conquest full of delight. A small matter, however, is that delight. His
Majesty regardeth as bearing much fruit that only which
concerneth the other world.

And for this purpose hath this scripture of the Law been
recorded, that my sons and grandsons who may be should
not regard it as their duty to carry out a new conquest.

If perchance a conquest should please them, they should take heed only of patience and gentleness, regarding as a conquest only that which is effected by the Law of Piety, for that availeth for both this world and the next.

The Borderers' Edict

Concerning the conquered province of Kalinga and the wild tribes dwelling on its borders.

Thus saith His Sacred Majesty: At Samapa the High Officers are to be addressed as follows:

All men are my children; [1] and just as I desire my children to enjoy all prosperity and happiness in this world and the next, so do I desire for all men the same.

If ye ask, With regard to the unsubdued borderers, What is the King's command? The King desireth that they should not be afraid of me, that they should trust me, and should receive from me kindness, not sorrow. Moreover, they should grasp the truth: The King will bear patiently with us, and that for my sake they should follow the Law of Piety and so gain both this world and the next.

Now do ye act accordingly and make these people to trust me and to grasp the truth: The King is to us even as a father; he loveth us even as he loveth himself; we are to the King even as his children.

And for this purpose hath this scripture been written here, that the high officers may strive without ceasing both to secure the confidence of these borderers and to set them moving on the path of piety.

Rock Edict II

Everywhere in his dominions the medical aid of His Sacred and Gracious Majesty the King hath been prepared in two kinds, medical aid for men and medical aid for beasts. Medicinal herbs also, medicinal herbs for men

[1] An echo of the saying ascribed to Buddha.

and medicinal herbs for beasts, wheresoever lacking, have been everywhere both imported and planted. Roots also and fruits, wheresoever lacking, have been everywhere both imported and planted.

Rock Edict VI

Thus saith His Sacred and Gracious Majesty the King: A long period hath elapsed during which in the past business was not carried on nor information brought in at all times. This therefore I have decreed, that at all times, when I am eating, or in my inner chamber, or in my conveyance, or in the pleasure-grounds, everywhere the persons appointed shall report the people's business to me.

Because I never feel satisfaction in my exertions and dispatch of business. For work I must for the welfare of all the people; and of that the root is energy and dispatch of business; for nothing is more essential than the welfare of all the people.

And whatsoever effort I make is made that I may be free from my debt to all creatures, so that while in this world I make some persons happy, they may win heaven in the world beyond. For that purpose have I caused to be written this scripture of the Law, that it may endure while my sons, grandsons, and great-grandsons take action for the welfare of all the people.

Rock Edict VII

His Sacred and Gracious Majesty the King desireth that in all places men of every sect may dwell, for they all desire mastery over their senses and purity of heart.

Rock Edict XII

His Sacred and Gracious Majesty the King doth reverence to men of all denominations, whether householders or ascetics, by gifts and manifold honours.

His Majesty, however, careth not so much for gifts or external reverence as that there should be a growth of the essence of the matter in all denominations. And the essence of the matter is restraint of speech: to wit, a man must not do reverence to his own denomination or disparage that of another without reason, because the sects of other people are all deserving of reverence.

By acting thus a man exalteth his own sect, and also doth service to the sects of others. By acting contrariwise a man hurteth his own sect and harmeth the sects of others.

Concord, therefore, is commendable.

ROCK EDICT IX

THUS saith His Sacred and Gracious Majesty the King: In sickness, at weddings, the birth of children, departure on journeys, on these and similar occasions people perform many ceremonies.

Ceremonies must be performed, though that kind beareth little fruit. This sort, on the other hand, the ceremonial of piety, beareth great fruit; to wit, proper treatment of servants and slaves, honour to teachers, gentleness toward living creatures, and liberality toward Brahmans and ascetics.

This will I perform, for the ceremonial of this world is of doubtful efficacy. But the ceremonial of piety is not temporal; because even though it fail to attain the desired end in this world, it surely produceth endless merit in the world beyond.

ROCK EDICT X

WHATSOEVER exertions His Majesty the King doth make are for the sake of life hereafter, so that all may be freed from peril, and that peril is vice.

Difficult, verily, it is to attain such freedom, whether by people of low or high degree, save by utmost exertion, giving up all other aims. That, however, for him of high degree, is hard.

Pillar Edict IV

To men who are bound with fetters, on whom punishment has been passed and who have been condemned to death have I granted three days as rightfully and exclusively their own; to stay their spiritual destruction they will give alms and observe fasts pertaining to the next world. For my desire is that even during the time of imprisonment they may try to win the bliss of the next world, and that manifold practices, self-restraint and liberality may grow among the people.

Pillar Edict VII

Thus saith His Sacred and Gracious Majesty the King: By what means can men be induced to conform to the Law of Piety? By what means can I lift up some of them at least through the growth of that law?

This thought occurred to me: Proclamation of the Law of Piety will I proclaim; with instruction in that Law will I instruct; so men hearkening thereto may conform, lift themselves up, and mightily grow with the growth of the Law of Piety.

For this my purpose proclamations of the Law of Piety have been proclaimed; manifold instructions in that Law have been diffused; my missioners, likewise my agents set over the multitude, will expound and expand my teaching.

On the roads too, to give shade to man and beast, I have had planted banyan-trees; groves of mango-trees I have had planted; at every half-kos wells have I had dug; rest-houses also have been raised; and numerous watering-places by me provided here and there for the enjoyment of man and beast.

With various blessings hath mankind been blessed by former kings, as also by me; by me, however, hath it been done with the intent that men may conform to the Law of Piety.

My High Officers of the Law of Piety, too, are employed on manifold objects of the royal favour affecting both householders and ascetics, among all denominations; and in the provinces they indicate in divers ways places where satisfaction may be given.

The practice of the Law of Piety is that whereby compassion, liberality, truth, purity, gentleness and saintliness will grow among mankind.

Whatsoever meritorious deeds have by me been done, those deeds mankind will imitate, whence followeth that they have grown and will grow in the virtues of hearkening to father and mother, hearkening to teachers, reverence to the aged, and the seemly treatment of Brahmans and ascetics, of the poor and wretched, yea, even of servants and slaves.

The superiority of reflection is shown by the growth of piety among men and the more complete abstention from killing animate beings and from the sacrificial slaughter of living creatures.

This scripture of the Law of Piety, where pillars of stone or tables of stone exist, must be written down that it may long endure.[2]

[2] The above selections from Asoka's Rock Edicts have been adapted from Vincent A. Smith's version.

SELECTIONS FROM

THE LAWS OF MANU

THE LAWS OF MANU

The Code of Manu is a Sanskrit work dating from before the Christian era. In the Indian legend of the Flood, Manu alone was saved; his oblations produced a woman through whom he generated the human race, thus becoming the Father of Mankind (Sanskrit manu—man. He was therefore considered as the founder of the moral and social order, and as a prophet to whom the sacred texts were revealed. In the Bhagavadgita, Krishna says: This unaltering Rule declared I to the Sun, the Sun declared it unto Manu.

SACRED Knowledge approached a Brahman and said to him: I am thy treasure; preserve me, deliver me not to a scorner; so shall I become extremely strong.   *II. 114.*

LET every Brahman, fixing his attention, recognize all nature, both visible and invisible, as existing in the Divine Spirit, the universe as resting in Him, Himself the whole assemblage of the gods and the Author of every human action.   *XII. 118, 119.*

WHEN Goodness, wounded by Injustice, cometh to a court of justice, and the judges extract not tenderly the dart, that very dart shall pierce them also.   *VIII. 12.*

THE only friend who followeth men even after death is justice; all else is lost when the body perisheth.   *VIII. 17.*

KNOWING what is expedient or inexpedient, what is pure justice or injustice, let the king examine the causes of suitors.

By external signs let him discover the internal disposition of men, by their voice, their colour, their aspect, their eyes, their gestures.

The internal mind is perceived through the aspect, the gait, the speech, the changes in the eye and in the face. *VIII. 24, 25, 26.*

THE sinful say in their hearts: None seeth us! But the gods distinctly see them and the Spirit within their breasts. *VIII. 85.*

IF thou think with respect to thyself: I am alone! Know that the Being who witnesseth all virtuous acts and crimes, resideth ever in thy heart. *VIII. 91.*

THE soul is its own witness, yea, the soul itself is its own refuge. Despise not thine own soul, the supreme witness of men! *VIII. 84.*

IF thou art not at variance with the Divinity who dwelleth in thy breast, thou needest not visit the Ganges' waters, nor go a pilgrim to the land of the Kurus. *VIII. 92.*

LET the king emulate the energetic action of Indra, of the Sun, of the Wind, of the Fire.

As Indra sendeth copious rains during the four months of the rainy season, even so let the king shower benefits upon his kingdom. *IX. 303, 304.*

LET a man say what is true, let him say what is pleasing, let him utter no disagreeable truth, let him utter no agreeable falsehood; this is the eternal law. *IV. 138.*

LET him bear patiently hard words; against an angry man let him not in return show anger; let him bless when he is cursed. *VI. 47, 48.*

LET him not, even in pain, speak words cutting to the quick; let him not injure others in thought or deed. *II. 161.*

LET him practise, as he is able, and with a cheerful heart, the duty of liberality; if he be asked, let him alway give, be it ever so little, grudging not; for a worthy recipient will be found. *IV. 227, 228.*

HAPPINESS hath contentment for its root; the root of misery is discontent. *IV. 12.*

EVEN from poison nectar may be taken, even from a child good counsel, even from a foe good conduct, and from an impure substance gold. *II. 239.*

THAT one plant should be sown and another be produced doth not occur; whatever seed be sown, even that kind cometh forth. *IX. 40.*

LET mutual fidelity continue until death; this may be held as the summary of the highest law for man and wife. *IX. 101.*

KNOW Goodness, Passion, and Darkness to be the three qualities of the Self, with which the Great One entirely pervadeth all existences.

Goodness is declared to have the form of knowledge, Darkness of ignorance, Passion of love and hatred.

When a man experienceth in his soul a feeling full of bliss, a deep calm, as it were, and a pure light, let him know that as Goodness.

The wise may know as Darkness every act a man is ashamed of having done, of doing, or being about to do. *XII. 24, 26, 27, 35.*

WHETHER among all these virtuous actions there be one which hath been declared more efficacious than the rest for securing the supreme happiness of man?

Yea, the knowledge of the Soul is the most excellent of them all; for that is the first of all sciences, because immortality is gained thereby.[1] *XII. 84, 85.*

---

[1] The above selections have been compiled from translations by Sir Monier Williams and Georg Bühler.

THE BHAGAVADGITA

THE SONG DIVINE

THE BHAGAVADGITA

THE SONG DIVINE

*A wonderful and holy dialogue between Krishna, an in-
carnation of the Deity, and his well-beloved Arjuna, son
of Pandu, King of India, accounted to have lived some
three thousand years before Christ. It forms part of the
Mahabharata, one of the two great Indian epics, and the
poet and prophet Vyasa is its reputed author. The pearl
of great price from the ocean of Brahmanical scriptures,
it dates from the beginning of the Christian era and is
the collected essence of all the Vedas which are the
earliest known record of religious truths. Its influence on
the spiritual life of India cannot be reckoned.*

*In this dialogue Arjuna is variously styled Son of Pritha,
or Kunti or Bharat, ancestors of the race. He has been
grieving over the imminent death of those dear to him.*

The Lord Spake:

THE wise grieve neither for the living nor the dead.
Never was I not, nor thou, nor these princes of the earth;
nor shall we after cease to be. As in this mortal frame
childhood, youth and age come to the embodied Soul, so
will It pass hereafter through other forms.

The contacts of the senses, O son of Kunti, whereby we
experience heat and cold, pleasure and pain, are passing,
they ever come and go. Bear them, thou of Bharat's race!
For the wise whom these do not disturb, merit immortality.

The unreal cannot be; the real can never cease to be.
Know that That cannot be destroyed which doth pervade
this world; the destruction of that unquenchable Principle none can bring about.

These bodies that enclose the everlasting Soul are known as finite; but It is eternal, deathless and infinite; It is not born, nor doth It ever die, nor having been, doth It ever cease to be. Unborn, unchangeable and primeval, It is not killed when the body is destroyed.

As a man casteth off old garments, putting on new, so the Soul, quitting its old bodies, goeth to others which are new.

Weapons cannot cleave It, nor flames consume; waters drench It not; the wind drieth It not up. It is all-pervading, constant, firm, unmanifest, unthinkable.

Wherefore knowing It to be such, thou shouldst not grieve. But if indeed thou believest It continually to be born and continually to die, still thou shouldst not grieve. For he that is born shall surely die, and he that dieth shall surely live.

The origin of creatures, O thou of Bharat's race, is unperceived, and unperceived their end; only their middle state is manifest. That which must befall, wherefore shouldst thou bemoan?

Do thou, Arjuna, be constant in goodness, neither gaining nor hoarding, equal in heat and cold, in pleasure and in pain, self-subdued.

Let not the fruit of thine action move thee to that action. Let not on inaction thine affection be fixed. Having recourse to devotion perform thine act, uncareful of the event, equal in gain and loss; such equality is named devotion.

Action is less excellent than the devotion of the mind. In that devotion seek thou shelter! The wise who have attained thereto do not regard the fruit of action; and released from bondage of repeated births, they attain the seat of bliss.

When thy mind hath crossed beyond delusion's maze, then shalt thou be unheedful of all thou heardest or shalt hear. When thy mind in contemplation shall stand firm and fixed, then hast thou reached devotion!

Arjuna said:

WHAT is the distinction, O Krishna, of him whose mind is steady, in contemplation fixed?

The Lord spake:

WHOSE heart in pain is undismayed, who longeth not for pleasure, from whom desire, wrath and fear have dropped, is called a sage of steady mind.

His mind is steady who draweth in his senses from their objects as a tortoise from all sides its limbs.

O son of Kunti! The boisterous senses bear away by force the mind even of the wise man striving for perfection. Curbing them, a man should live attuned with Me, making Me his one resort.

The man who pondereth objects of sense formeth attachment to them; from attachment cometh desire.

But he who moveth among natural things with senses self-subdued, free from affection, from aversion free, attaineth peace.

Such a man waketh when it is night for all things else; and when all beings wake, then is it night for the seeing sage.

He into whom all objects of desire enter as waters feed the ocean, which though replenished still, is fixed and changeless, he only gaineth peace.

From the Second Discourse.

The Lord spake:

IN this world there is a twofold path declared by Me of old: the devotion which is of wisdom and the devotion which is of action.

A man winneth not freedom from action solely by engaging not in action; nor doth he win perfection by mere renunciation. For none abideth for an instant without action.

Who, restraining his members from action, still pondereth in his mind objects of sense, is named a hypocrite. But who, restraining his senses by his mind, engageth his members in devotion of action, uncareful of the event, is better far.

Do thine allotted task, for work is better than inaction; thy body, too, by idleness cannot be maintained.

Wherefore unattached perform those acts which are to be performed. For the man acting thus attaineth to the Supreme.

As fire is enveloped by smoke, a mirror by dust, the foetus by the womb, so is wisdom by desire. Wisdom, O son of Kunti, is enveloped by this constant enemy of the wise, yea by desire, unsated like a flame of fire.

It hath been said, great are the senses, greater than the senses is the mind, greater than the mind the understanding. But greater than the understanding is the Supreme.

Thus knowing That which is higher than the understanding, thyself subduing thyself, do thou of mighty arms destroy desire, this foe perverse.

From the Third Discourse.

The Lord spake:

THIS unaltering Rule declared I to the Sun, the Sun declared it unto Manu,[1] and Manu made it known to Ikshavaku.[2] Thus in order handed down, it was learnt by royal sages. But that Rule, in course of time, was lost to the world. This same excellent Rule, greatest of mysteries, have I declared to thee today, seeing thou art my devotee and friend.

Arjuna said:

LATER is Thy birth; the birth of the Sun is prior. How then shall I understand that Thou declaredst this first?

[1] Manu, the son of the Sun-god and legendary author of *The Laws of Manu*, see p. 247.

[2] Ikshavaku, Manu's son, and the first King and founder of the Solar dynasty of Indian history.

The Lord spake:

Know, O Arjuna, I have passed through many births, and thou also. I know them all, but thou knowest them not. Though unborn and inexhaustible in My essence, and Lord of all created things, yet having dominion over My own nature, I am born by My own inscrutable power.

Whensoever piety languisheth, and impiety doth prevail, I create Myself. I am born age after age for the preservation of the righteous, the destruction of evil-doers, and the establishment of virtue.

Who truly knoweth My divine birth and works, casteth off this body and is not born again. O Arjuna, he cometh unto Me! Many from whom have dropt desire, wrath and fear, full of My spirit, making their home in Me, through penance of wisdom purified, have entered into Me.

However men may come to Me, thus even serve I them. By whatever path they come, O son of Pritha, that path is Mine!

But desirous of success in action in this life, men supplicate the gods; for success born of works in this world of men cometh speedily to pass.

The sacrifice of wisdom surpasseth far the sacrifice of substance; for all action, son of Pritha, is wholly in wisdom comprehended.

That wisdom thou shouldst learn by discipleship, questionings and service. Those wise ones who perceive the Truth will teach knowledge unto thee, which having learnt, O son of Pandu, thou shalt not again fall into folly and shalt see all beings first in thyself and then in Me.

For there is naught in this world in power of cleansing like unto wisdom; he who is perfected by right performance in due time findeth it in his own soul.

Actions fetter not him who is self-subdued, who hath by discernment renounced action, by wisdom destroyed doubt. Wherefore, O son of Bharat, destroy with the sword of wisdom this doubt, offspring of ignorance, which filleth thy mind. Engage in devotion! Arise!

From the Fourth Discourse.

Arjuna said:

O KRISHNA! Now Thou praisest renunciation of action, now its pursuit. Which of these twain is better, declare unto me with certainty.

The Lord spake:

RENUNCIATION and pursuit of action are both means of bliss. But of these twain, better is its pursuit than its renunciation. The simple, not the wise, think right performance and renunciation diverse; but whoso pursueth either well gaineth the fruit of both. Hard to obtain is true renunciation without right performance.

Whoso is fixed in holiness, pure in heart, victorious over his senses and his self, seeing all beings in himself, is not defiled by action.

The man of devotion, Knower of Truth, when he doth see, hear, touch, eat, move, sleep, breathe, will hold that he doth nothing of himself, but that the senses move amidst their objects.

Even in this world he hath gained eternity whose mind is ever equable.

He whose heart is unattached to objects of the senses, findeth that within which is very bliss; he who resteth in identity with the One Supreme, enjoyeth bliss eternal.

For the enjoyments born of contact of the senses with their objects are as wombs of future pain; they have a beginning and an end. The sage, O son of Kunti, delighteth not in these!

He whose happiness is within, whose diversion is within, whose light also is within, becoming one with the Supreme, attaineth His bliss supreme.

From the Fifth Discourse.

Raise thyself by thy self; debase not thyself, for a man's own self is his friend, a man's own self his foe.

A devotee should constantly exercise himself in abstraction, abiding in a secret place, his mind and self restrained, free from expectation or possessions. Planting his seat in a place undefiled, covered with deerskin and Kusa grass, he should practice devotion for the purification of his heart, and fix his mind on Me, his final Goal.

Devotion is not his, Arjuna, who eateth overmuch, nor his who eateth not at all; nor his who sleepeth overmuch or watcheth ever. That devotion that destroyeth misery is his who taketh due food and exercise, who toileth duly in all works, who sleepeth and waketh in due time.

That state of joy transcending the senses, to be grasped by reason only; adhering to which one swerveth never from the truth and is not shaken off by dire misery; acquiring which one thinketh no other acquisition higher; that should be named the devotion from which there is a severance of all pain.

Whoso seeth Me in everything, and everything in Me, for him I am never lost, nor is he lost for Me. Who worshippeth Me abiding in all beings, holding that all is one, liveth in Me.

Arjuna said:

O Krishna! The mind is fickle, boisterous, strong and obstinate; I think that to restrain it were as hard as to curb the wind.

The Lord spake:

Doubtless the mind is fickle and hard to be restrained. Still, O son of Kunti, it may be curbed by constant practice and by indifference to things of sense. Devotion is hard to be attained by him who hath not his soul in subjection. But by him who hath his soul in his own power, striving, by proper means it may be had.

Arjuna said:

WHAT is the end of him, O Krishna, who cometh in faith, but whose mind is shaken and not perfected in devotion, being not assiduous? Doth he, fallen from both paths, go to ruin like a broken cloud, without prop and bewildered on the road to Brahma?

The Lord spake:

O SON of Pritha! Neither here nor after is there ruin for him; for, O dear friend! none who worketh righteousness cometh to evil end. Though fallen from his first devotion, he yet attaineth to the regions of the righteous, and is reborn into a pure and blessed home. There he cometh into contact with the knowledge that was his in his former body, and there again he worketh for perfection.

From the Sixth Discourse.

The Lord spake:

O SON of Pritha know, of the whole universe, I am the Origin and End. There is nothing higher! All things hang upon Me as pearls upon a thread.

Moisture in the water am I, O Prince of Pandu, light of sun and moon; I am the essence of the Vedas, sound in space, humanity in men; I am the savour of the earth, refulgence in the fire; of living things I am the life, and in ascetics, penance I. I am the wisdom of the wise, the glory of the glorious, the strength of the strong. And I am love unopposed to righteousness.

O Arjuna! Workers of righteousness of four orders worship Me; the distressed, the searchers after truth, those desiring substance, and the wise. To the man of wisdom, I am passing dear, and he is dear to Me, yea, he is verily Myself.

Who through desires have been deprived of wisdom, follow other gods, observing various rites, by their own natures bound. Whatever god a worshipper may seek in earnest faith, that selfsame faith in his own god do I confirm.

Joined to that faith he laboureth for the worship of his chosen god, and gaineth the things he craveth, though by Me dispensed.

These undiscerning ones, not knowing My transcending and exhaustless essence, deem Me, the Unperceived, to be perceptible; but veiled by My mystic power, I am not manifest to all.

I know the things which have been, which are and are to be. But none, Arjuna, knoweth Me; for all beings are beguiled at birth by aversion and desire.

From the Seventh Discourse.

The Lord spake:

HE who in his last hour casteth off his mortal frame and goeth hence remembering Me, attaineth Me. Of this there is no doubt. Or what god else he call upon in quitting this mortal shape, he shall go unto him, having been used to ponder him. Wherefore, think thou on Me!

Who in reverence, with unwavering mind, in devotion fixed, remembereth at the hour of death the Ancient Seer, the Prime Director, than atom more minute, Preserver of all, of unthinkable form, whose countenance is like the sun, transcending gloom, he attaineth to that Soul Supreme, Divine.

Those high-souled ones who have gained supreme perfection, winning Me, come not again to transient life, mansion of woe. O son of Kunti, he who findeth Me returneth not again to birth.

From the Eighth Discourse.

The Lord spake:

I WILL now make known to thee that most mysterious knowledge knowing which thou shalt escape from evil. It is a sovereign mystery, conferring sanctity, easy to be performed.

By Me unmanifest is this whole world pervaded. Understand that all things rest in Me as the mighty air which passeth everywhere resteth in aetherial space.

At the end of a world-age, O son of Kunti, all things return to My primordial source; when beginneth a new world-age, I bring them forth again.

I am the Father and the Mother of this universe, the Sustainer and the Stay; I am the Goal; I am the Friend and Dwelling-place and Treasure-house; I am the deathless Seed. I cause the heat, I loose the rain and I stop the showers.

To those who worship Me and meditate on Me, who in undivided service wait on Me alone, I give new gifts and I secure their gains. Even those who bow to other gods, if but they bow in faith, involuntarily worship Me. For I am the Enjoyer and the Lord of every sacrifice.

Whoso in love doth offer leaf or flower, fruit or water unto Me, that given by him whose heart is pure, do I accept. Whatever thou doest, O son of Kunti, whatever thou eatest, whatever thou dost sacrifice or give, whatever penance thou dost perform, make each an offering to Me!

Who worship Me in love, they are in Me, and I in them.

From the Ninth Discourse.

The Lord spake:

Not the multitude of the gods, nor the great sages know My source; for I am indeed the origin of all the gods and sages.

Arjuna said:

The sages call Thee Parabrahman, the Supreme Abode, the Holiest of the holy, the Eternal Spirit, the Divine, Primeval God, unborn, pervading all. How shall I know Thee, O Thou of mystic power? And in what forms, O Lord, should I meditate on Thee?

The Lord spake:

I AM the self seated in the heart of every being. I am Vishnu [3] amongst the solar deities, the beaming sun amongst the stars; amongst the storm-gods I am Mariki, the moon amongst the constellations.

Of the senses I am mind, consciousness in living beings. Of aspiring mountains I am the Golden Mount, and I the ocean amongst floods of water.

I am never-failing Time, and I the Creator whose faces are in all directions. I am Death who seizeth all, and I the Source of what is to be.

I am Victory, I am Industry, I am the goodness of the good. I am the Rod of those that restrain, I am the Silence of the Secret. There is nothing animate or inanimate that without Me is. O Arjuna, My divine emanations are without end. Whatever is preëminent in glory or in strength, know that to be a product of but a portion of My power!   *From the Tenth Discourse.*

Arjuna said:

IF Thou deemest it may be beheld by me, O Lord, shew me Thine inexhaustible form!

The Lord spake:

IN hundreds and in thousands see My forms, O son of Pritha, various, divine, of divers shapes and colours! Behold wonders never seen before! Within My body see today the whole world, animate and inanimate, and all things else thou hast a mind to see. But thou canst not see Me with thy natural eye: I will give thee an eye divine. Behold My power as God!

(Having spoken thus, the Lord of great and mysterious power shewed to the son of Pritha His supreme form divine, anointed with heavenly essence, full of every

[3] Chief of the twelve Sun-gods.

marvellous thing, the infinite Lord whose countenance is turned on every side. If in the heavens the splendour of a thousand suns bursts forth at once, that may be likened to the lustre of that Mighty One. Then Arjuna, filled with amazement, bowed his head before the God, and spake, with joined hands:)

O Lord of the universe! O Thou of infinite forms! I cannot discover Thy beginning nor Thine end! I see Thee compact of glory, dazzling to behold, shining on all sides with the splendour of an immeasurable ardent fire or sun!

Thou art the inexhaustible, the supreme Goal of knowledge! The eternal Protector of everlasting piety! I believe Thee to be the Eternal Spirit.

I see Thee of infinite power, having the sun and moon for eyes, Thy mouth a flaming fire, with Thy fierce splendour warming the worlds! Heaven and earth and the space between are filled by Thee alone!

By Thy marvellous form of terror, O mighty Spirit, the three worlds are affrighted. Homage to Thee, O Greatest of the gods! O infinite Lord of gods! The world's Abode! That which is, which is not, and what is beyond. Thou art the primal God, the Ancient Being!

Thou art the Knower and the known. By Thee this universe was spread abroad. Obeisance be to Thee a thousand times, again and again obeisance unto Thee from every side! Thou pervadest all, wherefore Thou art all!

The Lord spake:

O Arjuna, being well-pleased with thee, I have by Mine own inscrutable power shewn thee My form supreme, all-embracing, infinite, primeval, which hath not yet been seen by any other. Be not afraid, be not perplexed at seeing this My form of terror!

(Having spoken thus, the Lord took again his milder shape and comforted him who had been sore afraid.)

Arjuna said:

O KRISHNA! Seeing this gentle human form of Thine, I am come now to my right mind and to my natural state!

The Lord spake:

EVEN the gods are ever anxious to behold this form of Mine which thou hast seen. I cannot be seen as thou hast seen Me, by study of the Vedas, nor by penance, nor by gifts, nor yet by sacrifice.

But, O Arjuna, by devotion to Me alone, can I in this form be truly known, seen, and entered into. He who performeth unto Me his acts, to whom I am the Highest, who is My servant, from attachment free, who hath no enmity towards any being, he, O son of Pandu, cometh unto Me!   *From the Eleventh Discourse.*

THOSE who commit their every act to Me and worship Me as their highest goal, and meditate on Me with devotion on naught else, and whose minds are fixed on Me, I presently raise them up from the ocean of this world of death.

Place then thy heart on Me alone; in Me let thy faith dwell. Thou shalt hereafter dwell in Me, there is no doubt.

That servant of Mine who is friendly and compassionate, free from self-love and thought of *me* and *mine,* forgiving and content, continually devout, self-subdued, and firm in his resolves, he is dear to Me!

He my servant is dear to Me who is unexpecting, pure, assiduous, impartial; who worketh not for reward.

Who grieveth not, desireth not, who is alike to friend and foe, as also in honour and dishonour, in heat and cold, in pleasure and in pain; to whom praise and blame are one, that man is dear to Me!
                    From the Twelfth Discourse.

The Lord spake:

As by reason of its subtlety space passing everywhere remaineth without soil, so the omnipresent Spirit is not defiled though abiding in the body.

He seeth indeed who seeth the Lord Supreme abiding alike in all things, not destroyed though they be destroyed. When he perceiveth all natural species to be comprehended in the One and to emanate from the One, then he becometh one with Brahma.

From the Thirteenth Discourse.

I AM the embodiment of the Brahman, of indefeasible immortality, of eternal piety and unbroken bliss.

From the Fourteenth Discourse.

HE who with highest devotion to Me shall recite among my servants this mystery sublime, shall assuredly come to Me. And whoso shall study this sacred dialogue of ours shall have offered to Me the sacrifice of knowledge.[4]

From the Eighteenth Discourse.

[4] After the translation by Kashinath Telang with alterations suggested by the renderings of Charles Wilkins, C. C. Caleb, Lionel D. Barnett, and Mohini Chatterji.

THE BOOK OF SOCRATES

BEING SELECTIONS FROM THE WORKS OF XENOPHON AND PLATO

If you open him, you will find within admirable temperance and wisdom. For he cares not for mere beauty, but despises more than anyone can imagine all external possessions, whether it be beauty or wealth, or glory, or anything for which the multitude felicitates the possessor. . . . I know not whether anyone of you have ever seen the divine images which are within, when he has been opened. I have seen them, and they are so supremely beautiful, so golden, so divine and wonderful, that everything which Socrates commands surely ought to be obeyed, even like the voice of a god. . . . But if any should see his discourse opened, and get within the sense of his words, he would then find that they alone of all that enters the mind of man to utter had a profound and persuasive meaning, and that they were most divine and presented to the mind innumerable images of every excellence; and that they tended towards objects of the highest moment. Alcibiades' description of Socrates in Plato's Symposium.

To me, being such as I have described him, so pious that he did nothing apart from the will of heaven; so just, that he wronged no man, but was of service in the most important matters to those who enjoyed his society; so temperate, that he never preferred pleasure to virtue; so wise, that he never erred in distinguishing better from worse; so able to explain and settle such questions by argument; and besides, so capable of discerning character, of confuting those that were in error, and of exhorting them to virtue and honour, he seemed the very impersonation of human perfection and happiness. Xenophon's Memorabilia, Book I. i. 15; Book IV. viii. 11.

And truly, when I consider the wisdom and greatness of soul, so essential to this man, I find it not more out of my power to forget him than to remember and not praise him. Xenophon's Defence of Socrates.

THE BOOK OF SOCRATES

*Socrates, the great seeker after a knowledge of virtue,
which he identified with knowledge, may be said to have
created the science of ethics, and renouncing speculation
on celestial things to have placed religion on the basis of
pure humanity. He was born at Athens about 470 B.C.;
and in 399 he was accused by members of the democratic
party of denying the gods the city held sacred, of introducing new divinities, and of corrupting the youth. He
was tried and condemned to drink the hemlock. His disciple Plato was present at the trial, and the following
accounts of Socrates and his teachings are from Plato's
Dialogues and the works of his other noted disciple
Xenophon (430(?)-355(?)B.C), for he left no writings
of his own.*

LEARN, my good youth, that your mind, existing within
your body, directs your body as it pleases; and it becomes you therefore to believe that the Intelligence pervading all things directs all things as may be agreeable
to It, and not to think that while your eye can extend its
sight over many furlongs, that of the Divinity is unable
to see all things at once; or that while your mind can
think of things here, or things in Egypt or Sicily, the
mind of the Deity is incapable of regarding everything
at the same time.

Xenophon, Memorabilia I. iv. 16, 17.

To want nothing is to resemble the gods, and to want
as little as possible is to make the nearest approach to
the gods. *I. vi. 10.*

OF what is valuable and excellent, the gods grant nothing
to mankind without labour and care; and if you wish

the gods, therefore, to be propitious to you, you must worship the gods; if you seek to be beloved by your friends, you must serve your friends; if you desire to be honoured by any city, you must benefit that city; if you claim to be admired by all Greece for your merit, you must endeavour to be of advantage to all Greece; if you are anxious that the earth should yield you abundance of fruit, you must cultivate the earth; if you wish to be vigorous in body, you must accustom your body to obey your mind, and exercise it with toil and exertion.

II. i. 27.

A GOOD friend interests himself in whatever is wanting on the part of his friend, assists him with his means; if any apprehension alarms him, he lends him his aid, sometimes co-operating with him, frequently cheering him when he is successful, and supporting him when he is in danger of falling.

What the hands do, what the eyes foresee, what the ears hear, what the feet accomplish for each individual, his friend, of all such services, fails to perform no one; and ofttimes what a person has not effected for himself, or has not seen, or heard, or accomplished, a friend has succeeded in executing for his friend; and yet, while people foster trees for the sake of their fruit, the greater portion of mankind are heedless and neglectful of that most productive possession which is called a friend.

II. iv. 6.

THE shortest, safest, and best way, Critobulus, is to strive to be really good in that in which you wish to be thought good. *II. vi. 39.*

A PERSON being angry because, on saluting another, he was not saluted in return: It is an odd thing, said Socrates to him, that if you had met a man ill-conditioned in body, you would not have been angry, but to have met a man rudely disposed in mind provokes you!

III. xiii. 1.

Tell me, Euthydemus, have you ever gone to Delphi? Yes, twice, replied he. And did you observe what is written on the temple wall,—KNOW THYSELF? I did. And did you take no thought of that inscription, or did you attend to it and try to examine yourself, to ascertain what sort of character you are? I did not indeed try, for I thought I knew very well already, since I should hardly know anything else if I did not know myself.

But whether does he seem to know himself who knows his own name merely, or he who having ascertained how he is adapted for the service of mankind, knows his own abilities? Is it not evident that men enjoy a great number of blessings in consequence of knowing themselves, and incur a great number of evils through being deceived in themselves? *IV, ii. 24-26.*

Tell me, Euthydemus, do you regard liberty as an excellent and honourable possession for an individual or a community? The most honourable and excellent that can be, replied he.

Do you consider him, who is held under control by the pleasures of the body, and is rendered unable, by their influence, to do what is best for him, to be free? By no means, replied Euthydemus.

Do not the intemperate appear to you, then, to be absolutely without freedom? Yes, by Jupiter!

And do the intemperate appear to you to be merely prevented from doing what is best, or to be forced also to do what is most dishonourable? They appear to me to be no less forced to do the one than they are hindered from doing the other.

And what sort of masters do you consider those to be who hinder men from doing what is best, and force them to do their worst? The very worst possible, by Jupiter! replied he.

And what sort of slavery do you consider to be the worst? That, said he, under the worst masters.

Do not the intemperate, then, endure the very worst slavery?[1] *IV. v. 2-6.*

My good friend, consider whether that which is noble and good is not something else than to save and be saved; and whether the principle that one is to live as long as one can is not to be given up by one who is truly a man, and life not to be too fondly loved, but that leaving these things to the care of the Deity, one should consider this, by what means one may pass the remainder of one's life in the best possible manner.

Now I, Callicles, am persuaded of the truth of these things; and I consider how I shall present my soul whole and undefiled before the judge.

Wherefore, disregarding the honours that most men value, and looking to the truth, I shall endeavour to live as virtuously as I can, and when I die, to die so. And I invite all other men, to the utmost of my power, and you too I in turn invite to take part in the great combat which is the combat of life and greater than every other earthly conflict.

But now, amongst so many arguments, while others have been refuted, this alone remains unshaken, that we ought to beware of committing injustice rather than of being injured, and that above all, a man ought to study not to appear good, but to be so, both privately and publicly.

Let us use as our guide then the reasoning that has been made clear to us, that this is the best mode of life, to live and to die in the exercise of justice and the other virtues. This then let us follow and invite others to do the same. *The Gorgias of Plato.*[2]

Hermogenes, Socrates' intimate friend, having observed him choosing rather to discourse on any other subject than the business of his trial, asked him if it was not necessary to be preparing for his defence.

---

[1] From the translation by Rev. J. S. Watson.

[2] Compiled from the translations of Henry Cary and Benjamin Jowett.

And what! said he, my Hermogenes, suppose you I have not spent my whole life in preparing for this very thing?

Hermogenes desiring that he would explain himself; I have, said he, steadily persisted, throughout life, in a diligent endeavour to do nothing which is unjust; and *this* I take to be the best, the most honourable preparation.

Apollodorus being present, one who loved Socrates extremely, he said to him: But it grieveth me, my Socrates, to have you die so unjustly!

Socrates, with much tenderness laying his hand upon his head, answered smiling; And what, my much-loved Apollodorus! wouldst thou rather they had condemned me justly?   *The Apology of Xenophon.*[3]

MELETUS asserts; Socrates is guilty of corrupting the young and of not believing in the gods in whom the city believes, but in some strange divinities.
                    The Apology of Plato I. xi.

(BUT) I have gone about doing one thing and one thing only,—exhorting all of you, young and old, not to care for your bodies or for money above or beyond your souls and their welfare, telling you that virtue does not come from wealth, but wealth from virtue, even as all other goods, public or private that man can need;

One who clings to the city at God's command, as a gadfly clings to a horse. And God, I think, has set me here as something of the kind, to stir you up and urge you, and prick each one of you, and never cease, sitting close to you all day long;

Trying to persuade every one of you not to think of what he has, but rather of what he is, and how he may grow wise and good.   *I. xvii. xviii: II. xxvi.*

MANY a time in battle the soldier could avoid death if he flung away his arms and turned to supplicate his pursuers, and there are many devices in every hour of danger for escaping death, if we are prepared to say and do anything whatever.

But, sirs, it may be that the difficulty is not to flee from death, but from guilt. Guilt is swifter than death.

And now I am to go away under sentence of death from you; but on my accusers truth has passed sentence of unrighteousness and injustice.   *III. xxix.*

And you, too, my judges, must think of death with hope, and remember this at least is true, that no evil can come to a good man in life or death, and that he is not forgotten of God.

But now it is time for us to go, I to death, and you to life; and which of us goes to the better state is known to none but God.[4]

III. xxxiii.

Phædo, the beloved disciple, relates to Echecrates the tale of the last hours of Socrates, with whom were present at the time Apollodorus, Cebes, Simmias, Crito and others.

Were you personally present with Socrates, Phædo, on that day when he drank the poison in prison? I was there myself, Echecrates.

Take the trouble then to tell me what passed as clearly as you can.

I will try to give you a full account; for to call Socrates to mind, whether speaking myself or listening to some one else, is always the greatest delight to me.

I was indeed wonderfully affected by being present; for the man appeared to me to be happy, Echecrates, both from his manner and discourse, so fearlessly and nobly did he meet his death; so much so, that it occurred to me that in going to the other world he was not going without

_____
[4] From the translation by Miss F. M. Stawell.

a divine destiny; but that when he arrived there he would be happy, if any one ever was.

For this reason I was entirely uninfluenced by any feeling of pity, as would seem likely to be the case with one present on so mournful an occasion; nor was I affected by pleasure from being engaged in philosophical discussions; for our conversation was of that kind. But an altogether unaccountable feeling possessed me, a kind of mixture compounded of pain and pleasure together, when I considered that he was immediately about to die.

On the preceding days we were constantly in the habit of visiting Socrates, meeting early in the morning at the court-house where the trial took place, for it was near the prison. Here we waited conversing with each other; but as soon as the prison was opened we went in to Socrates and usually spent the day with him.

On that occasion, however, we met earlier than usual, and the porter who was used to admit us, coming out, told us to wait; For, he said, The Eleven are now freeing Socrates from his chains and announcing to him that he must die today. But in no long time he returned and bade us enter.

When we entered we found Socrates just freed from his bonds and Xantippe [5] sitting by him, holding his little boy in her arms. As soon as Xantippe saw us she wept aloud and said: Socrates, your friends will now converse with you for the last time and you with them!

But Socrates, sitting up in bed, said: Perhaps, my friends, as I am going to another place, it is meet for me to enquire about the journey thither, what kind we think it is. What else can one do in the interval before sunset?

If I were not persuaded that I should go first of all amongst deities who are both wise and good, and next, amongst men who have departed this life, better than any here, I should be wrong in not grieving at death. On this account I am not troubled, but I entertain a good hope

[5] His wife.

that something awaits those who die, and that it will be far better for the good than for the bad.

But now I wish to render an account to you of the reason why a man who has really devoted his life to philosophy, when he is about to die, appears to me on good grounds to have confidence and to entertain a firm hope that the greatest good will befall him in the other world.

Is death anything else than the separation of the soul from the body? First of all then, does not the philosopher above all other men evidently free his soul as much as he can from communion with the body?

Simmias: It appears so.

Socrates: And surely the soul then reasons best when none of these things disturb it, neither sound, nor sight, nor pain, nor pleasure of any kind, but it retires as much as possible within itself, taking leave of the body, and, as far as it can, not communicating or having contact with it, but aspiring after true being.

And while we live, we shall thus, as it seems, approach nearest to knowledge, if we hold the least possible intercourse or communion with the body and do not suffer ourselves to be polluted by its nature, but keep ourselves pure until God himself shall release us.

And thus being pure and freed from the folly of the body, we shall hold converse with the pure and shall of ourselves know the whole real essence which is no other than the light of truth.

If this then is true, my friend, there is great hope for one who arrives where I am going, there, if anywhere, to acquire that in perfection for the sake of which we have taken so much pains during our past life; so that the journey now appointed me is set out upon with good hope, and will be so by any other man who thinks that his mind has been as it were purified.

Then would it not be ridiculous for a man who has endeavoured throughout his whole life to live as near as possible to death, when death arrives, to grieve?

Simmias: How should it not be?

Cebes: Socrates, all the rest appears to me to be said rightly, but what you have said respecting the soul will occasion much incredulity in many from the apprehension that when it is separated from the body it may no longer exist anywhere, but be destroyed on the very day on which a man dies and dispersed like breath or smoke, vanishing into nothingness. This probably needs no little persuasion and proof, that the soul of a man who dies exists and possesses activity and intelligence.

Socrates: Let us consider this, then; whether it is necessary that all things which have a contrary should be produced from nothing else than their contrary. As, for instance, when anything becomes greater, is it not necessary that, from being previously smaller, it afterwards became greater? And if it becomes smaller, will it not, from being previously greater afterwards become smaller? And from stronger, weaker? And from slower, swifter?

Certainly.

We have then, he said, sufficiently determined this; that all things are thus produced, contraries from contraries?

Certainly.

What next? Is there also between two contraries a mutual process from one to the other and from the other back again? for between a greater thing and a smaller there is increase and decrease.

Yes.

What then? Has life any contrary, as waking has its contrary, sleeping?

Certainly; death.

And from sleeping waking is produced, and from waking sleeping?

Certainly.

What then is produced from life?

Death, he replied.

What then is produced from death?

I must confess, he replied, that life is!

From the dead, then, O Cebes, living things and living men are produced. This being the case, there appears to me sufficient proof that the souls of the dead must necessarily exist somewhere, from whence they are again produced.

For if one class of things were not constantly given back in the place of another, revolving as it were in a circle, but generation were direct from one thing alone into its opposite, and did not retrace its course, all things would at length have the same form and cease to be produced.

Cebes: According to that doctrine,[6] Socrates, which you are frequently in the habit of advancing, if it be true that our learning is nothing else than reminiscence, it is surely necessary that we must at some former time have learned what we now remember. But this is impossible unless our soul existed somewhere before it came into this human form; so that from hence also the soul appears to be something immortal.

Socrates: If those things which we are continually talking about really exist, absolute beauty, absolute good, and an absolute essence of things, and if to this we refer all things that come under the senses, as finding it to have a prior existence and to be our own; and if we compare these things to it, it necessarily follows that as these exist, so likewise our soul exists even before we are born.

Simmias: But whether when we are dead it will still exist does not appear to me to have been demonstrated, Socrates; but that popular doubt which Cebes just now mentioned still stands in our way, whether when a man

---

[6] Comp. extract from *The Meno* of Plato, p. 305, and *The Meno* itself, where the theory that "inquiry and learning is reminiscence all" is fully set forth. Socrates is there represented as eliciting from a slave-boy by questions geometrical truths of which he at first appeared ignorant; from which Socrates educed: If, then, he had this knowledge within him, not having acquired it in this present life, it is plain that in some other time he had actually possessed it.

dies the soul is not dispersed, and this is the end of its existence.

For what hinders its being born and formed from some other source and existing before it came into a human body, and yet when it has come and is separated from this body, its then dying also itself and being destroyed?

Socrates: This has been even now demonstrated. For if the soul exists before and is produced from nothing else than death, how is it not necessary for it also to exist after death, since it must needs be produced again?

However, you appear to wish to sift this argument more thoroughly, and to be afraid like children lest on the soul's departure from the body the winds should blow it away and disperse it. We ought then to ask ourselves to what kind of thing it appertains to be dispersed and to what not.

Does it not, then, appertain to that which is compounded to be dissolved in the same manner as that in which it was compounded; and if there is anything not compounded, does it not appertain to this alone, if to anything, not to be thus affected?

Cebes: It appears to me to be so.

Socrates: Is it not most probable then that the things which are always the same, and in the same state, are uncompounded, but that things which are constantly changing and are never in the same state are compounded?

Cebes: To me it appears so.

Socrates: These then you can touch or see or perceive by the other senses; but those that continue the same, you cannot apprehend in any other way than by the exercise of thought; for such things are invisible?

Cebes: You say what is strictly true.

Socrates: What then shall we say of the soul, that it is visible or not visible?

Cebes: Not visible.

Socrates: And did we not some time since say this too, that the soul when it employs the body to examine anything, either by means of the sight or hearing or any other sense, is then drawn by the body to things that never continue the same, and wanders and is confused, and reels as if intoxicated through coming in contact with things of this kind?

Cebes: Certainly.

Socrates: But when it examines anything by itself, does it approach that which is pure, eternal, immortal and unchangeable, and, as being allied to it, continue constantly with it, so long as it is not let or hindered; and does it cease from its wandering and continue constantly the same, being in communion with the unchanging? And is this state of the soul called wisdom?

Cebes: You speak in every respect well and truly, Socrates.

Socrates: Consider it also thus: when soul and body are together, nature enjoins the latter to be subservient and obey, the former to rule and exercise dominion. And which of the two appears to you to be like the divine, and which the mortal? Does it not appear to you to be natural that the divine should rule and command, but the mortal be subservient?

Consider then, Cebes, whether from all that has been said, these conclusions follow, that the soul is most like that which is divine, immortal, intelligent, uniform, indissoluble, and which always continues in the same state, but that the body on the other hand is most like that which is human, mortal, unintelligent, multiform, dissoluble, and which never continues in the same state.

Can the soul, then, which is invisible, and which goes to another place like itself, excellent, pure, and invisible, to the presence of a good and wise God (whither, if God will, my soul must shortly go!), can this soul of ours, being such and of such a nature, when separated from

the body be immediately dispersed and destroyed? Far
from it, my dear Cebes and Simmias!

Does not the soul then, when in this state, depart to that
which resembles itself, the invisible, the divine, immortal
and wise? And on its arrival there, is it not its lot to be
happy, free from error, ignorance, fears, wild passions,
and all other evils to which human nature is subject; and
does it not in truth pass the rest of its time with the
gods?

But I think, if it departs from the body polluted and
impure, as having constantly held communion with the
body and having served and loved it, and been bewitched
by it through desires and pleasures, so as to think that
there is nothing real except what one can touch and see
and drink and eat, do you think that a soul thus affected
can depart from the body pure and unalloyed?

Cebes: By no means whatever!

Socrates: But I think it will be impressed with that which
is corporeal, which the intercourse and communion with
the body through constant association have made natural to it.

We must think, my dear Cebes, that this is ponderous
and heavy, earthly and visible, by possessing which a
soul is weighed down and drawn again into the visible
world through dread of the invisible, wandering, as it is
said, amongst monuments and tombs about which indeed
certain shadowy phantoms of souls have been seen.

When Socrates had thus spoken, a long silence ensued;
and he was pondering upon what had been said, as he
appeared, and so were most of us; but Cebes and Simmias were conversing a little with each other. At length
Socrates perceiving them, said; What think you of what
has been said? Does it appear to you to have been proved
sufficiently?

Upon this Simmias said: Indeed, Socrates, I will tell you
the truth; for some time each of us being in doubt has
been urging and exhorting the other to question you,

but we were afraid lest it should be disagreeable to you in your present circumstances.

But he hearing this, gently smiled, and said; Bless me, Simmias! With difficulty indeed could I persuade other men that I do not consider my present condition a calamity since I am not able to persuade even you that I am no worse off now than at any other time of my life! But tell me in what respect it was not sufficiently proved?

Simmias: In this: because anyone might use the same argument with respect to harmony and a lyre; that harmony is something invisible and incorporeal, very beautiful and divine, in a well-modulated lyre; but the lyre and its chords are bodies, of corporeal form, compounded and earthly, akin to that which is mortal.

When anyone, then, has either broken the lyre or cut the chords, he might maintain from the same reasoning as yours, that it is necessary the harmony should still exist and not be destroyed.

For I think, Socrates, that you yourself have arrived at this conclusion, that we consider the soul to be pretty much of this kind, namely, that our body being compacted and held together by heat and cold, dryness and moisture, and other such qualities, our soul is the fusion and harmony of these, when they are well and duly combined with each other.

If then the soul is a kind of harmony, it is evident that when our body is unduly relaxed or strained through diseases and other maladies, the soul must of necessity perish, although it is most divine.

Socrates, therefore, looking steadfastly at us, as his manner was, and smiling, said: Simmias indeed speaks justly. Come then, Cebes, say what it is that disturbs you.

Cebes: The argument seems to me to rest where it was, and to be liable to the same objection that we mentioned before. For that our soul existed even before it came into this present form, I do not deny has been very fully demonstrated: but that it still exists anywhere when we are dead, does not appear to me to have been clearly proved.

For, though one should concede that not only did our soul exist before we were born, but that even when we die nothing hinders the souls of some of us from still existing and continuing to exist hereafter, and from being often born and dying again; for so strong is it by nature that it can hold out against repeated births; though he granted this, he would not yet concede that it does not exhaust itself in its many births, and at length perish altogether in some one of its deaths.

Socrates: Simmias, I think is in doubt lest the soul, though more divine and beautiful than the body, should perish before it, as being a species of harmony. What then do you say about that argument in which we asserted that knowledge is reminiscence, and that this being the case our soul must necessarily have existed somewhere before it was enclosed in the body?

Cebes: I was indeed both then wonderfully persuaded by it, and now persist in it as in no other argument.

Simmias: And I too am of the same mind, and should very much wonder if I should ever think otherwise on that point.

Socrates: Then you must needs think otherwise, my Theban friend, if this opinion holds good, that harmony is something compounded and that the soul is a kind of harmony that results from the parts compacted together in the body. For surely you will not allow yourself to say that harmony was composed prior to the things from which it required to be composed?

Simmias: By no means, Socrates.

Socrates: Do you perceive then that this results from what you say, when you assert that the soul existed before it came into a human form and body, but that it was composed from things that did not yet exist?

For harmony is not such as that to which you compare it; but first the lyre and the chords and the sounds yet unharmonized exist, and last of all harmony is produced and first perishes. How then will this argument accord with that?

Simmias: Not at all.

Socrates: Consider then, which of these two statements do you prefer, that knowledge is reminiscence, or the soul harmony?

Simmias: The former by far, Socrates.

Socrates: Be it so, then, we have already, it seems, sufficiently appeased this Theban harmony! [7]

But Cebes, you require it to be proved that our soul is imperishable and immortal. To show that the soul is something strong and divine and that it existed before we were born, you say may evince, not its immortality, but that the soul is durable and existed an immense space of time before and knew and did many things. But that, for all this, it was not at all the more immortal, and at last perishes in that which is called death.

Cebes: That is what I mean.

Socrates: I lay down as a hypothesis then that there is a certain abstract beauty and goodness and magnitude, and so of all other things; which if you grant me and allow that they exist, I hope that I shall be able from these to explain to you that the soul is immortal.

For it appears to me that if there be anything else beautiful besides beauty itself, it is not beautiful for any other reason than that it partakes of that abstract beauty; and I say the same of everything.

And by magnitude great things become great, and greater things greater; and by littleness lesser things become less. For it appears to me not only that magnitude itself is never disposed to be at the same time great and little, but that magnitude in us never admits the little. But further consider whether you will agree with me in this. Do you call heat and cold the same as snow and fire?

[7] Simmias was from Thebes.

Cebes: By Jupiter, I do not!

Socrates: But this, I think, is apparent to you, that snow, while it is snow, can never when it has admitted heat continue to be what it was, snow and hot, but, on the approach of heat, it must either withdraw or perish?

Cebes: Certainly.

Socrates: And again, that fire when cold approaches it must either depart or perish; but that it will never endure, when it has admitted coldness, to continue what it was, fire and cold?

Cebes: You speak truly.

Socrates: It appears then not only that contraries do not admit each other, but that they do not admit that idea which is contrary to the idea that exists in themselves, but that when it approaches they perish or depart. For you know surely that whatever things the idea of three occupies must of necessity not only be three but also odd?

Cebes: Certainly.

Socrates: On such a thing, then, the contrary idea will never intrude.

Cebes: It cannot.

Socrates: But did the odd give it its impress?

Cebes: Yes.

Socrates: And is the contrary to this the idea of the even?

Cebes: Yes.

Socrates: Three, then, has no part in the even?

Cebes: None whatever.

Socrates: Tell me then, what that is which when it is in the body, the body will be alive?

Cebes: The soul.

Socrates: Does the soul, then, always bring life to whatever it occupies?

Cebes: It does indeed.

Socrates: Whether, then, is there any contrary to life or not?

Cebes: Death.

Socrates: The soul, then, will never admit the contrary of that which it brings with it?

Cebes: No.

Socrates: Is the soul, then, immortal?

Cebes: Immortal.[8]

Socrates: When, therefore, death approaches a man, the mortal part of him may be supposed to die, but the immortal portion departs safe and uncorrupted, having withdrawn itself from death?

Cebes: It appears so.

Socrates: The soul, therefore, Cebes, is most certainly immortal and imperishable, and our souls will really exist in another world.

But it is right, my friends, that we should consider this, that if the soul is immortal, it requires our care not only for the present time which we call life, but for all time; and the danger would now appear to be dreadful if one should neglect it.

For if death were a deliverance from everything it would be a great gain for the wicked when they die to be at the same time delivered from the body and from their vices together with the soul; but now since it appears to be immortal, it can have no release or salvation from evil except by becoming as good and wise as possible.

For the sake of these things which we have described we should use every endeavour, Simmias, to acquire virtue and wisdom in this life; for the reward is noble and the hope great!

[8] Snow	contrary to	Fire	Odd No.	contrary to	Even No.	Soul	contrary to	Body
brings with it	does not admit	brings with it	brings with it the idea of	does not admit	brings with it the idea of	brings with it	does not admit, inhere in	brings with it
Cold	contrary to	Heat	Odd	contrary to	Even	Life	contrary to	Death

Wherefore, I say, let a man be of good cheer about his soul who having cast away the pleasures and ornaments of the body as alien to him and working harm rather than good, has sought after the pleasures of knowledge; and has arrayed the soul, not in some foreign attire, but in her own proper jewels, temperance, and justice, and courage, and nobility and truth; and thus waits for his passage to the other world as one who is ready to depart whenever destiny shall summon him.

You then, Simmias and the rest, will each depart at some future time; but now destiny summons me.

When he had thus spoken, Crito said: Socrates, what commands have you to give to these or to me either respecting your children or any other matter, in attending to which we can most serve you?

What I always say, Crito, he replied; nothing new: That by taking care of yourselves you will render a service to both me and mine and yourselves; but if you neglect yourselves, and will not live as it were in the footsteps of what has now and formerly been said, even though you should promise much at present, and that earnestly, you will do no good at all.

We will endeavour to do so, he said. But in what way shall we bury you? [9]

Just as you please, he said, if only you can catch me, and I do not escape from you! And at the same time smiling gently and looking round on us, he said: I cannot persuade Crito, my friends, that I am that Socrates who is now conversing with you; but he thinks that I am he whom he will shortly behold dead, and asks how he should bury me!

But that which I some time since argued at length, that when I have drunk the poison I shall no longer remain with you, but shall depart to some happy state of the

[9] Compare with the closing scene in Buddha's life: What are we to do, Lord, with the remains of the Tathagata? Hinder not yourselves, Ananda, by honouring the remains of the Tathagata. Be earnest, be zealous, intent on your own good.

blessed, this I seem to have argued to him in vain, though I meant at the same time to console both you and myself.

When he had spoken thus he rose and went into a chamber to bathe, and Crito followed him. We waited, talking about what had been said and thinking of the greatness of our sorrow, and that like those who are deprived of a father, we should pass the rest of our life as orphans.

And it was now near sunset, for he spent a considerable time within. When he came out he sat down and did not speak much afterwards.

Then the officer of the Eleven came in and standing near him said: Socrates, I shall not have to find that fault with you that I do with the others, that they are angry with me and curse me when, by order of the archons, I bid them drink the poison.

But you I have ever found to be the most noble, gentle and excellent man of all that ever came to this place: and therefore I am now convinced that you will not be angry with me, for you know who are to blame. Now then, farewell, and try to bear as well as possible what needs must be. You know my errand. Then bursting into tears he turned away and went out.

And Socrates looked after him and said: And thou too, farewell, we will do as thou dost direct. At the same time, turning to us, he said: How courteous the man is! During the whole time I have been here he has often visited me and conversed with me and proved the worthiest of men; and now how generously he weeps for me! But come Crito, let us obey him and let someone bring the poison.

Then Crito said: But I think, Socrates, that the sun is still on the mountains, and has not yet set. Do not hasten then, there is yet time.

Upon this Socrates replied: Go then, obey, and do not resist! Crito having heard this nodded to the servant who stood near. And the servant having gone out returned bringing with him the man that was to administer the poison. And he held out the cup to Socrates.

And he having received it very cheerfully, neither trembling nor at all changing colour or countenance, but as he was wont looking steadfastly at the man, said: My good friend, what say you of this potion with respect to making a libation to any god? May I or not?

We pound only so much, Socrates, as we deem enough.

I understand, he said. But it is certainly both lawful and right to pray to the gods that my journey hence to that other world may be happy; which therefore I pray, and so may it be! And as he said this he drank off the potion readily and calmly.

Hitherto most of us were with difficulty able to restrain ourselves from weeping, but when we saw him drinking, we could no longer forbear, but in spite of myself my tears came flowing fast, so that, covering my face, I wept for myself, for I did not weep for him, but at the thought of my sad fortune in being bereft of such a friend.

Crito, even before me, when he could not restrain his tears, had risen up. But Apollodorus even before this had not ceased weeping; and then, bursting into an agony of grief, he pierced the heart of us all except Socrates alone. But he said: What are you doing, my admirable friend? I indeed for this reason chiefly sent away the women that they might not commit any folly of this kind. Be quiet, therefore, and have patience!

When we heard this we were ashamed and restrained our tears. But he, having walked about, lay down, for so the man directed him. Then Socrates touched himself and said when the poison reached his heart he should depart. When, uncovering his face, for he had been covered over, he said, and they were his last words; Crito, we owe a cock to Æsculapius; pay it therefore, and do not neglect it! [10]

[10] Socrates' last words, often misunderstood, called upon his friend to offer a sacrifice of thanksgiving to the god of health and resurrection, as if to show that to him death was life, and burial of the body a new arising to a higher and fresh youth. C. Loring Brace.

This, Echecrates, was the end of our friend, a man whom I may truly call the best of all that I have ever known, and the most wise and just![11]

From the Phædo of Plato.

[11] Compiled from the translations of Henry Cary and Benjamin Jowett.

THE BOOK OF PLATO

BEING SELECTIONS FROM THE PHÆDRUS, REPUBLIC, TIMÆUS,
MENO, SYMPOSIUM, AND LAWS

It is said Socrates in a dream seemed to be holding on his knees a cygnet which suddenly grew wings and flew aloft, singing sweetly. The next day Plato came to him; and Socrates said he was the bird.

Diogenes Laertius.

A Moses speaking in Attic.

Numenius, of Plato.

Audiamus enim Platonem quasi quendam deum philosophorum.

Cicero.

THE BOOK OF PLATO

Plato, first of philosophers, from whom all nobler forms of mysticism derive, was born at Athens, 427 B.C., and died there 347 B.C. His writings may be regarded as partly the outcome of the profound impression made upon him by Socrates; and with mingled devotion and freedom he used Socrates as the mouthpiece for his own views. Two great forces are persistent in Plato, the love of truth and zeal for human improvement; and after the lapse of more than twenty centuries, Platonism, so vital a part of Christian theology, may still be regarded as the greatest exposition of idealism and, in a sense, one of the leading religions of the world, "an emphatic witness to the unseen, the transcendental, the beauty which is not for the bodily eye." [1] *In the following selections, unless otherwise indicated, it is supposedly Socrates who speaks.*

ENOUGH of the soul's immortality. Of her nature, though her true form be ever a theme of large and more than mortal discourse, let me speak briefly and in a figure. And let the figure be composite, a pair of winged horses and a charioteer.

Now the winged horses and the charioteers of the gods are all of them noble, and of noble breed, while those of other races are mixed; the human charioteer drives his steeds in a pair, and one of them is noble and of noble origin, and the other is ignoble and of ignoble origin; and as might be expected, there is a great deal of trouble in managing them.

I will endeavour to explain to you in what way the mortal differs from the immortal creature. The soul or animate

[1] Walter Pater.

293

being has the care of the inanimate, and traverses the whole heaven in divers forms appearing; when perfect and fully winged she soars upward, and orders the whole world; while the imperfect soul loses her feathers, and drooping in her flight, at last settles on the solid ground; there finding a home, she receives an earthly frame; and this composition of soul and body is called a living and mortal creature.

The reason why the soul loses her feathers is as follows: The wing is to soar aloft and carry that which gravitates downward into the upper region which is the dwelling of the gods; and this is the element of the body most akin to the divine. The divine is beauty, wisdom, goodness and the like; and by these the wing of the soul is nourished and grows apace; but when fed upon evil and foulness, wastes and falls away.

Now the chariots of the gods, self-balanced, glide in obedience to the rein; but the others labour, for the vicious steed, when not thoroughly trained by the chari-oteer, goes heavily, weighing him down to the earth; and this is the hour of agony and extremest conflict of the soul.

For the immortal souls, when they are at the end of their course, go out and stand upon the outside of heaven, and the revolution of the spheres carries them round, and they behold the world beyond.

Now of the heaven of heavens no earthly poet has sung or ever will sing worthily; but this is the fashion of it. There abides real Being, in very truth of the soul; the colourless, formless, intangible essence, visible only to the mind, the pilot of the soul.

The divine intelligence, being nurtured upon mind and pure knowledge, and the intelligence of every other soul capable of receiving the food proper to it, rejoices at beholding reality, and once more gazing upon truth is replenished and made glad, until the revolution of the worlds brings her round again to the same place.

In that journey round, she looks upon Justice itself, and Temperance, and Knowledge absolute, not in the form of generation or of relation, which men call existence, but knowledge absolute in existence absolute; and beholding the other things that really are in like manner, and feasting upon them, she passes down into the interior of the heavens and returns home.

Such is the life of the gods; but of other souls, that which follows God best and is likest to Him lifts the head of the charioteer into the outer world, and is carried round in the revolution, troubled indeed by the steeds, and with difficulty beholding true being; while another only rises and falls, and sees, and again fails to see by reason of the unruliness of the steeds.

The rest of the souls are also longing after the upper world, and they all follow, but not being strong enough, they are carried round below the surface, plunging, treading on one another, each striving to be first, in extremest turmoil and struggle; and many of them are lamed or have their wings broken through the ill-driving of the charioteers; and all of them after fruitless toil, without being blessed by admission to the spectacle of truth, go away and feed thenceforth on mere opinion.

The reason of the exceeding eagerness of the souls to behold the plain of truth is that pasturage is found there which is suited to the highest part of the soul; and the wing on which the soul soars is nourished with this.

Every man's soul has by the law of his birth been a spectator of eternal truth, or it would never have passed into this our mortal frame.

There is a law that the paths of darkness beneath the earth shall never again be trodden by those who have so much as set their foot on the heavenward road, but that walking hand in hand they shall live in light always.

If the ends be glorious, all that befalls us in seeking them is glorious also.[2]   *The Phædrus.*

[2] Compiled from the translations of Jowett and J. Wright.

BEAUTY of expression and fine consonance and grace and rhythm all minister to goodness of nature, a mind that is truly adorned with a beautiful and fine temper.

And the absence of grace and rhythm and harmony is closely allied to an evil style and an ill sentiment.

Ought we not then to seek out artists who by the power of genius can trace out the nature of the fair and graceful, that our young men, dwelling, as it were, in a healthful region, may drink in good from every quarter, whence any emanation from noble works may strike upon their eye or ear like a breeze wafting health from salubrious lands, and win them unaware from their earliest childhood into likeness, love and harmony with the true beauty of reason?

On these grounds is not education in music of the greatest importance, because more than anything else rhythm and harmony make their way down into the inmost part of the soul and take hold upon it with the utmost force, bringing with them rightness of form if one be rightly nurtured?[3]   *The Republic, Book III.*

THE just man will not permit the several principles within him to do any work but their own, nor allow the distinct classes in his soul to interfere one with the other, but will really set his house in order, and having gained the mastery over himself, will so regulate his own character as to be on good terms with himself, and to set those three principles[4] in tune together as if they were verily three chords of a harmony.

And after he has bound all these together, and reduced the many elements of his nature to a real unity, as a temperate and duly harmonized man, he will at length proceed to do whatever he may have to do; in all which he will believe and profess that the just and honourable

[3] Compare with the Chinese Shu-king, the *Canon of Shun;* and Li Chi, *Yao Chi,* pages 124, 139.

[4] The rational principle, or knowledge; the irrational or concupiscent principle, desire; the spirited principle, emotion (the natural ally of the rational principle, if it be not corrupted by training).

course is that which preserves and assists in creating the aforesaid habit of mind, and that the genuine knowledge which presides over such conduct is wisdom.   *Book IV.*

THEN shall we not be making a reasonably good defence if we say that the natural tendency of the real lover of knowledge is to strain every nerve to reach real existence; and far from resting at those multitudinous particular phenomena which are the objects of opinion, he presses on, undiscouraged, and desists not from his passion till he has apprehended the nature of each thing as it really is, with that part of his soul whose property it is to lay hold of such objects in virtue of its affinity to them; and that having, by means of this, verily approached and held intercourse with that which verily exists, he begets wisdom and truth, so that then, and not till then, he knows, enjoys true life, receives true nourishment, and is at length released from his travail-pangs.

For surely he who has his thoughts truly set on the things that really exist cannot even spare time to look down upon the occupations of men, and by disputing with them, catch the infection of malice and hostility.

On the contrary, he devotes all his time to the contemplation of certain objects orderly and uniform; and beholding how they are all obedient to order and in harmony with reason, he studies to imitate and resemble them as closely as he can. Or do you think it possible for a man to avoid imitating that with which he reverently associates?

The essential Form of the Good is the highest object of learning, and this essence, by blending with just things and all other created objects, renders them useful and advantageous.

Whenever the soul has fastened upon an object over which truth and real existence are shining, it seizes that object by an act of reason, and knows it, and thus proves itself to be possessed of reason; but whenever it has fixed upon objects that are blent with darkness, the world of birth and death, then it rests with opinion, and its sight grows dim, as its opinions shift backwards and forwards, and it has the appearance of being destitute of reason.

Now this power which supplies the objects of real knowledge with the truth that is in them, and which renders to him who knows them the faculty of knowing them, you must consider to be the essential Form of Good, and you must regard it as the origin of science, and of truth, so far as the latter comes within the range of knowledge; and though knowledge and truth are very beautiful, you will be right in looking upon Good as distinct from these and still more beautiful.

And just as it is right to regard light and vision as resembling the sun, but wrong to identify them with the sun; so, in the case of science and truth, it is right to regard both of them as resembling good, but wrong to identify either of them with Good; because the quality of the Good itself is worthy of greater honour.

Book VI.

COMPARE our natural condition to a state of things like the following. Imagine men living in an underground cavernous chamber, with an entrance open to the light, extending along the entire length of the cave, in which they have been confined from their childhood with their legs and necks so shackled that they are obliged to sit still and look straight forwards, because of their chains being incapable to turn their heads round; and imagine a bright fire burning some way off, above and behind them, and a roadway above them passing between the fire and the prisoners, with a low wall built along it.

I have, replied Glaucon.[5]

Also figure to yourself persons walking behind this wall carrying statues of men, together with various other articles which appear over the wall.

[5] A brother of Plato, one of the group in the house of Cephalus where the discussion takes place.

You are describing a strange scene and strange prisoners!

They resemble us, I replied. For let me ask whether persons so confined could have seen anything of themselves or of each other beyond the shadows thrown by the fire upon the opposite part of the cave?

Certainly not.

And is not their knowledge of the things carried past them equally limited? And if they were able to converse with one another, do you not think that they would be in the habit of giving names to the objects which they saw before them?

Doubtless they would.

Again, if their prison-house returned an echo from the part facing them, whenever one of the passers-by opened his lips, to what could they refer the voice, if not to the shadow which was passing?

Unquestionably they would refer it to that.

Then surely such persons would hold the shadows of those images to be the only realities.

Without doubt.

Now consider what would happen if the course of nature brought them a release from their fetters in the following manner. Suppose that one of them has been released and compelled suddenly to stand up and turn his neck round and walk with open eyes towards the light; he will go through all these actions with pain, and the dazzling splendour will render him incapable of discerning those objects of which he used formerly to see the shadows.

What answer would you expect him to make if some one were to tell him that in those days he was watching foolish phantoms, but that now he is approaching real Being, and has a truer sight of things? Should you not expect him to be puzzled and to regard his old visions as more real than the objects which are now shown him?

Yes.

And if he were further compelled to gaze at the light itself, would not his eyes, think you, be distressed, and would he not shrink and turn away to the things which he could see distinctly, and consider them to be really clearer than the things pointed out to him?

And if some one were to drag him violently up the rough and steep ascent from the cave and out into the light of the sun, would he not, think you, be vexed and indignant, and on reaching the light find his eyes so dazzled by the glare as to be incapable of making out so much as one of the objects that are now called true?

Yes.

Hence, I suppose, habit will be necessary to enable him to perceive objects in that upper world. At first he will be most successful in distinguishing shadows; then he will discern reflections of men and things in water, and afterwards the realities; after this, he will raise his eyes to encounter the light of the moon and stars. Last of all he will be able to observe and contemplate the nature of the sun. His next step will be to reason that the sun is the author of the seasons and the years, the guardian of all things in the visible world, and in a manner the cause of all those things which he and his companions used to see.

What then! When he recalls to mind his first habitation and the wisdom of the cave, and his fellow-prisoners, do you not think he will felicitate himself on the change, and pity them? And if it was their practice in those days to receive honour and commendation one from another, and to give prizes to him who had the keenest eye for a passing object, do you fancy that he will covet these prizes, and envy those who receive honour and exercise authority among them?

Now this imaginary case, my dear Glaucon, you must apply to our former argument, by comparing the world of sight to the prison-house, the light of the fire to the sun; and if by the upward ascent and contemplation of the upper world you understand the mounting of the soul into the intellectual region, you will apprehend my meaning.

In the world of knowledge, the essential Form of Good appears last of all, and can barely be perceived; but when perceived, we cannot help concluding that it is in every case the source of all that is bright and beautiful, in the visible world giving birth to light and its principle the sun, and in the intellectual world dispensing truth and reason; and that whoso would act wisely must set this Form of Good before his eyes.

Our present argument shows us that there is a faculty residing in the soul, and an instrument enabling each of us to learn; and that this faculty or instrument must be wheeled around, in company with the entire soul, from the perishing world, until it be enabled to endure the contemplation of the real world and the brightest part thereof, which is the Form of the Good. Am I not right?

This is a question involving the revolution of a soul, which is the traversing of a road leading from a kind of night-like day up to a true day of real existence; and this road we shall doubtless declare to be true philosophy.

Book VII.

WHEN any one, being healthfully and temperately disposed towards himself, turns to sleep, having stirred the reasonable part of him with a feast of fair thoughts and high inquiries, collecting himself in meditation; and has, on the other hand, indulged his appetites neither too much nor too little, to the end that they may slumber well and by their pain or pleasure cause no trouble to that part which is best in him, but may suffer it, alone by itself, in its pure essence, to behold and aspire towards some object, and apprehend what it knows not; and in like manner has soothed hostile impulse, so that falling to no hostile thoughts against any, he goes not to rest with a troubled spirit, but with those two parts at peace within, and with that third part, wherein reason is engendered, aroused; I think that in sleep of this sort he lays special hold on truth, and then least of all is there lawlessness in the visions of his dreams.   *Book IX.*

To understand the real nature of the soul we must look at it not after it is marred by association with the body and other ills; but we must carefully contemplate it by the aid of reasoning when it appears in unsullied purity; then its surpassing beauty will be discovered and the nature of justice and injustice will be far more clearly discerned.

We have looked at it in a state like that of the sea-god Glaucus whose original nature can no longer be readily discerned because the members of his body have either been broken or crushed and marred by the action of the waves; and extraneous substances, like shell-fish and sea-weed and stones have grown to him. The soul has been reduced to a similar state by a thousand ills. But we ought to fix our attention on one part of it exclusively, Glaucon.

On which part?

On its love of wisdom, that we may learn to what it clings, and with what it desires to have intercourse, in virtue of its close connexion with the divine, the immortal and the eternal; and what it would become if it invariably pursued the divine, and were, by the impulse thence derived, lifted out of the sea in which it now is, and disencumbered of the stones and shell-fish and that uncouth multitude of earthy and rocky substances with which, because earth has been its food, it is now overgrown. And then we should behold its true nature and everything concerning it.

Indeed, believing the soul to be immortal, we shall ever cleave to the upward path and follow after righteousness and wisdom by every means within our power, that we may be dear to ourselves and to the gods not only while remaining here, but also when, like victors in the games collecting their rewards, we receive the prizes in store for virtue.[6] *Book X.*

Timaeus: All men, Socrates, who have any degree of right feeling, at the beginning of any enterprise, whether small or great, call upon God. And we, too, who are going to discourse of the nature of the universe, how created, or how existing without creation, must invoke the aid of gods and pray that our words may be acceptable to them and consistent with themselves.

First then, we must make a distinction and ask, What is that which always is and has no becoming; and what is that which is always becoming and never is? That which is apprehended by intelligence and reason is always in the same state, but that which is conceived by opinion with the help of sensation and without reason, is always in a process of becoming and perishing and never really is.

Now everything that becomes or is must of necessity be created by some cause, for without a cause nothing can be created. The work of the Creator, whenever He looks to the unchangeable and fashions the form and nature of His work after an unchangeable pattern, must necessarily be made fair and perfect; but when He looks to the created only, and uses a created pattern, it is not fair or perfect.

Was heaven then or the world always in existence and without beginning? Or created, and had it a beginning? Created, I reply, being visible and tangible and having a body, and therefore sensible; and all sensible things are apprehended by opinion and sense and are in a process of creation and created.

But the Father and Maker of all this universe is past finding out; and even if we found Him, to tell of Him would be impossible. And there is still a question to be asked about Him: Which of the patterns had the Artificer

---

* The above selections from The Republic are compiled from the translations of Davies and Vaughan, Spens, and Jowett.

in view when He made the world? The pattern of the unchangeable, or of that which is created?

Everyone will see that He must have looked to the eternal; for the world is the fairest of creations and He is the best of causes. And having been created in this way, the world has been framed in the likeness of that which is apprehended by reason and mind and is unchangeable, and must therefore of necessity be a copy of something.

God desired that all things should be good as far as attainable. Wherefore also, finding the whole visible sphere not at rest, but moving in an irregular and disorderly fashion, out of disorder He brought order.

And the Creator, reflecting on the things which are by nature visible, found that no unintelligent creature taken as a whole was fairer than the intelligent taken as a whole; and that intelligence could not be present in anything which was devoid of soul.

For which reason, when he was framing the universe, He put intelligence in soul, and soul in body, that He might be the creator of a work which was by nature fairest and best. Wherefore we may say that the world became a living creature truly endowed with soul and intelligence by the providence of God.

It would be an unworthy thing to liken it to any nature which exists as a part only; for nothing can be beautiful which is like any imperfect thing; but let us suppose the world to be the very image of that whole of which all other animals both individually and in their tribes are portions. For the original of the universe contains in itself all intelligible beings, just as this world comprehends us and all other visible creatures.

27-31, Timæus.

THERE are three kinds of soul located within us, having each of them motions, and one part, if remaining inactive and ceasing from its natural motion, must necessarily become very weak, but that which is trained and exercised, very strong. Wherefore we should take care that the movements of the different parts of the soul should be in due proportion.

And we should consider that God gave the sovereign part of the human soul to be the divinity of each one, being that part which, inasmuch as we are a plant not of an earthly but of a heavenly growth, raises us from earth to our kindred who are in heaven.

When a man is always occupied with the cravings of desire and ambition, and is eagerly striving to satisfy them, all his thoughts must be mortal, and as far as it is possible altogether to become such, he must be mortal every whit, because he has cherished his mortal part.

But he who has been earnest in the love of knowledge and of true wisdom, and has exercised his intellect more than any other part of him, must have thoughts immortal and divine, if he attain truth, and in so far as human nature is capable of sharing in immortality, he must altogether be immortal; and since he is ever cherishing the divine power, and has the divinity within him in perfect order, he will be perfectly happy.

Now there is one way of taking care of things, and this is to give to each the food and motion which are natural to it. And the motions which are naturally akin to the divine principle within us are the thoughts and revolutions of the universe.

These each man should follow, and by learning the harmonies and revolutions of the universe, should assimilate the thinking being to the thought, renewing his original nature, and having assimilated them should attain to that perfect life which the gods have set before mankind, both for the present and the future.[7]   *90.*

I HAVE heard from certain wise men and women who spoke of things divine that the soul of man is immortal; that sometimes it has an end which is called dying; and that afterwards it is born again, but never is dissolved;

[7] After Jowett's translation.

and that for this reason we ought to live always in perfect holiness.

The soul then being immortal, having often been born, having beheld the things which are here, which are in the world below, and all things, there is nothing of which she has not gained the knowledge.

No wonder, therefore, that she is able to recollect, with regard to virtue as to other things, what formerly she knew. For as all nature is akin, and the soul has known all things, nothing hinders but that any man who has recalled to mind, or as men say, learnt, one thing only, should of himself recover all this ancient knowledge, if he have but courage and faint not.

For inquiry and learning is reminiscence all. This way of thinking makes men diligent, sets them at work, and puts them upon inquiry.

If the truth of things therefore is always in the soul, then the soul is immortal. So that whenever you happen now not to know, that is, not to remember, you ought to undertake with confidence to seek within yourself, and recall it to your mind.[8]   *The Meno.*

Agathon: Love is the divinity who creates peace among men, and calm upon the sea, the windless silence of storms, repose and sleep in sadness. Love divests us of all alienation from each other, and fills our vacant hearts with overflowing sympathy.

Yes, Love, who showers benignity upon the world, and before whose presence all harsh passions flee and perish; the author of all soft affections; the destroyer of all ungentle thoughts; merciful, mild, the object of the admiration of the wise, and the delight of the gods; possessed by the fortunate, and desired by the unhappy, therefore unhappy because they possess him not.

The father of grace, and delicacy, and delight and persuasion; the cherisher of all that is good, the abolisher

[8] Compiled from Jowett's and Floyer Sydenham's translations.

of all evil; our most excellent pilot, defence, saviour and guardian in labour and in fear, in desire and in reason; the ornament and governor of all things human and divine; the best, the loveliest; in whose footsteps every one ought to follow, celebrating him excellently in song, and bearing each his part in that divinest harmony which Love sings to all things which live and are, soothing the troubled minds of gods and men.

Diotima: Love interprets between human and divine. Through Love all the intercourse and converse of God with man, whether asleep or awake, is carried on.

Love may be described generally as the desire in men that good should be for ever present to them. Love is the desire of generation in the beautiful, whether of body or soul. Because to the mortal creature generation is something eternal and immortal.

It necessarily follows that we must desire immortality together with what is good, since Love is the desire that good be for ever present to us. Wherefore Love must also be the desire for immortality.

For the mortal nature seeks, so far as it is able, to become deathless and eternal. But it can accomplish this desire only by generation which forever leaves another new in place of the old.

In this way, O Socrates, does what is mortal, the body and all other things, partake of immortality. Those whose bodies only are pregnant with this principle of immortality beget children; but they whose souls are more pregnant than their bodies conceive and produce that which is more suitable to the soul.

And what is suitable to the soul? Wisdom and every other power and excellence of the mind; of which all poets and all other artists who are creative and inventive, are the authors. The greatest and most admirable wisdom is that which regulates the government of families and states, and which is called moderation and justice.

Whosoever, therefore, from his youth feels his soul pregnant with the conception of these excellencies, is divine; and when due time arrives, desires to bring forth; and wandering about, he seeks the beautiful in which he may propagate what he has conceived.

And if he meets, in conjunction with loveliness of form, a beautiful, generous, and gentle soul, he embraces both at once. For by the intercourse with, and as it were, the very touch of that which is beautiful, he brings forth and produces what he had formerly conceived; and nourishes and educates that which is thus produced together with the object of his love, whose image, whether absent or present, is never divided from his mind.

So that those who are thus united are linked by a nobler tie and a firmer love, as being the common parents of a lovelier and more enduring progeny than the parents of other children.

And every one who considers what posterity Homer and Hesiod, and the other great poets have left behind them, the sources of their immortal memory and renown; or what children of his soul Lycurgus has appointed to be the guardians, not only of Lacedaemon, but of all Greece; or what an illustrious progeny of laws Solon has produced, and how many admirable achievements, both among the Greeks and barbarians, men have left as pledges of that love which subsisted between them and the beautiful, would rather choose to be the parent of such children than of those in a human shape.

He who aspires to love aright ought from his earliest youth to seek intercourse with beautiful forms, and first to make a single form the object of his love, and therein to generate fair thoughts.

Soon he will of himself perceive that the beauty of one form is akin to the beauty of another, and he would therefore remit much of his ardent love of the one and become a lover of all beautiful forms.

In the next stage he would consider the beauty of the soul more excellent than that of form. So that one endowed with an admirable soul, though the flower of the form were withered, would suffice him as the object of his love and care and the companion with whom to seek and bring to birth such thoughts as may improve the young; until he might be led to observe the beauty of institutions and laws, and to esteem little mere beauty of the outward form.

He would then go on to science, that he might look upon the loveliness of wisdom; and that contemplating thus the universal Beauty, he would no longer unworthily enslave himself to the attractions of one form of love, but would turn toward the wide ocean of Beauty, and from the sight of the lovely and majestic forms which it contains, would abundantly bring forth many fair and noble thoughts in boundless love of wisdom, until, strengthened and confirmed, he would at length steadily contemplate one science, which is the science of universal Beauty.

He who has been instructed thus far in Love, by seeing the beautiful in due order and succession, now arriving at the end of all that concerns Love, on a sudden sees a beauty wondrous in its nature. And for this, O Socrates, all the former labours were endured.

It is eternal, unproduced, indestructible, waxing and waning not; not, like other things, beautiful in one way, unbeautiful in another; at one time beautiful and at another not; beautiful in this relation, unlovely in that; nor can this supreme beauty be figured to the imagination like a beautiful face or hands, or speech or knowledge.

Nor does it subsist in any other being that lives or is, either in earth or heaven; but it is Beauty absolute, separate, simple and everlasting. All other things are beautiful through participation in it, though while they are subject to decay it becomes neither more nor less, nor suffers any change. He who, ascending under the influence of true Love, begins to contemplate this supreme Beauty, already touches the consummation of his labour.

Such a life as this, spent in the contemplation of the Beauty absolute, is the life above all others for men to live; which, if you chance ever to experience, you will esteem far beyond gold and rich garments, and even those lovely persons whose presence does now entrance you.

What then shall we imagine to be the aspect of the supreme Beauty itself, simple, pure, uncontaminated with the intermixture of human flesh and colours and all other idle and unreal shapes attendant on mortality; the true Beauty simple and divine? What must be the life of him who dwells with and gazes on that which it becomes us all to seek?

Think you not that he alone will be enabled to bring forth not mere images of virtue, for he is in contact not with a shadow but with reality; but virtue itself, in the production and nourishment of which he becomes the friend of God, and himself immortal, if any being may?[9]
197, 202-212, The Symposium.

THEN what life is agreeable to God and becoming in his followers? One only, expressed once for all in the old saying: Like agrees with like, with measure measure. Now God ought to be to us the measure of all things, and not man,[10] as men commonly say. And he who would be dear to God must, as far as is possible, be like Him and such as He is.   *716, The Laws.*

TRUTH is the beginning of every good thing, both to gods and men; and he who would be blessed and happy, should be from the first a partaker of the Truth.   *731.*

LET us say: The Ruler of the universe has ordered all things with a view to the excellence and preservation of the whole, and each part, as far as may be, has an action and passion appropriate to it. And one of these portions of the universe is thine own which, however little, con-

[9] Compiled from the translations of Shelley and Jowett.
[10] The Greek philosopher Protagoras (480-411 (?) B. C.) taught that man was the measure of all things.

tributes to the whole; and you do not seem to be aware that this and every other creation is for the sake of the whole, and in order that the life of the whole may be blessed; and that you are created for the sake of the whole, and not the whole for the sake of you.

For every physician and every skilled artist does all things for the sake of the whole, directing his effort toward the common good, executing the part for the sake of the whole, and not the whole for the sake of the part.

O youth or young man, who fancy that you are neglected by the gods, know that if you become worse you shall go to the worse souls, or if better, to the better; and in every succession of life and death you will do and suffer what like may fitly suffer at the hands of like!

This is the justice of heaven, which neither you nor any other unfortunate will ever glory in escaping, and which the ordaining powers have specially decreed; take good heed thereof, for it will be sure to take heed of you!

If you say: I am small and will creep into the depths of the earth, or: I am high and will fly up to heaven, you are not so small or so high but that you shall pay the fitting penalty, either here or in the world below.

903-905.

Now we must believe the legislator when he tells us that the soul is in all respects superior to the body, and that even in life what makes each one of us to be what we are is only the soul; and that the body follows us about in the likeness of each of us, and therefore, when we are dead, the bodies of the dead are quite rightly said to be our shades or images, for the true and immortal being of each one of us which is called the soul goes on her way to other gods, before them to give an account, which is an inspiring hope to the good.[11]   *959.*

[11] The above selections from The Laws are from Jowett's translation. All the quotations from Jowett in this volume are from his *Dialogues of Plato*, permission to reprint having been kindly granted by the publishers, the Oxford University Press.

SELECTIONS FROM

THE ENNEADS OF PLOTINUS

The utterance of Plato, the most pure and bright in all philosophy, scattering the clouds of error, has shone forth most of all in Plotinus who has been deemed so like his master that one might think them contemporaries if the length of time between them did not compel us to say that in Plotinus Plato lived again.

Augustine, Contra Academicos III. 18.

Celestial! Man at first, but now nearing the diviner ranks! The bonds of necessity are loosed for you and, strong of heart, you beat your eager way from out the roaring tumult of the fleshly life to the shores of that wave-washed coast free from the thronging of the guilty, thence to take the grateful path of the sinless soul:

Where glows the splendour of God, where Right is throned in that stainless place, where all is unison and winning tenderness and guileless joy, where dwells Plato, consecrated power, and stately Pythagoras and all else that form the choir of Immortal Love, there where the heart is ever lifted in joyous festival.

O Blessed One, you have fought your many fights; now, crowned with unfading life, your days are with the Ever-Holy.

Thus much I could but tell, to my golden lyre, of Plotinus, the hallowed soul.

Oracle rendered upon Plotinus by Apollo.

Often having been awakened from the body to my true self, and having come to be outside of all other things, but within myself, I saw a marvellous light and beauty; then there came over me an absolute certainty that my destiny was a great one; for when I lived my highest life, and coöperated with the Deity in it, then I established myself above all intellectual things.

When after such a sojourn in the divine spheres, I descend to the material realm, I am wont to question with myself how the descent occurred, and how my soul ever insinuated itself into the body, in view of the fact that even while she dwells in the body, she remains the divine being which she appeared while yet separate from it.

Plotinus, Ennead IV. viii. 1.

THE ENNEADS OF PLOTINUS

The most divine *Plotinus, apostle of mysticism and classical exponent of Neo-Platonism, now a vital part of the structure of Christian theology, was born at Lycopolis, 205* A.D., *"a being wise without the usual mixture of human darkness, great without the usual combination of human weakness and imperfection." His system revolved round the idea of a threefold Principle; the Absolute, or the Good; the Divine Mind or Intelligence radiating like light from the Absolute and of whose Ideal-Forms the appearances of this visible world are but the image; and the World-Soul emanating from the Divine Intelligence and in turn giving birth to all things. He proclaimed the identity of knowledge with the thing known, the unreality of the material, the reality of the Spiritual, and unity with God to be the one essential. Ever a bit ashamed to find his soul in body, he murmured with his dying breath: Now I endeavour that my divine part may return to that Divine Nature which flourishes throughout the universe.*

FEAR must be entirely removed:—the purified soul will fear nothing. *Ennead* [1] *I. ii. 5.*

ON HAPPINESS

THE contentment of the Sage does not hang upon actions and events: it is his own inner habit that creates at once his felicity and whatever pleasure may accompany it.

To put happiness in actions is to put it in things that are outside virtue and outside the Soul; for the Soul's expression is not in action but in wisdom, in a contemplative operation within itself; and this, this alone, is Happiness. *Ennead I. v. 10.*

---

[1] Each of the six Enneads contains nine chapters, hence the name, from the Greek *ennea*, nine.

As for violent personal sufferings, the Sage will bear them as well as he can; if they overpass his endurance they will carry him off.

And so in all his pain he asks no pity; there is always the radiance in the inner soul of the man, untroubled like the light in a lantern when fierce gusts beat about it in a wild turmoil of wind and tempest.

We cannot be indolent: this is an arena for the powerful combatant holding his ground against the blows of fortune, and knowing that, sore though they be, they are little to him, nothing dreadful, nursery terrors.

It is precisely to meet the undesired when it appears that he has the virtue which gives him, to confront it, his passionless and unshakable soul.

Happiness is centered in Soul, is an Act of the Soul. He who is to be wise and to possess happiness draws his good from the Supreme, fixing his gaze on That, becoming like to That, living by That.

He will give to the body all that he sees to be useful, but he himself remains a member of another order, and necessarily leaving it at nature's hour, he himself always the master to decide in its regard,—the thing he tends and bears with as the musician cares for his lyre as long as it can serve him.

When the lyre fails him, he will give it up, as having another craft, one that needs no lyre; and then he will let it lie unregarded at his side while he sings on without accompaniment. But it was not idly that the instrument was given him; he has found it useful until now, many a time.   *I. iv. 8-16.*

ON THE BEAUTIFUL

WHAT is it that gives comeliness to material forms and draws the ear to the sweetness perceived in sounds, and what is the secret of the beauty there is in all that derives from Soul?

Is there some One Principle from which all take their grace? Finally, one or many, what should such a Principle be?

What is it that attracts the eyes of those to whom a beautiful object is presented, and calls them, lures them towards it, and fills them with joy at the sight?

Undoubtedly this Principle exists; it is something which the soul names as from an ancient knowledge, and recognizing, welcomes it, enters into unison with it.

Our interpretation is that the soul by the very truth of its nature, by its affiliation to the noblest Existents in the hierarchy of Being, when it sees anything of that kin, or any trace of that kinship, thrills with an immediate delight, takes its own to itself, and thus stirs anew to the sense of its nature and of all its affinity.

But is there any such likeness between the loveliness of this world and the splendours in the Supreme? What is there in common between beauty here and beauty There?

This then is how the material thing becomes beautiful, by communicating in the thought that flows from the Divine.

And the soul includes a faculty peculiarly addressed to Beauty, one incomparably sure in the appreciation of its own, never in doubt when any lovely thing presents itself for judgment.

And harmonies unheard create the harmonies we hear and wake the soul to the consciousness of beauty, showing it the one essence in another kind.

Thus far of the beauties of the realm of sense, images and shadow-pictures, fugitives that have entered into Matter to adorn and to ravish where they are seen.

As it is not for those to speak of the graceful forms of the material world who have never seen or known their grace, so those may not tell of the splendour of virtue who have never known the face of Justice and of Moral-Wisdom, beautiful beyond the beauty of Evening and Dawn.

Such vision is only for those who see with the Soul's sight, and at the vision they will rejoice, for they are now moving in the realm of Truth.

This is the spirit that Beauty must ever induce, wonderment and a delicious trouble, longing and love and a trembling that is all delight.

What do you feel in presence of the grace you discern in actions, in all the works and fruits of virtue, in the beauty of souls? What is this Dionysiac exultation that thrills through your being, this straining upwards of all your Soul, this longing to break away from the body and live sunken within the veritable self?

These are no other than the emotions of souls under the spell of love.

But what is it that awakens all this passion? No shape, no colour, no grandeur of mass: all is for a Soul, for the moral wisdom the Soul enshrines and all the other hueless splendour of the virtues.

It is that you find in yourself, or admire in another, loftiness of spirit; righteousness of life; disciplined purity; courage of the majestic face; gravity; modesty that goes fearless and tranquil and passionless; and, shining down upon all, the light of godlike Intellection.

And it is just to say that in the Soul's becoming a good and beautiful thing is its becoming like to God, for from the Divine comes all the beauty and all the Good in beings.

The beauty in things of a lower order—actions and pursuits—comes by operation of the shaping Soul which is the author of the beauty found in the world of sense. For the Soul, a divine thing, a fragment of the Primal Beauty, makes beautiful to the fulness of their capacity all things whatsoever that it grasps and moulds.

Therefore we must ascend again towards the Good, the desired of every Soul. Anyone who has seen This, knows It is beautiful. To attain It is for those that take the upward path, who will set their faces towards It, who will divest themselves of all that we have put on in our descent.

So to those that approach the Holy Celebrations of the Mysteries there are appointed purifications and the laying aside of the garments worn before, and the entry in nakedness, until each in the solitude of himself shall behold that solitary-dwelling Existence, the Apart, the Unmingled, the Pure, That from which all things depend, for Which all look and live and act and know, the Source of Life and of Intellection and of Being.

And one that shall know this vision, with what passion of love shall he not be seized, with what pang of desire, what longing to be molten into one with This, what wonddering delight!

If he that has never seen this Being must hunger for It as for all his welfare, he that has known must love and reverence It as the very Beauty; he will be flooded with awe and gladness; he loves with a veritable love, with sharp desire; all other loves than this he must despise, and disdain all that once seemed fair.

Beholding this Being, the Choragos [2] of all Existence, resting rapt in the vision and possession of so lofty a Loveliness, growing to Its likeness, what Beauty can the Soul yet lack? For This, the Beauty supreme, the absolute and the primal, fashions Its lovers to Beauty and makes them also worthy of love.

And for This the sternest and uttermost combat is set before the Souls; for all our labour is for This, lest we be left without part in this noblest vision, which to attain is to be blessed, which to fail of is to fail utterly.

For not he that has failed of the joy that is in visible forms, not he that has failed of power or of honours or of kingdom has failed, but only he that has failed of only This, for whose winning he should renounce kingdoms and command over earth and ocean and sky, if only,

[2] The leader of the chorus.

spurning the world of sense from beneath his feet, and straining to This, he may see.

But what must we do? How lies the path? How come to vision of the inaccessible Beauty, dwelling as if in consecrated precincts, apart from the common ways where all may see?

He that has the strength, let him arise and withdraw into himself, foregoing all that is known by the eyes, turning away for ever from the material beauty that once made his joy. When he perceives those shapes of grace that show in body, let him not pursue: he must know them for copies, vestiges, shadows, and hasten away towards That they tell of.

Let us flee then to the beloved Fatherland. But what is this flight? The Fatherland to us is There whence we have come, and There is the Father.

This is not a journey for the feet; the feet bring us only from land to land; nor need you think of coach or ship to carry you away: you must close the eyes and call instead upon another vision which is to be waked within you, a vision, the birthright of all, which few turn to use.

Newly awakened it is all too feeble to bear the ultimate splendour. The Soul must be trained to the habit of remarking, first, all noble pursuits; then the works of beauty produced by the virtue of men known for their goodness; lastly you must search the souls of those that have shaped these beautiful forms.

Withdraw into yourself and look. And if you do not find yourself beautiful yet, act as does the creator of a statue that is to be made beautiful: he cuts away here, he smoothes there, he makes this line lighter, this other purer, until a lovely face has grown upon his work.

So do you also; cut away all that is excessive, straighten all that is crooked, bring light to all that is overcast, labour to make all one glow of beauty, and never cease chiselling your statue until there shall shine on you from it the godlike splendour of virtue, until you shall see the perfect goodness established in the stainless shrine.

When you know that you have become this perfect work, nothing now remaining that can shatter that inner purity, nothing from without clinging to the authentic man; when you find yourself wholly that only veritable Light which is not measured by space, but ever unmeasurable as something greater than all measure and more than all quantity; when you perceive that you have grown to this, you are now become very vision: call up all your confidence, strike forward yet a step (you need a guide no longer), strain and see!

This is the only eye that sees the mighty Beauty. If the eye that ventures the vision be dimmed by vice, impure or weak, unable in its cowardly blenching to see the uttermost brightness, then it sees nothing, though another point to what lies plain to sight. Never did eye see the sun unless it had first become sunlike; never can the soul have vision of the First Beauty unless itself be beautiful.

Therefore, let each become godlike and beautiful who cares to see God and Beauty: the Primal Good and the Primal Beauty have one dwelling-place, and thus, always, Beauty's seat is There. *I. vi. 1-9.*

If life is a good, is there good for all that lives?

No, in the vile, life limps: it is like the eye to the dim-sighted; it fails of its task.

But if the mingled strand of life is to us, though entwined with evil, still in the total a good, must not death be an evil?

Evil to what? There must be a subject for the evil: but if the possible subject is no longer among beings, is devoid of life, why a stone is not more immune.

If, on the contrary, after death life and soul continue, then death will be no evil but a good; Soul, disembodied, is the freer to ply its own act. If it be taken into the All-Soul, what evil can reach it There?

Life is a partnership of a Soul and body; death is the dissolution; in either life or death, then, the Soul will feel itself at home.   *I. vii. 3.*

As to our own Soul, it stands, in part, always in the presence of the Divine Beings, while in part it is concerned with the things of this sphere. The Soul's disaster falls upon it when it ceases to dwell in the perfect Beauty, its appropriate dwelling-place.

There it rests free from all solicitude. For the measure of its absorption in that vision is the measure of its grace and power, and what it draws from this contemplation it communicates to the lower sphere, illuminated and illuminating always.

For it is of the essence of things that each gives of its being to another: without this communication, the Good would not be Good, nor would soul itself be what it is: the law is, some life after the Primal Life, a second where there is a first; all linked in one unbroken chain; all eternal. Matter itself must receive the Divine light.

What reflection of that world could be conceived more beautiful than this of ours? And what globe more minutely perfect, or more admirably ordered in its course? And for a sun figuring the Divine Sphere, if it is to be more splendid than the sun visible to us, what a sun it must be!

This universe exists by God and looks to Him, and tells of Him to men, all alike revealing the plan and will of the Supreme.

To say, Look to God, is not helpful without instruction as to what this looking imports. One can look and still sacrifice no pleasure, still be the slave of impulse, repeating the word *God* but held in the grip of every passion and making no effort to master any. Virtue linked with thought, occupying a Soul, makes God manifest: God on the lips without a good conduct of life, is a word.

To despise this sphere or anything else that is lovely, is not the way to goodness. Where we love, our hearts are

warm to the kin of the beloved. Now every Soul is a child
of that Father; but in the heavenly bodies there are
Souls, intellective, holy, much closer to the Supernal Beings than are ours; for how can this Kosmos be a thing
cut off from That? How deny that the Lord of Providence
is here? If He is absent from the Universe, He is absent
from yourselves.

Surely no one seeing the loveliness lavish in this world
of sense, this vast orderliness, the form which even the
stars in their remoteness display, no one could be so
dull, so immovable, as not to be carried by all this to
recollection, and gripped in reverent awe in the thought
of all this, so great, sprung from that greatness. Not to
answer thus could only be to have neither fathomed this
world nor had any vision of that other.   *II. ix. 2-16.*

THE Intellectual Principle or Divine Intelligence, in
its unperturbed serenity has brought the universe into
being by communicating from its own store (of reason)
unto Matter; do but survey it and this is the pleading
that you shall hear:

> I am made by a God: from that God I came per-
> fect above all forms of life, adequate to my
> function, self-sufficing, lacking nothing: for I
> am the container of all, of every plant and ani-
> mal, of all created things and nations of Spirit-
> Beings and lofty souls and men happy in their
> goodness.

> And do not think that while earth is ornate with
> all its growths and living things of every race,
> and while the very sea has answered to the
> power of Soul, that the great air and the ether
> and the far-spread heavens remain void of it:
> there it is that all good Souls dwell, infusing
> life into the stars and into the orderly circuit of
> the heavens which in their conscious movement
> ever about the one Centre are a faithful copy of

the Divine Mind.[3] And all that is within me
strives towards the Good; and each, to the measure of its faculty, attains. For from that Good
all the heavens depend, with all my own Soul and
the Gods that dwell in my every part, and all
that lives and grows, and even all in me that you
may judge inanimate.

As the actors of our stages get their masks and cos-
tume, robes of state or rags, so a Soul is allotted its
fortunes, not at haphazard but always under a Reason;
it adapts itself to the fortunes assigned to it, ranges
itself rightly to the drama; then it speaks out its business,
exhibiting at the same time all that a Soul can express of
its own quality, as a singer in a song.

A voice, a bearing naturally fine may increase the charm
of a piece; on the other hand, an actor may make a sorry
exhibition of himself: the dramatist disgraces one, taking his part from him, with perfect justice: another he
promotes to more serious rôles.

Just so the Soul, entering this drama of the Universe,
bringing to its acting its personal excellence or defect
and accepting from the Author its entire rôle, receives in
the end its punishment and reward.

But these actors, Souls, hold a peculiar dignity: They act
in a vaster place than any stage: the Author has made
them masters of all this world; they themselves determine the honour or discredit in which they are agents,
since their place and part are in keeping with their
quality.

They therefore fit into the Reason-Principle of the Universe, as every string of the lyre is set in the right position. All is just and good in the Universe in which every
actor is set in his own appropriate place, though it be to
utter in the Darkness and in Tartarus the dreadful
sounds whose utterance there is well.

[3] The Divine Mind has no progress in any region; for It turns upon
Itself. This is why the All, circling as it does, is at the same time at rest.
Ennead II. ii. 3.

We may perhaps think of actors having the right to add
something to the poet's words: the drama as it stands is
not perfectly filled in, and they are to supply where the
Author has left blank spaces here and there; the actors
are to be something else as well; they become parts of
the poet, who on his side has a foreknowledge of the
word they will add, and so is able to bind into one story
what the actors bring in and what is to follow.

III. ii. 2, 3, 17, 18.

CONSIDER the performers in a choral dance; they sing
together though sometimes one voice is heard while the
others are silent; each brings to the chorus something of
his own; it is not enough that all lift their voices together; each must sing choicely his own part to the music
set for him.

Exactly so in the case of the Soul; there will be harmony
when each faculty performs its appropriate part.

Thus far we have been meeting those who identify body
with real being and find assurance of truth in the phan-
tasms that reach us through the senses, those, in a word,
who, like dreamers, take for actualities the figments of
their sleeping vision.

The sphere of sense (is for) the Soul in its slumber;[4]
for all of the Soul that is in body is asleep and the true
getting up is not bodily but from the body: in any movement that takes the body with it there is no more than a
passage from sleep to sleep, from bed to bed; the veritable waking or rising is from corporeal things.

III. vi. 2, 6.

THE Souls of men, seeing their images in the mirror of
Dionysus as it were, have entered into that realm in a
leap downward from the Supreme: yet even they are not
cut off from their origin; though they have descended
even to earth, yet their higher part holds forever above
the heavens.

[4] Sensation is the slumber of the soul, for in so far as soul dwells in
body it is asleep.

Their initial descent is deepened since that mid-part [5] of
theirs is compelled to labour in care of the care-needing
thing into which they have entered.

But Zeus, the Father, takes pity on their toil and makes
the bonds in which they labour soluble by death, freeing
them from the body, that they too may come to dwell
there where the Universal Soul, unconcerned with earthly
needs, has ever dwelt.

Each several entity is overruled to go towards that place
and kind to which it characteristically tends, that is,
towards the image of its primal choice and constitution.

Now comes the question of the soul leaving the body;
where does it go?

The space open to the soul's resort is vast and diverse;
the divine law is ineluctable, carrying bound up, as one
with it, the foreordained execution of its doom.

Souls, body-bound, are apt to body-punishment; clean
souls no longer drawing to themselves any vestige of
body are, by their very being, outside of the bodily
sphere; there where Essence is, and Being, and the
Divine within the Divinity, among Those, within That,
such a soul must be.

If you still ask Where, you must seek otherwise than
with the sight.

As the soul hastens to the things that are above, it will
ever forget the more; unless its life on earth leave a
memory of things done well. For even here may man
do well if he stand clear of the cares of earth. And he
must stand clear of their memories too; so that one may
rightly speak of a noble soul as forgetting those things
that are behind.   *IV. iii. 12-32.*[6]

[5] Plotinus imagines the head, or intelligent part of the soul, as remaining
in heaven, for the intelligence cannot be completely incarnated. The lower
parts of the soul,—what Plato calls the spirited and appetitive parts—
alone come down, and these are supposed to be situated in the middle
regions of the body.

[6] The above excerpts from Plotinus, except En. I. ii. 5 and IV. iii, 32,
have been condensed from the rendering by Stephen Mackenna: *Plotinus*,
Medici Society of London and Boston.

First then let every soul consider that it is the universal Soul which created all things, breathing into them the breath of life,—into all living things which are on the earth, in the air, and in the sea, and the divine stars, the sun, and the great heaven, Itself conducting all their rhythmic motion.

The Soul must be more honourable than they, since they are born and perish as the Soul grants them life and leaves them; but the Soul lives forever and never ceases to be.

So let the soul that is not unworthy of that vision contemplate the Great Soul; freed from deceit and every witchery and collected into calm. Calmed be the body for it in that hour, and the tumult of the flesh; ay, all that is about it, calm: calm be the earth, the sea, the air, and let heaven itself be still. Then let it feel how into that silent heaven the Great Soul floweth in.

Even as the bright beams of the sun enlighten a dark cloud and give it a golden border, so the Soul when it enters into the body of the heavens gives it life and immortality and awakens it from sleep.

So the world, guided in an eternal movement by the Soul which directs it, becomes a living and blessed being; and the heaven, when the Soul has made it Its habitation, becomes a thing of worth.

The Soul is not divided, nor does It split Itself up in order to give life to each individual. All things live by the Soul in Its entirety; It is all present everywhere, both in Its unity and Its universality.

The heaven, vast and various as it is, is one by the power of the Soul, and by It is this universe of ours divine. The sun too is divine, being the abode of the Soul, and so are the stars; and we ourselves, if we are worth anything, are so in virtue of the Soul.

Now our soul is of one form with the Universal Soul; and if you remove from it all that is adventitious, and consider it in its state of purity, you will see how precious the essence of the soul is, far more precious than anything bodily.

Since then the soul is so precious and divine a thing, be persuaded that by it thou canst attain to God; with it raise thyself to Him. Be sure that thou wilt not have to go far afield; there is not much between.

Take as thy guide in the ascent that which is more divine than this divine,—that part of the soul which is next neighbor to That which is above, after which and through which the soul exists. For though the soul is so great a thing, it is no more than an image of the Divine Mind.

After having admired the world of sense, its grandeur and beauty, the eternal regularity of its movements, the celestial spirits and animals and plants which it contains, we may rise to the archetype of this world, a world more real than ours; we may there contemplate all the spiritual objects which are of their own nature eternal, and which exist in their own knowledge and life, and the pure Spirit which presides over them, and infinite Wisdom.

For It embraces in Itself all that is immortal, all Spirit, all that is God, all Soul, eternally unchanging. For why should That seek to change, in which all is well? And whither should That move which holds all things within?

V. i. 2-4.[7]

It is in truth unspeakable; for if you say anything of It, you make It a particular thing. Now That which transcends all things, even the most august Divine Mind, cannot be regarded as one of them; nor can we give It a name or predicate aught of It.

We speak indeed about It, but Itself we do not express; nor have we knowledge or intellection of It. But though It escapes our knowledge, It does not entirely escape us; for we can say what It is not, if not what It is.

We are like men inspired and possessed, who know only that they have in themselves something greater than

---

[7] Adapted from the rendering by Dean Inge.

themselves, they know not what. So it is with our relation to the Absolute.

When we use pure intelligence, we recognize that It is the Mind within the mind, the Source of being and of all things of the same order with Itself; but we see too that the One is not identified with any of them, but is greater than all we call being, greater and better than reason and intelligence and sense, though it is That which gives them whatsoever reality they have.

And we may think that the One is present when He illumines the house of him who calls upon Him; for there would be no light without His presence. The soul is dark that does not behold Him; but when illumined by Him, it has what it desired.

And this is the true end and aim of the soul, to apprehend that Light, and to behold It by that Light Itself, which is no other than the light by which it sees; even as we can only see the sun by the light of the sun.

How then can this come to us? *Let all else go!*[8]

V. iii. 13-17.

THE Supreme will be heralded by some ineffable beauty: before the great King in His progress there comes first the minor train, then rank by rank the greater and more exalted, close to the King the kinglier; next His own honoured company, until suddenly appears the Supreme Monarch Himself, and all prostrate themselves and hail Him.

The King is of another order from those that go before Him; He holds that most just of governances, rooted in nature, the veritable kingship, for He is King of Truth, holding sway by reason over a host that shares His divinity, King over kings and Father of Gods.

V. v. 3.

ALL IS CONTAINED IN THE SOURCE

THE Source, having no prior, cannot be contained; uncontained by other forms of being, It is orbed around all;

[8] After the renderings by Caird and Inge.

It possesses, but is not possessed. Holding all—Itself nowhere held—It is omnipresent.

We cannot think of something of God here and something else there, nor of all God gathered at some one spot; there is an instantaneous presence everywhere.

Soul is not in the universe, on the contrary the universe is in the Soul; bodily substance is not a place to the Soul; Soul is the container of body.[9]   *V. v. 9.*

A PLEASANT life is theirs who dwell in heaven; they have Truth for mother, nurse, real being, and nutriment; they see all things, not the things that are born and die, but those which have real being; and they see themselves in others.

For them all things are transparent, and there is nothing dark or impenetrable, but everyone is manifest to everyone internally, and all things are manifest; for light is manifest to light.

For everyone has all things in himself and sees all things in another; so that all things are everywhere and all is all and each is all, and the glory is infinite.

Each of them is great, since the small also is great. The sun too which is there is all the stars, and again each and all are the sun. Rest is also perfect there, because no principle of agitation mingles with it. There is likewise no weariness of vision; but the life there is wisdom.

V. viii. 4.[10]

FROM their birth men exercise their senses earlier than their intelligence, and are by necessity forced to direct their attention to objects of sense. Some stop there, and spend their life without progressing further; like those heavy birds who, having weighted themselves down by picking up too much from earth, cannot take flight, though by nature provided with wings.

[9] This and the preceding passage after the rendering by Mackenna.
[10] After renderings by Taylor and Inge.

Others indeed do lift themselves a little above the earth because their soul withdraws from pleasures to seek something higher; but they have not the power to see the highest.

But there is a third order,—those godlike men endowed with piercing vision, whose penetrating glance contemplates the splendours of the world above and who rise unto it, taking their flight above the clouds and darkness of this world.

Then, full of scorn for terrestrial things, they remain and reside in their true fatherland with the unspeakable bliss of the man who, after long journeying, returns at last home.   *V. ix. 1.*[11]

It is then that the soul takes fire and is carried away by love. The fullest life is the fullest love; and the love comes from the celestial light which streams forth from the Absolute One, the Absolute Good, that Supreme Principle which made life, and made spirit, the Source and Beginning, which gave spirit to all spiritual things and life to all living things.

For it is not possible to see Him or to be in harmony with Him while one is occupied with anything else. The soul must remove from itself everything, that it may receive the One alone as the One is alone.

When the soul is so blessed and is come to Him, or rather when He manifests His presence; when the soul turns away from visible things and makes itself as beautiful as possible and becomes like the One; and sees the One suddenly appearing in itself (for there is nothing between, nor are they any longer two, but one); it is that union of which the union of earthly lovers is but the reflection.

The soul is no longer conscious of body, for the contemplation of such things would seem unworthy, and it has no leisure for them; but when, after having sought

[11] After the rendering by Guthrie.

the One, it finds itself in His presence, it goes to meet Him and contemplates Him instead of itself.

When in this state the soul would exchange its present condition for nothing, no, not for the very heaven of heavens; for there is nothing better, nothing more blessed than this. For it can mount no higher; all other things are below it, however exalted they be.

It fears no evil while it is with the One, or even while it sees Him; though all else perish around it, it is content, if it can only be with Him; so happy is it.

When the soul has intuition of God it abandons everything else. It is like a visitor introduced into a lordly dwelling who for a while is content to gaze upon its varied beauties, but who forgets them all when the master of the house presents himself.

Upon him, therefore, the visitor will steadfastly fix his eyes till he no longer sees the object he contemplates, but his vision becomes, as it were, incorporate therewith.

But we must think of the master of the house not as a man, but as a God, and again, we must think of this God as not merely appearing to the eyes of the visitor, but as filling his soul.

For this alone will fitly illustrate the difference between that lower power of intelligence by which it contemplates what is in itself and that higher power by which in a flash of intuition and inspiration it grasps that which is beyond itself, first seeing it, and then becoming one with what it sees.

For it is just when it has drunk of this nectar which deprives it of understanding that it is reduced by love to that simple unity of being which is the perfect satisfaction of our souls. *VI. vii. 23, 34, 35.*[12]

GOD is neither to be expressed in speech nor in written discourse; but we speak and write of Him in order to direct the soul to Him and to stimulate it to rise from

[12] After renderings by Caird and Inge.

thought to vision, like one who points the upward road which they who would behold Him have to traverse. Our teaching only indicates the way in which they should go, but the vision itself must be their own achievement.

The One does not lie in one place and not in another, but is present everywhere to him who can touch Him. God is not far from every one of us; He is present with all, though they know Him not.

Bodies by their nature cannot enter into real communion with other bodies; but incorporeal things are not kept apart by body; they are separated not by distance but by otherness and difference. Where no unlikeness is, they are immediately present with each other.

So we become present to God when we put away all unlikeness to Him. He does not revolve about us, but we always move round Him, though we do not always fix our gaze upon Him.

As a choir of singers encircling the leader may for a time have their attention drawn from him and so sing out of tune, yet when they turn to him they sing in perfect harmony; so do we encircle God.

But near as He is to us, we often do not look towards Him. When we do turn to Him, our utmost wish is crowned, our souls have rest, our song is no longer a discord but a hymn divine.

And in this choral dance we behold the Well of Life, the Fountain of the Spirit, the Source of Being, the Primal Good and the Root of the Soul.

We more truly live when we turn towards Him, and near Him lies our well-being, while far from Him our souls grow lonely and fall into a decline.

In Him our soul rests; it has ascended to a region pure of evil; there it has spiritual vision, and is exempt from passion and suffering; there it truly lives.

For our present life without God is a mere shadow and mimicry of the true life, a falling away, an exile, a loss of the soul's wings. Because the soul springs from God it must in its natural state love Him, desiring to be united with Him.

Let him who has not had this experience consider how blessed a thing it is in earthly love to obtain what one most desires, although the objects of earthly loves are mortal and injurious and loves of mere shadows which change and pass.

But yonder is the true object of our love which it is possible to grasp and live and truly possess, since no envelope of flesh separates us from it.

Whoso has seen it knows what I say, that the soul then has another life when it comes to God and knows that it is in the presence of the Dispenser of true life and needs nothing more.

On the contrary, we must strip off all else, as it were husks, and hasten to depart hence indignant of the bodily bonds that fetter us; and embrace God with all our being, leaving no part of us which is out of touch with Him.

Then indeed we know ourselves divine, aflame with the glowing fire of Life, a radiance which would flicker and die should we grow heavy again with earthly desire. Why then does not the soul abide yonder?

In this state the seer does not see or distinguish two things; he becomes another, he belongs to God and is one with Him; Like two concentric circles, they are one when they coincide and two only when they are separated.

Caught up in an ecstasy, tranquil and alone with God, he enjoys an imperturbable calm. He who seeks God in any other manner will find nothing.

These are but figures by which prophets indicate how we may see God. But the wise priest, understanding the symbol, may enter the sanctuary and make the vision real.

Such is the life of the Gods and of godlike and blessed men; a liberation from all earthly bonds, a flight of the alone to the Alone.[13]   *VI. ix. 7-11*

[13] After the renderings by Inge, Caird, Guthrie and Taylor.

THE BOOK OF SENECA

BEING SELECTIONS FROM HIS EPISTLES,
DE VITA BEATA, DE PROVIDENTIA, DE IRA
AND OTHER DIALOGUES

I would fain lead you to the study of philosophy, the true place of refuge for all who are flying from the cruelty of Fortune: this will heal your wounds and take away all your sadness.

Seneca, De Consolatione ad
Helviam Matrem.

Are you willing to have great honour? I will give you a great empire; obtain dominion over yourself!   Seneca.

Testimonium animae naturaliter Christianae.

Tertullian, of Seneca.

THE BOOK OF SENECA

The great Roman moralist and Stoic philosopher, Lucius Annæus Seneca, tutor of Nero, was born at Cordova about 4 B. C. Brother of that Gallio who as Governor of Achaia when St. Paul was accused by the Jews "cared for none of these things," Seneca may have come into contact with the great Apostle; though doubtless the parallelisms between their writings are due rather to a similar response to the spirit of their times. However, standing as he did on the very threshold of Christianity, the primitive Church regarded him as practically a Christian, naming him one of the Fathers of the Church; and in Spain he is still styled St. Seneca. In 69 A. D. he was falsely accused by Nero of complicity in Piso's conspiracy and condemned to death.

Is there any better end to it all than to glide off to one's proper haven when nature slips the cable? I shall leave it to Death to determine what progress I have made.

Therefore with no faint heart, I am making ready for the day when, putting aside all stage artifice and actor's rouge, I am to pass judgment on myself, whether I am merely declaiming brave sentiments, or whether I really feel them; whether all the bold threats I have uttered against fortune are a pretence and a farce.

Put aside the opinion of the world! Death will deliver the final judgment in your case. Your debates and learned talks, your maxims gathered from the teachings of the wise, your cultured conversation, all these afford no proof of the strength of your soul.

What you have done in the past will be manifest only when you draw your last breath. This is what I say to myself, but I would have you think that I say it to you also. *Epistle XXVI.*[1]

WHAT then is good? The knowledge of things. If you seize this good, you begin to be the associate of the gods, and not their suppliant.

But how, you ask, does one attain that goal?

You do not need to cross the Pennine or Graian hills, or traverse the Candavian waste, or face Syrtes, or Scylla, or Charybdis; the journey for which nature has equipped you is safe and pleasant.

She has given you such gifts that you may, if you do not prove false to them, rise level with God.

Your bordered robe will not place you on a level with God; for God is not clad in raiment; nor will your reputation, nor a display of self, nor a knowledge of your name widespread throughout the world. The throng of slaves which carries your litter along the city streets will not help you; for this God of whom I speak carries all things on His shoulders. Neither can beauty or strength make you blessed.

What we have to seek for, then, is that which does not each day pass more and more under the control of some power which cannot be withstood. And what is this? It is the soul,—but the soul that is upright, good, and great.

What else could you call such a soul than a god dwelling as a guest in a human body? A soul like this may descend into a Roman knight as well as into a freedman's son or a slave. One may leap to heaven from the very slums. Only rise.

And mould thyself to kinship with thy god![2]
Epistle XXXI.

---

[1] The Epistles from which these excerpts are drawn are addressed to Lucilius, a Roman knight prominent in civil service, and, at the time the letters were written (63-65 A. D.), Procurator of Sicily.
[2] Virgil, Æneid, viii, 364.

WE break up life into little bits and fritter it away. Hasten ahead, then, and reflect how greatly you would quicken your speed if an enemy were at your back and pressing hard upon your steps as you fled.

It is true; the enemy is indeed pressing upon you; you should increase your speed and escape away and reach a safe position, remembering what a noble thing it is to round out your life before death comes.

Epistle XXXII.

YOU have promised to be a good man; you have enlisted under oath. Any man will be but mocking you if he declares that this is an effeminate and easy kind of soldiering. I will not have you deceived. The words of this most honourable compact are: Through burning, imprisonment, or death by the sword.

The gladiator may lower his weapon and test the pity of the people; but you will neither lower your weapon nor beg for life. You must die erect and unyielding. What profit is it to gain a few days or years?

There is no discharge for us from the moment we are born. Proceed with a steady step, and if you would have all things under your control, put yourself under the control of reason; if reason becomes your ruler, you will become ruler over many. *Epistle XXXVII.*

WE do not need to uplift our hands towards heaven, or to beg the keeper of the temple to admit us to his idol's ear. God is near you, He is with you, He is within you. A holy spirit dwells within us [3] who marks our good and evil deeds and is our guardian.

If ever you have come upon a grove that is full of ancient trees grown to an unusual height, shutting out a view of the sky by a veil of pleached and intertwining branches, then the loftiness of the forest, the seclusion of the spot will prove to you the presence of the Deity.

Or if a cave holds up a mountain on its arch, a place not built with hands, but hollowed out into such spaciousness

[3] Comp. St. Paul, I Cor. III. 16.

by natural causes, your soul will be deeply moved by a certain intimation of the existence of God.

If you see a man unterrified in the midst of dangers, untouched by desires, happy in adversity, peaceful amid the storm, will you not say: A divine power has descended upon that man?

Just as the rays of the sun do indeed touch the earth, but still abide at the source from which they are sent; even so the great and hallowed soul does indeed associate with us, but still cleaves to its origin; on that source it depends, thither it turns its gaze and strives to go.

Epistle XLI.

THIS friend in whose company you are jesting is in fear! Help him, and take the noose from about his neck.

Men are stretching out imploring hands to you on all sides; lives ruined and in danger of ruin are begging for some assistance; men's hopes, men's resources depend upon you. They ask that you deliver them from all their restlessness, that you reveal to them, scattered and wandering as they are, the clear light of truth.

Tell them how simple are the laws which nature has laid down, how pleasant and unimpeded life is for those who follow these laws, how bitter and perplexed for those who have put their trust in opinion rather than in nature.

Epistle XLVIII.

A GOOD man will hasten unhesitatingly to any noble deed; though confronted by the hangman, the torturer, and the stake, he will persist, regarding not what he must suffer, but what he must do; he will entrust himself as readily to an honourable deed as he would to a good man; he will consider it advantageous to himself, safe, propitious.

Epistle LXVI.

WHEN we have assigned to our wise man that field of public life which is worthy of him, in other words, the universe, he is not then apart from public life, even if he withdraws.

Nay, perhaps he has abandoned only one little corner thereof and has passed over into greater and wider regions; and when he has been set in the heavens, he understands how lowly was the place in which he sat when he mounted the curule chair or the judgment-seat.

Lay this to heart, that the wise man is never more active in affairs than when things divine as well as human have come within his ken. I do recommend retirement to you, but only that you may use it for greater and more beautiful activities than those which you have resigned.

Epistle LXVIII.

WE have sailed past life, Lucilius, as if we were on a voyage, and just as when at sea, lands and towns are left astern, even so, we put below the horizon first our boyhood and then our youth, and then the space which lies between young manhood and middle age, and next, the best years of old age itself.

Last of all we begin to sight the general bourne of the race of man. Fools that we are, we believe this bourne to be a dangerous reef; but it is the harbour where we must some day put in; and if a man has reached this harbour in his early years, he has no more right to complain than a sailor who has made a quick voyage.

For some sailors are tricked and held back by sluggish winds, and grow weary and sick of the slow-moving calm; while others are carried quickly home by steady gales.

Mere living is not a good, but living well.

It is folly to die through fear of dying.

Epistle LXX.

LET great souls comply with God's wishes, and suffer unhesitatingly whatever fate the law of the universe ordains; for the soul at death is either sent forth into a better life, destined to dwell with Deity amid greater radiance and calm; or else, at least, without suffering any harm to itself, it will be mingled with nature again, and will return to the universe.   *Epistle LXXI.*

Do you marvel that man goes to the gods? God comes to men; nay, He comes nearer, He comes *into* men. No mind that has not God, is good. Divine seeds are scattered throughout our mortal bodies; if a good husbandman receives them, they spring up in the likeness of their Source.   *Epistle LXXIII.*

It is thus that we should live, as if in plain sight of all men; and it is thus that we should think, as if there were someone who could look into our inmost souls; and there is One who can so look.

For what avails it to keep something hidden from man? Nothing is hid from the sight of God. He is witness of our souls, and He comes into the very midst of our thoughts.[4]   *Epistle LXXXIII.*

All this universe which encompasses us is one, and it is God; we are associates of God; we are His members. Our soul has capabilities, and just as it is the nature of our bodies to stand erect and look upward to the sky, so the soul was framed by nature to this end, that it should desire equality with the gods.

It would be a great task to journey heavenwards; the soul but returns thither. When once it has found the road, it marches boldly on, scornful of all things. It casts no backward glance at wealth; it knows that riches are stored elsewhere than in men's treasure-houses; that it is the soul, and not the strong-box, which should be filled.   *Epistle XCII.*

Pray let us see to it, my dear Lucilius, that our lives, like jewels of great price, be noteworthy not because of their width, but because of their weight. Let us measure them by their performance, not their duration.

[4] Comp. St. Paul, Heb. IV. 13.

Would you know wherein lies the difference between this hardy man who, despising Fortune, has served through every campaign of life and has attained to life's Supreme Good, and that other over whose head merely many years have passed? The former exists even after his death; the latter has died even before he is dead.

We should therefore number in the company of the blest that man who has invested well the portion of time, however little, that has been allotted to him. He has not only lived, but flourished. Sometimes he enjoyed fair skies; sometimes it was only through clouds that there flashed to him the radiance of the mighty star.

Why do you ask: How long did he live? He still lives! At one bound he has passed over into posterity and has consigned himself to the guardianship of memory.

Just as one of small stature can be a perfect man, so a life of small compass can be a perfect life. This is the only thing you have the right to require of me, that I shall cease to measure out an inglorious age as it were in darkness, and devote myself to living instead of being carried along past life. *Epistle XCIII.*

IF you would wield a command that is profitable to yourself and injurious to nobody, clear your own faults out of the way. *Epistle XCIV.*

WE are mad, not only individually, but nationally. We check manslaughter and isolated murders; but what of war and the much-vaunted crime of slaughtering whole peoples? There are no limits to our greed, none to our cruelty.

As long as such crimes are committed by stealth and by individuals, they are less harmful and less portentous; but cruelties are practised in accordance with acts of senate and popular assembly, and the public is bidden to do what is forbidden to the individual.

Deeds that would be punished with loss of life when committed in secret, are praised by us because uniformed generals have carried them out. Man, naturally the gentlest class of being, is not ashamed to revel in the blood of others, to wage war.

I can lay down for mankind a rule, in short compass, for our duties in human relationships: all that you behold, that which comprises both god and man, is one; we are parts of one great body.[5] Nature produced us related to one another, since she created us from the same source to the same end.

She engendered in us mutual affection, and made us prone to friendships. She established fairness and justice; according to her ruling, it is more wretched to commit than to suffer injury. Through her orders, our hands are ready to help in the good work.

Let this verse be in your heart and on your lips:

> I am a man; and nothing in man's lot do I deem foreign to me.[6]

Let us possess things in common; for birth is ours in common. Our relations with one another are like a stone arch, which would collapse if the stones did not mutually support each other.   *Epistle XCV.*

WHEN everything seems to go hard and uphill, I have trained myself not merely to obey God, but to agree with His decisions. I follow Him because my soul wills it, and not because I must.

Nothing will ever happen to me that I shall receive with ill humour or with a wry face. I shall pay up all my taxes willingly. Now all of the things which cause us to groan or recoil, are part of the tax of life; things, my dear Lucilius, which you should never hope and never seek to escape.   *Epistle XCVI.*

ALL things that Fortune looks upon become productive and pleasant only if he who possesses them is in possession also of himself, and is not in the power of that which belongs to him.

[5] Comp. St. Paul, Rom. XII. 5.   [6] Terence, *Heautontimorumenos,* 77.

For men make a mistake, my dear Lucilius, if they hold that anything good, or evil either, is bestowed upon us by Fortune; it is simply the raw materials of good and ill that she gives to us, the sources of things which, in our keeping, will develop into good and ill.

For the soul is more powerful than any sort of Fortune; by its own agency it guides its affairs in either direction, and of its own power can produce a happy life or a wretched one. *Epistle XCVIII.*

He only is anxious about the future, to whom the present is unprofitable. But when I have paid my soul its due, when a soundly-balanced mind knows that a day differs not a whit from eternity, whatever days or problems the future may bring, then the soul looks forth from lofty heights and laughs heartily to itself when it thinks upon the ceaseless succession of the ages.

For what disturbance can result from the changes and instability of Chance, if you are sure in the face of that which is unsure?

Therefore, my dear Lucilius, begin at once to live, and count each day a separate life. *Epistle CI.*

The human soul is a great and noble thing; it permits of no limits except those which can be shared even by the gods. It does not consent to a lowly birthplace, like Ephesus or Alexandria.

The soul's homeland is the whole space that encircles the height and breadth of the firmament, the whole rounded dome within which lie land and sea, and where all the sentinel stars are taking their turn on duty.

Again, for the soul a narrow span of existence will not suffice. All the years, says the soul, are mine; no epoch is closed to great minds; all time is open for the progress of thought.

When the day comes to separate the heavenly from its earthly blend, I shall leave the body where I found it, and shall of my own volition betake myself to the gods.

As the mother's womb holds us for months, making us ready for the existence into which we seem to be sent forth when at last we are fitted to draw breath and live in the open; just so , throughout infancy and old age, we are making ourselves ready for another birth.

Survey everything that lies about you as if it were luggage in a guest-chamber: you must travel on. Nature strips you as bare at your departure as at your entrance. What is more, you must throw away the major portion of that which you brought with you into life; you will be stripped of the very skin which covers you, of bones and sinews, the framework of these transitory parts.

That day which you fear as being the end of all things, is the birthday of your eternity. *Epistle CII.*

If we had the privilege of looking into a good man's soul, oh what a fair, holy, magnificent, gracious and shining face should we behold; radiant on the one side with justice and fortitude, on another with temperance and wisdom!

And besides these, moderation, endurance, refinement, affability and love of one's fellow-men, all these would be shedding their glory over that soul. What a wonderful combination of sweetness and power! No one could call such a face lovable without also calling it worshipful.

If we might behold such a face, more exalted and radiant than the mortal eye is wont to behold, would we not pause as if struck dumb by a visitation from above, and utter a silent prayer, saying: May it be lawful to have looked upon it? And then should we not bow down and worship?

And such a vision will indeed be a present help and relief to us, if we are willing to worship it. But this worship does not consist in slaughtering fattened bulls, or in offerings of gold and silver; rather does it consist in a will that is reverent and upright.[7] *Epistle CV.*

[7] The quotations from Seneca's *Epistles* are after the translation by Richard M. Gummere.

LET us bear with magnanimity whatever the system of the universe makes it needful for us to bear. We have been born into a monarchy: our liberty is to obey God.
De Vita Beata XV. 6.

I WILL look upon death or a comedy with the same countenance: I will submit to labours, however great, upholding my body by my mind: riches present or absent I will equally contemn, no sadder if I have them not, nor gayer if they sparkle round me: Fortune coming or going I will not heed.

I will view all lands as my own, my own as though they belonged to all: I will live as though I were born for others, and will thank Nature therefor: she has given me alone to all, all to me alone.

Whatever I have, I will neither hoard it greedily nor squander it recklessly, believing I possess nothing more really than what I well bestow: I will reckon my beneficences neither by their magnitude nor number, nor by anything save their value to him who receives them, considering no gift large which is bestowed upon a worthy object.

I will do nothing because of opinion, everything because of conscience. I will be agreeable to my friends, mild and gentle to my foes, granting pardon before I am asked for it, running to meet the wishes of the honourable. I will know that the world is my native city and the gods its governors, and that they stand above and about me, censors of my words and deeds.

Whenever Nature demands my breath again, I will quit this life calling all to witness that I have loved a good conscience and good pursuits; that no one's freedom, least of all my own, has been by me impaired.
De Vita Beata XX.

NATURE bids me do good to mankind, be they freemen or slaves. Wherever there is a human being, there is an opportunity for a benefit.   *De Vita Beata XXIV.*

BETWEEN good men and the gods there is friendship and union, virtue conciliating. Friendship, do I say? Nay rather, affinity and likeness; since the good man differs from a god in time alone, and is his disciple and true offspring. *De Providentia I.*

JUST as so many rivers, so many showers of rain from above, so many medicinal springs do not alter the taste of the sea, so the pressure of adversity does not affect the mind of the brave man, for it maintains its balance, and over all that happens it throws its own complexion because it is more powerful than external circumstance. *De Providentia II.*

CONCEIVE, therefore, that God says: You, who have chosen righteousness, what complaint have you to make of me? I have encompassed other men with unreal good things; to you I have given sure and lasting things.

I have granted to you to scorn danger, to disdain passion. I have placed every good thing within your own breasts; it is your good fortune not to need good fortune. *De Providentia VI.*

FORTUNE takes away nothing save what she gave. Now Fortune does not give virtue, hence she does not take it away. Virtue is free, inviolable, not to be moved or shaken, and so hardened against misfortunes that she cannot be bent, much less overcome by them.

The wise man, therefore, can lose nothing of whose loss he will be sensible, for he is in the possession of virtue from which he can never be driven. If injury can hurt none of those things which are the peculiar property of the wise man, then it is impossible that an injury should be done to a wise man. *De Constantia Sapientis V.*

DEMETRIUS took Megara, and the philosopher Stilbo, when asked by him whether he had lost anything, answered: No, I carry all my property with me. His inheri-

tance had been given up to pillage, his country had fallen
under a foreign dominion: yet he struck the victory out
of the king's hands, and though the city was taken, he
bore with him those true goods which no one can lay
hands upon.

Amid the flash of swords, the riot of plundering soldiery,
the flames and blood and ruin of the fallen city, the crash
of temples falling on their gods, one man was at peace.
I have, says he, I hold, whatever of mine I ever had!

See then, that the perfect man, full of virtues human and
divine, can lose nothing; his goods are surrounded by
strong and impassable walls. The ramparts which protect the wise are safe from fire and incursion; they afford
no passage; they are lofty, impregnable, divine.
De Constantia Sapientis V, VI.

CONSOLATION to Polybius on the Death of his Brother.

We are flung, as it were, into this deep and rough sea,
whose tides ebb and flow, at one time raising us aloft by
sudden accession of fortune, at another bringing down
low by still greater losses, and for ever tossing us about.

Do not, then, grudge your brother his rest; he has at last
become free, safe, and immortal, and ranges joyous
through the boundless heavens; he has left this low-
lying region and has soared upwards to that place which
receives in its happy bosom the souls set free from the
chains of matter.

Your brother has not lost the light of day, but has obtained a more enduring light. He has not left us, but has
gone on before.   *Consolatio ad Polybium IX.*

THE spirit should be brought up for examination daily.
It was the custom of Sextius, when the day was over,
and he had betaken himself to rest, to enquire of his
spirit; What bad habit of yours have you cured today?
What vice have you checked? In what respect are you
better?

Anger will cease and become more gentle if it knows that every day it will have to appear before the judgment seat. How sweet is the sleep that follows this self-examination! How calm, how sound, how careless!

I make use of this privilege, and daily plead my cause before myself: when the lamp is taken out, and my wife, who knows my habit, has ceased to talk, I pass the whole day in review, and repeat all that I have said and done: I conceal nothing from myself, omit nothing.

De Ira XXXVI.

LET us therefore briskly and cheerfully hasten with undaunted steps whithersoever circumstances call us; let us wander over whatever countries we please; no place of banishment can be found in which man cannot find a home.

I can raise my eyes from the earth to the sky in one place as well as another; the heavenly bodies are equally near to mankind: as long as my eyes are not deprived of that spectacle of which they can never have their fill, as long as I am allowed to gaze on the sun and the moon, to see so many stars glittering throughout the night;

While I am permitted to commune with these, and to hold intercourse, as far as a human being may, with all the company of heaven, while I can raise my spirit aloft to view its kindred sparks above, what does it matter upon what soil I tread?

Should that lowly barn be entered by the virtues, it will straightway become more beautiful than any temple, because within it will be seen justice, self-restraint, prudence, love, a right division of all duties, a knowledge of things in heaven and on earth.

No place can be narrow, if it contains such a company of the greatest virtues; no exile irksome in which one is attended by these companions.

It is the mind that makes men rich: this it is that accompanies them into exile and in the most savage wilderness enjoys its own overflowing resources.

From this it follows that no free-born man, who is akin
to the gods, and fit for any world and age, can ever be in
exile: for his thoughts are directed to all the heavens and
to all times past and future: this trumpery body, the
prison and fetter of the spirit, may be tossed to this
place or to that; upon it tortures, robberies, disease may
work their will: but the spirit itself is holy and eternal,
and upon it none may lay their hands.[8]

De Consolatione ad Helviam Matrem VIII, IX, XI.

[8] The above extracts from Seneca's *Dialogues* are after the translation
of Aubrey Stewart.

THE BOOK OF EPICTETUS

BEING SELECTIONS FROM HIS DIS-
COURSES, APHORISMS, AND ENCHIRIDION

How few words it requires to say that man's end is to follow the gods, and that the nature of good is a proper use of appearances.

Epictetus, Discourses I. xx.

We see that the carpenter when he has learned certain things becomes a carpenter; the pilot by learning certain things becomes a pilot. May it not then in philosophy also not be sufficient to wish to be wise and good, and that there is also a necessity to learn certain things? You are rich, you have children and a wife perhaps and many slaves: Cæsar knows you, in Rome you have many friends, you render their dues to all, you know how to requite him who does you a favour, and to repay him who does you a wrong. If then I shall shew you that you lack the things most necessary for happiness and that you have looked after everything rather than what you ought, that you know neither what God nor man is, that you know nothing about yourself, how is it possible that you should endure me and bear the proof? Yet what harm have I done you? Unless the mirror also injures the ugly man because it shows him himself such as he is; unless the physician also insults the sick man, when he says: You have a fever. No one says: What an insult! But if you say to a man, Your desires are inflamed, your intentions inconsistent, your pursuits not conformable to nature, your opinions false, the man immediately goes away and says: He has insulted me!

Epictetus, Discourses II, XIV.

THE BOOK OF EPICTETUS

The Stoic philosopher Epictetus, a native of Hierapolis in Phrygia, was born before the middle of the 1st cent. A. D. and lived in Rome in the time of Nero as a slave—a lame one at that—of the profligate freedman Epaphroditus; he was among the philosophers exiled by Domitian in the year 89 A. D. The Discourses *from which most of the following excerpts are taken were set down as nearly as possible in Epictetus' own words by his affectionate disciple Arrian. Freedom from slavery of circumstance won by the domination of the will is the burden of their clarion call.*

From the Discourses, Book I

That which is the most excellent and superior of all, the right use of appearances, is, as was right, the only thing which the gods have put in our power; over other matters they have given us no control. For, placed upon earth, and confined to such a body and such companions, how was it possible that with respect to these things we should not be hindered by externals?

But what says Zeus? Epictetus, do not now mistake! The body is not your own, but only finely tempered clay. But I have given you a certain portion of Myself, the faculty of pursuing an object or avoiding it, of desire and aversion, in a word, the use of appearances.

If you will take care of this faculty, and consider that in its exercise lies all that is really your own, you will never be checked or hindered. You will not groan, nor complain, nor flatter any one.

What then is to be done? To make the best use of what is in our power and take the rest as it happens. And how is that? As it pleases God! *Chapter I.*

355

You look upon yourself as one thread only of many that make up the garment. Accordingly, it is fitting that you should consider how to be like the rest of mankind, just as one thread desires to be in no way distinguished from the other threads.

I, on the contrary, would be the purple border of the garment, that small and brilliant part which gives luster and beauty to the rest. Why do you bid me resemble the multitude, then? If I do, how shall I be the purple?

This Priscus Helvidius also saw, and acted conformably. For when Vespasian sent to forbid his going to the senate, he replied: It is in your power to prevent my remaining a senator, but as long as I am one, I must go.

Well, then, at least be silent there, said the Emperor.

Do not ask my opinion and I will be silent.

But I must ask it!

And I must say what I think right!

But if you do, I will put you to death.

Did I ever tell you that I was immortal? You will do your part, and I mine. It is yours to kill, mine to die intrepid; yours to banish, mine to depart untroubled.

What good then did Priscus do, who was but a single person? Why, what good does the purple do to the garment? What else but to be beautiful in itself, and to give an example of beauty to others?   *Chapter II.*

If a person could be persuaded of this principle as he ought, that we are all descended from God, and that He is the Father of gods and men, I conceive he would never think meanly or degenerately of himself.

Suppose Caesar were to adopt you, there would be no bearing your haughty looks; and will you not be elated on knowing yourself to be the son of Zeus?   *Chapter III.*

Most of us dread a bodily paralysis, and would use every means to avoid it; but none of us is troubled about a paralysis of the soul!   *Chapter V.*

IF God had made colours, and had not made the faculty of seeing them, what would have been their use? None. On the other hand, if He had made the faculty of vision without objects to be seen, what would have been the use of that? None. Again, if He had formed both the faculty and the objects, but had not made the light? Neither in that case would they have been of any use.

Who is it then, that has fitted this to that, and that to this?

Who is it that has fitted the sword to the scabbard, and the scabbard to the sword? Is it no one? From the very construction of a complete work, we are used to declare it must be the work of some artificer, and not the effect of mere chance. Does every such work, then, demonstrate an artificer, and do not visible objects, and the faculty of vision, and light, demonstrate one?

God has introduced man to be a spectator of God and of His works; and not only a spectator of them, but an interpreter.

You take a journey to Olympia to behold the work of Phidias, and think it a misfortune to die without a knowledge of such things. But when there is no need to travel, since, there where he is, one has the works of God before him, will you not desire to see and understand them? Will you never perceive what you are, nor for what you were born, nor why you received the faculty of sight?

But there are some things unpleasant and difficult in life!

And are there none at Olympia? Are you not heated? Are you not pressed by the crowd? Are you not wet when it rains? Have you not uproar and clamour? But I suppose by setting the magnificence of the spectacle against all these things, you do bear and endure them.

Well, have you not received faculties by which you may support every event of life? Have you not received greatness of soul? Have you not received manliness? Endurance? What matters to me anything while I have great-

ness of soul? What shall disconcert or trouble or appear
grievous to me?　　　　　　　　　　　　　　*Chapter VII.*

IF what philosophers say of the kinship between God and
men be true, what can one do but follow the example of
Socrates, who, when asked of what country he was, never
said that he was a citizen of Athens, or of Corinth, but
of the world? For why do you say that you are of Athens,
and not of that little corner of it only where your body
was laid at birth?

Is it not, plainly, from something more authoritative,
which comprehends not only that corner and your whole
family, but even that whole country from which the stock
of your progenitors has been derived down to you, that
you call yourself an Athenian or Corinthian?

He, then, who has learned that the greatest and most
comprehensive of all commonwealths is this system of
men and God, and that from Him are descended the seeds
of being, not only to one's father and grandfather, but
also to all things that are produced and born on earth,
and especially to rational natures, since these alone are
by nature formed to have communion with God,—why
may not such a one call himself a citizen of the world?
Why not a son of God?

And why shall he fear anything that happens among
men? Shall kindred with Caesar, or any other of the great
at Rome, enable a man to live secure, above contempt and
void of fear, and shall not the fact that God is our
Maker, Father and Guardian free us from terror and
griefs?

You say: Epictetus, we can no longer bear being
bound to this paltry body, feeding it and giving it drink,
on its account obliged to humour these and those. Are
not these things indifferent and nothing to us and death
no bane? Are we not God's kindred, and came we not
from Him?

Suffer us to go back thither from whence we came. Suffer
us to be freed from these fetters that chain and weigh

us down. Here are thieves and robbers, and tyrants think to have power over us because of the body and its possessions. Permit us to show them that they have no real power over any man!

My friends, wait for God! Wait till He gives the signal and releases you from this service, then go to Him. For the present, be content to remain at the post where He has placed you. For what tyrant, what robber, what thief is formidable to those who thus account the body and its possessions as naught? Wait then, depart not without a reason! *Chapter IX.*

True instruction is this: to learn to will that things should happen as they do. And how do they happen? As He who orders them has disposed.

Can we escape from mankind? Can we, by associating with men, change them? What then remains, or what method of commerce with them can be found? You, if you are alone, term it a desert; if with men, you call them knaves and robbers. You find fault too with your parents and children, brothers and neighbors.

Whereas you ought, if you live alone, to call that repose and freedom, and to regard yourself as like the gods; and when you are in company, not to call it a crowd and a tumult and trouble, but an assembly and a festival, and thus to take all with content. *Chapter XII.*

God has assigned to each man a director, his own good genius, and committed him to his care, a director who never sleeps and cannot be deceived. To what better, more careful guardian could He have committed us?

So when you have shut your doors and darkened your room, remember never to say that you are alone, for you are not. God is within, and your genius is within, and what need have they of light to see what you are doing?

To this God you likewise ought to swear such an oath as the soldiers swear to Caesar. For do they, in order to receive their pay, swear to prefer before all things the safety of Caesar; and will not you swear, who have received so many and so great favours; or if you have sworn, will you not abide by your oath?

And what must you swear? Never to disobey, nor find fault, nor murmur at any of the things appointed by Him, nor be unwilling to do or suffer anything that is necessary. In the first oath, men swear not to honour any other more than Caesar; in the last, not to honour any other more than themselves. *Chapter XIV.*

ANY one thing of those which exist would be enough to make a man perceive the providence of God. And speak not now to me of great things, but only of this, that milk is produced from grass, and cheese from milk, and wool from skins. Who made these things or devised them? Are these the only works of Providence toward us? And what words can adequately express their praise?

For if we had understanding, ought we to do anything else both jointly and severally than to sing hymns to God and to laud Him and tell of His benefits? Ought we not when we are digging and ploughing and eating to sing this hymn to God: Great is God?

For what else can, I, a lame old man, do but sing hymns to God? Were I a nightingale, I would act the part of a nightingale; a swan, the part of a swan; but since I am a reasonable creature, it is my duty to praise God. Nor will I ever desert this post as long as it is vouchsafed me; and I exhort you to join me in the same song. *Chapter XVI.*

I LATELY had an iron lamp burning before my household gods. Hearing a noise at the door, I ran down, and found that my lamp was stolen. But it did not strike me that he who stole it had done anything surprising. What then? Tomorrow, I said, you shall find an earthen one; for a man loses only what he has.

But I have lost my coat! Aye, because you had a coat. I have a pain in my head! You could not well have a pain in your horns! Why then are you out of humour? For loss and pain can be only of such things as possessed.

Who then is the invincible? It is he whom none of those things disturb which are independent of the will.

Chapter XVIII.

DIFFICULTIES are the things that show what men are. For the rest, remember, in any difficulty, that God, like a trainer of athletes, has matched you with a rough antagonist. For what end? That you may be a conqueror in the Olympic games; and this does not happen without toil.

So now, if you should come and tell us, Things are in a fearful way at Rome! Death is terrible; banishment terrible, calumny, poverty terrible! Run, friends, the enemy is at hand! We will answer; Get you gone, and prophesy for yourself! Our only fault is that we have sent such a spy.

Diogenes [1] was sent as a spy before you: he brought us other tidings. He says that death is no evil, for it is nothing base; and that calumny is but the noise of madmen. That nakedness is better than a purple robe, and for sleep the bare ground is the softest bed. And he gives as proof of all that he says his own courage, tranquillity, freedom, and bodily health and vigour. No enemy is near, he says, All is profound peace.

Chapter XXIV.

IF neither honour nor judgment is destroyed, the man himself is preserved likewise; but when either of these is demolished, he is lost also.

Paris, they say, was undone because the Greeks invaded Troy and laid it waste, and his family were slain in battle! By no means: for no one is undone by an action that is not his own. His true undoing was when he lost the modest, the faithful, the hospitable, the decent character. This is human undoing, this the siege, this the

---

[1] One of the lesser Socratics, 414 (?)-324 (?) B. C.

overthrow, when right principles are ruined and destroyed.   *Chapter XXVIII.*

How was it that Socrates suffered such things from the Athenians?

Imbecile! Why do you say *Socrates?* State the fact as it is: How was it that the paltry *body* of Socrates was dragged to prison by those who were stronger; that one gave hemlock to the *body* of Socrates, so that it died?

Had Socrates, then, no equivalent for these things? What does he say? Anytus and Meletus may indeed kill me, but hurt me they cannot. If it so pleases God, so let it be!

         Chapter XXIX.

WHEN you are going in to any great personage, remember that Another also from above sees what is going on, and that you ought to please Him rather than the other.

He then who sees from above asks you: In the schools what used you to say about exile and bonds and death and disgrace?

I used to say that they are things indifferent.
What then do you say of them now? Are they changed at all?
No.
Are you changed then?
No.
Tell me then what things are indifferent.
The things which are independent of the will.
Tell me also what follows from this.
The things which are independent of the will are nothing to me.

Then go into the great person boldly and remember these things. I imagine that you will have such thoughts as these: Is this the thing which men name power? This the antechamber? The men of the bedchamber? The armed guards? All this is nothing: but I have been preparing myself as for something great!

         Chapter XXX.

Book II

WHAT is death? A tragic mask. Turn it and be convinced. See, it does not bite! This poor body and the spirit must be separated either now or later. Why, then, are you troubled if it be now? For if not now, it will be hereafter. Why? To complete the revolution of the world; for that has need of some things present, others to come, others already completed.

What is pain? A mask. Turn it too, and be convinced.

Chapter I.

(WHEN a person maintains his proper station in life, he does not gape after externals[2]). If you gape after externals you must of necessity ramble up and down in obedience to the will of your master. And who is the master? He who has the power over the things which you seek to gain or try to avoid.

Chapter II.

THUS then in life the chief business is this: distinguish and separate things and say: Externals are not in my power, will is in my power. Where shall I seek the good and the bad? Within, in the things which are my own. But in what does not belong to you, call nothing either good or bad.

We should act as we do in the case of a voyage. I can choose the master of a ship, the sailors, the day, the opportunity. Then comes a storm. What more have I to care for? My part is done. The business belongs to another, the master.

But the ship is sinking! What then have I to do? I do the only thing I can,—not to be drowned full of fear, nor screaming nor blaming God, but knowing that what has been produced must also perish;[3] for I am not an immortal being, but a man, a part of the whole, as an

[2] Inserted from Book 1, Chapter XXI.
[3] Comp. The Book of Buddha, pp. 186, 218.

hour is part of the day. I must be present like the hour, and past like the hour.   *Chapter V.*

You are a distinct portion of the essence of God, and contain a certain part of Him in yourself. Why then are you so ignorant of your noble birth? Why do you not consider whence you came? Why do you not remember when you are eating, who you are who eat and whom you feed? When you are conversing, when you are exercising, when you are disputing, do you not know that it is God you feed, God you exercise? You carry God about with you, wretch, and know nothing of it.

Do you suppose I mean some god without you, of gold or silver? It is within yourself you carry Him and profane Him without being sensible of it, by impure thought and unclean actions.

If even the image of God were present, you would not dare to act as you do; and when God is within you, and hears and sees all, are you not ashamed to think and act thus, insensible of your own nature and hateful to God? Have you not God? Do you seek any other while you have Him?

If you were a statue of Phidias, either Zeus or Athena, you would remember both yourself and the artist, and if you had any sense, you would endeavour to do nothing unworthy of Him who formed you, or of yourself, nor to appear in an unbecoming manner to spectators.

And are you now careless how you appear, because you are the workmanship of Zeus? And yet, what comparison is there, either between the artists or the things they have formed? What work of any artist contains in itself those faculties which are shown in forming it? Is it anything but marble, or brass, or gold or ivory?

The Athena of Phidias, when its hand is once extended and a Victory placed in it, remains in that attitude forever. But the works of God are endued with motion, breath, and the use of appearances, judgment.

Being, then, the work of such an artist, will you dishonour Him, especially when He has not only formed you, but has entrusted you and given the guardianship of you to yourself? Will you not only be forgetful of this, but also dishonour the trust?

If God had committed some orphan to your charge, would you have been thus careless of him? He has delivered you to your own care, and says: I had no one fitter to be trusted than you. Keep this person for me just what he is by nature, modest, faithful, noble, unterrified, dispassionate, tranquil.

And will you not keep him such? *Chapter VIII.*

CONSIDER who you are. In the first place you are a *man,* and this is one who has nothing superior to the faculty of the will, but all other things subjected to it; and the faculty itself he possesses unenslaved and free from subjection. Consider then from what things you have been separated by reason. You have been separated from wild beasts: you have been separated from domestic animals.

Further, you are a *citizen of the world,* and not one of the subservient, but one of the ruling parts, for you are capable of comprehending the divine administration and of considering the connexion of things.

What then does the character of a citizen promise? To hold nothing as profitable to himself; to deliberate about nothing as if one were detached from the community, but to act as the hand or foot would, if they had reason, for they would never put themselves in motion nor desire anything otherwise than with reference to the whole.

After this remember that you are a *son.* What does this character promise? To consider that everything that is the son's belongs to the father, to obey him in all things, never to blame him to another, not to say or do anything which does him injury, cooperating with him as far as you can.

After this know that you are a *brother* also, and that to this character it is due to make concessions; to be easily persuaded, to speak good of your brother, never to claim in opposition to him any of the things which are independent of the will. For see what a thing it is, in place of a lettuce, if it should so happen, or a seat of superiority, to gain for yourself goodness of disposition! How great is the advantage!

And if instead of a man, who is a tame animal and social, you are become a mischievous wild beast, treacherous, biting, have you lost nothing? Must you lose a bit of money that you must suffer damage? And does the loss of nothing else do a man damage?

Is there then no energy of the soul which is an advantage to him who possesses it, and a damage to him who has lost it? Have we not a natural modesty, fidelity, affection?

A natural disposition to help others, a natural disposition to forbearance? The man then who allows himself to be damaged in these matters, can he be free from harm and uninjured?

What then? Shall I not hurt him who has hurt me? Consider first what hurt means. For if the good consists in the will, and the evil also in the will, see if what you say is not this: What then? Since that man has hurt himself by doing an unjust act to me, shall I not hurt myself by doing an unjust act to him?   *Chapter X.*

WHAT, then, is the world? Who governs it? Has it no governor? How is it possible, when neither a city nor a house can remain ever so short a time without someone to govern and take care of it, that this vast and beautiful universe should be administered in a fortuitous and disorderly manner? There is, then, a governor.
Chapter XIV.

GIVE me but one who cares *how* he does anything, who does not regard the success of what he is doing, but his own manner of acting.

Ah, when shall I see Athens and the citadel again?

Wretch, are you not content with what you see every day? Can you see anything better than the sun, the moon, the stars, the whole earth, the sea? But if, besides, you comprehend Him who administers the whole, and carry Him about in yourself, do you still long after pebbles and a fine rock?

Boldly make a desperate push, man, for prosperity, for freedom, for magnanimity. Lift up your head at last, as free from slavery. Dare to look up to God and say: Make use of me for the future as Thou wilt. I am of the same mind as Thou art; I am one with Thee. I refuse nothing which seems good to Thee. Lead me whither Thou wilt. Clothe me in whatever dress Thou wilt. Is it Thy will that I should hold a public or a private station, dwell here or be banished, be poor or rich? Under all these circumstances I will defend Thee before men. I will show what the nature of each condition is.

Chapter XVI.

EVERY habit and faculty is preserved and increased by correspondent actions, as the habit of walking by walking, of running, by running. In general, then, if you would make anything habitual, practise it; if you would not make it habitual, do not practise it, but accustom yourself to something else.

It is the same with regard to the operations of the soul. Whenever you are angry, be assured that you have not only suffered a present evil, but have also strengthened a habit and added fuel to a fire.

For it is impossible but that habits and faculties must either be first produced, or strengthened and increased, by correspondent actions.

Be willing to approve yourself to yourself; be willing to appear beautiful in the sight of God; be desirous to converse in purity with your own pure mind and with God.

Chapter XVIII.

SHOW me one who is sick, and happy; in danger, and happy; exiled, and happy; disgraced and happy. Show him to me, for, by Heaven, I long to see a Stoic!

All I ask is that someone should show me a human soul willing to be of one mind with God; to accuse neither God nor man; not to be disappointed at anything; not to look upon anything as an injury; not to be angry; not to be envious; not to be jealous,—in a word, desirous from a man to become a god, and to aim, in his poor mortal body to have fellowship with Zeus. Show me such a one.

Chapter XIX.

BE not deceived, no living being is attached to anything so strongly as to its own interest. Whenever, therefore, anyone regards his interest as identical with sanctity, virtue, country, parents, and friends, all these are saved; but if he places on one side self-interest and on the other friends, country, family, and justice itself, all these give way, borne down by the weight of the former.

For wherever *I* and *mine* are placed, thither must every being incline. If in the body, that will sway us; if in the will, that; if in externals, these. Only, then, if I recognize that my interest lies in rightness of choice, shall I be the son, the friend, or the father that I ought.

Chapter XXII.

Book III

As it is the nature of every mind to assent to truth, and to dissent from falsehood, so it is by nature affected by desire of good and aversion from evil.

For just as a money-changer or seller of herbs is not at liberty to reject Caesar's coin, but is obliged, whether he will or not, to deliver what is sold for it, so it is in the mind. Apparent good as soon as it is seen attracts, and evil repels. Nor will the mind any more reject what seems to be good than it will refuse Caesar's coin.

For this reason the good is preferred to every intimate relationship. This is the coin which God has given me.

Chapter III.

Do you not know that when sickness and death overtake us we must be engaged in doing something? The husbandman will be overtaken at his plow, the sailor on his voyage. At what employment, then, would you be surprised?

For my part, (I would have death find me at some humane, beneficent, public-spirited, gallant action. If, however, I cannot be doing any such great things) [4] I would be found studying this, that I may be able to say to God: Have I transgressed Thy commands? Have I perverted the powers, the senses, the principles, which Thou hast given me? Have I ever accused Thee or censured Thy dispensations?

I have been poor, since it was Thy will, but with joy. I have not held positions of power, because it was not Thy will; and power I have never desired. Hast Thou ever seen me out of humour on this account? Have I not always approached Thee with a cheerful countenance ready to follow Thy commands and the intimations of Thy will?

It is now Thy pleasure that I depart from this assembly. I depart, and I give Thee thanks that Thou hast thought me worthy to have a share in it with Thee, to see Thy works and to comprehend Thine administration. May death overtake me while I am thinking, while I am writing, while I am reading such thoughts as these!

Chapter V.

WHAT, then, do I need?
What you lack,—constancy, a mind conformable to nature, freedom from perturbation. Whether I have a patron or not, what care I? I am richer than you. I am not anxious what Caesar will think of me. I flatter no one on that account.

This I have instead of vessels of silver and gold. You have your vessels of gold, but your discourse, your principles, your assents, your pursuits, your desires, are nothing but earthenware.

[4] Inserted from Book IV, Ch. X.

When I have all these in conformity with nature, why should I not bestow some study upon my reasoning too?

You, when you have nothing to do are restless; you go to the theatre, or perhaps to bathe. Why should not the philosopher polish his reason? You have fine murrhine vases, I have accurate forms of reasoning. Your appetite is insatiable; mine is satisfied.

When children thrust their hand into a narrow jar of nuts and figs they cannot get their full hand out again. Then they fall to crying. Drop a few of the nuts and you will get out the rest! And do you too drop some of your desires. Do not covet many things, and some you will obtain.   *Chapter IX.*

EACH of us ought to say upon every occasion of difficulty: It was for this that I exercised, it was for this that I prepared myself. God says to you: Give me a proof that you have gone through the preparatory combats, that you have followed the proper diet, the proper exercise; that you have obeyed the trainer.

And after this, do you faint when the time for action comes? Now is the time for a fever; bear it well! For thirst; bear it well! Is it not in your power? Who shall hinder you?   *Chapter X.*

SOLITUDE is a certain condition of a helpless man. For because a man is alone, he is not for that reason also solitary; just as, though he be among numbers, he is not for that reason not solitary. We ought, however, to be prepared for this also, to be self-sufficient and able to bear our own company.

For as Zeus dwells with Himself, is tranquil by Himself, contemplates His own administration, and is employed in thoughts worthy of Himself, so should we too be able to talk with ourselves, and not to need the conversation of others, nor be at a loss for employment; to observe the divine administration; to consider our relation to other beings; how we have formerly been

affected by events, how we are affected now; if anything
wants completing, to complete it according to reason.

Shall not a man who enjoys this peace be content when
he is alone? When he sees and reflects: Now no evil can
happen to me; for there is no robber, no earthquake,
everything is full of peace, full of tranquillity: every
way, every city, every neighbor, companion is harmless.

One whose business it is supplies me with food; another
with raiment; another with perceptions and preconcep-
tions. And if he does not supply what is necessary, God
gives the signal for retreat, opens the door, and says to
you: Go!

Go whither? To nothing terrible, but to the place whence
you came, to friends and kinsmen, to the elements. What
there was in you of fire goes to fire, of earth, to earth;
of air, to air; of water, to water: no Hades, nor Acheron,
nor Cocytus, but all is full of gods.

He who can have such thoughts, and can look upon the
sun, moon and stars, and enjoy the earth and sea, is
no more solitary than he is helpless.

As bad actors cannot sing alone, but only in a chorus,
so some persons cannot walk alone. Friends, if you are
anybody, walk alone, talk by yourself, and do not skulk
in the chorus! Think a little at last; look about you,
examine yourself, that you may know what you are.

Chapter XIII.

BOOK IV

WHEN you have received all, even your very self, from
another, are you angry and do you blame the Giver
if He takes something away from you? Was it not He
who brought you here? Was it not He who showed you
the light? Has He not given you fellow-workers? Has
He not given you senses? Has He not given you reason?

And as whom did He bring you here? Was it not as
one subject to death? Was it not as one to live with a
little portion of flesh upon earth and to observe His ad-

ministration and to watch the spectacle with **Him for a**
short time? After having beheld the spectacle then, will
you not depart when He leads you out, adoring and
thankful for what you have heard and seen?

No, you reply; I want to enjoy the feast still longer!

So might the spectators at Olympia desire to see more
combatants. But the solemnity is over. Go away. Depart
like a grateful and modest person, and make room for
others.　　　　　　　　　　　　　　　　　*Chapter I.*

PROVINCES are being distributed, money, military command, a consulship. Let children scramble for them!
To me such things are nothing but figs and nuts.

If you miss them while Caesar is throwing them about,
do not let that trouble you; if, however, a fig should
happen to fall into your lap, take it and eat it, for one
may pay so much regard even to a fig.

But if I must overthrow one rival or be overthrown by
another, and flatter those who have pushed their way
into Caesar's favour, this is too dear a price to pay for
a fig.　　　　　　　　　　　　　　　　　*Chapter VII.*

APHORISMS

BE not so much ashamed of what is thought to be dis-
graceful as studious to shun what is so in truth.

In every feast remember that there are two guests to
be entertained, the body and the soul; and that what
you give the body you presently lose, but what you give
the soul remains forever.

It is better, by yielding to truth, to conquer mere opinion,
than, by yielding to opinion, to be defeated by truth.

You will commit the fewest faults in judging if you are
faultless in your own life.

Let not him think that he is loved by any who loves none.

Neither should a ship rely on one small anchor, nor
should life rest on a single hope.

Think of God oftener than you breathe.

From the Enchiridion (*Manual*) [5]

MEN are disturbed, not by things, but by the principles and notions which they form concerning things.   *V.*

EVERYTHING has two handles, one by which it may be carried, another by which it cannot. If your brother acts unjustly, do not lay hold on the action by the handle of his injustice, for by that it cannot be carried; but by the opposite, that he is your brother, that he was nurtured with you; thus you will lay hold of it in such a way that it can be borne.   *XLIII.*

IT is characteristic of a vulgar person that he never expects either benefit or harm from himself, but from externals. The characteristic of a philosopher is that he expects all harm and all benefit from himself.

The marks of one who is making progress are that he censures no one, praises no one, blames no one, accuses no one, says nothing about himself as being anybody or knowing anything. When he is hindered or restrained, he accuses himself; if he is praised, he secretly laughs at the person who praises him, and if he is censured, he makes no defence.   *XLVIII.*

How long, then, will you defer thinking yourself worthy of the noblest things, and in no instance transgressing the distinctions of reason? You have received the rules to which you ought to assent, and you have assented to them. What other master, then, do you wait for, that you defer to him the reforming of yourself?

If you will always add procrastination to procrastination, purpose to purpose, and fix day after day in which to attend to yourself, you will insensibly continue without proficiency, and living and dying, persevere in being one of the vulgar.

[5] The *Enchiridion* was adopted as a manual by the early Christian Church.

This instant, then, think yourself worthy of living as a grown-up man and a proficient. Let whatever appears to be the best be to you an inviolable law. And if any instance of pain or pleasure, or glory or disgrace be set before you, remember that now the Olympic contest is on, and cannot be put off; and that by once being worsted and giving way, proficiency is lost.

Thus Socrates became perfect, improving himself in all things, attending to nothing but reason. And though you are not yet a Socrates, you ought to live as one who desires to become a Socrates.[6]

[6] The above quotations from the *Discourses*, the *Aphorisms*, and the *Enchiridion* of Epictetus are compiled from Benjamin E. Smith's edition (1900) based upon Elizabeth Carter's translation (1807), and the version by George Long (1890).

THE MEDITATIONS OF MARCUS AURELIUS

My city and country as I am Antoninus is Rome; as a man, the whole world. Marcus Aurelius, VI. **xxxix.**

Everything harmonizes with me which is harmonious to thee, O Universe! Nothing for me is too early or too late which is in due time for thee. Everything is fruit to me which thy seasons bear, O Nature! From thee are all things, in thee are all things, to thee all things return. Could the poet say of Athens, Thou lovely city of Cecrops; and shalt not thou say of the world, Thou lovely city of God? Marcus Aurelius, IX. **xix.**

THE MEDITATIONS OF MARCUS AURELIUS

The Emperor Marcus Aurelius Antoninus, "unspotted by pleasure, undaunted by pain," was born at Rome A.D. 121. Amidst the cares of state and the coarse clangour of arms he learned to retire into the sanctuary of his own soul and renew his calm and courage by the Meditations, a form of diary written solely for his own use. A Stoic, drawing his inspiration from Epictetus among others, he stressed the distinction between the things which are in our power to control and those which are not, and insisted on the unity of the universe and man's duty as a member of the great whole. Upon his death in A.D. 180, he received the honour of deification, and his statue or bust was added to the Dei Penates of the Roman household.

It is high time for thee to understand both the true nature of the world whereof thou art a part; and of that Lord [1] and Governor of the world from Whom as a channel from the spring thou thyself didst flow;

And that there is but a certain limit of time appointed unto thee, which if thou shalt not make use of to calm and allay the many distempers of thy soul, it will pass away and thou with it, and never after return.   II. i.

Whatsoever thou dost affect, whatsoever thou dost project, so do, and so project all as one who, for aught thou knowest, may at this very present depart out of this life.

As for death, if there be any gods,[1] it is no grievous thing to leave the society of men. But if there be no gods, why

---

[1] Marcus Aurelius, like Plato, Aristotle and Epictetus, speaks sometimes of God, sometimes of *the gods*, in his use of the latter term accommodating himself to the ordinary language of the day.

should I desire to live in a world devoid of divine providence?   *II. viii.*

IT is sufficient for a man to apply himself wholly, and to confine his thoughts and cares to the tendance of that spirit which is within him, and really and truly to serve him.   *II. xi.*

OUR life is but a point in time; our bodies hasten to their decreed decay; dull the perception and the soul confused; the future, a mystery, and glory, vanity. In brief, the things of the body are a stream; the things of the soul a dream and a mist; life itself a battle, the sojourn of a traveler, and fame, oblivion! What, then, shall guide man aright? One thing, one thing alone, the love of wisdom.

And this is wisdom, for a man to preserve that divine spirit which is within him serene and undefiled, and above all pains or pleasures;

Never to do anything rashly or feignedly; wholly to depend upon himself and his own proper actions; all things that happen to him to embrace contentedly, as coming from Him from whom he also came; and above all things, with all meekness and calm cheerfulness to expect death, as being nothing else but a resolution of those elements of which every creature is composed.   *II. xv.*

THOU must hasten therefore; not only because thou art every day nearer unto death than other, but also because that intellective faculty in thee whereby thou art enabled to know the true nature of things and to order all thy actions, doth daily waste and decay; or may fail thee before thou die.   *III. i.*

THOU must use thyself to think only of such things of which if a man were of a sudden to ask thee: What is that thou art now thinking? thou mayst answer, This and That, freely and boldly;

That so by thy thoughts it may presently appear that in thee all is sincere and peaceable; free from all covetousness, envy, suspicion, and from whatever else thou wouldst blush to confess thy thoughts were set upon.   *III. iv.*

AND further, let the deity which is in thee be the guardian of a living being, manly and mature, engaged in matters political, a Roman and a ruler who has taken his post like a man waiting for the signal which summons him from life; and ready to go, having need neither of oath nor of any man's testimony.

Be cheerful also, and seek not external help nor the tranquillity which others give. A man must stand erect, not be kept erect by others.   *III. v, vi.*

Do thou therefore absolutely and freely make choice of that which is best, and stick unto it.   *III. vii.*

NEVER esteem anything as profitable which shall ever constrain thee either to break thy faith or to lose thy modesty; to hate any man, to suspect, to curse, to dissemble, to lust after anything that requireth the secret of walls or veils.   III. viii

IF thou workest at that which is before thee, following right reason seriously, vigorously, calmly, without allowing anything else to distract thee, but keeping thy divine part pure, as if thou shouldst be bound to give it back immediately; if thou holdest to this, expecting nothing, fearing nothing, in all things that thou shalt either do or speak, contenting thyself with heroical truth, thou shalt live happily; and from this, there is no man that can hinder thee.   *III. xiii.*

WITHOUT relation unto God thou shalt never speed in any worldly actions; nor on the other side, in any divine, without some respect had to things human.   *III. xiv.*

MEN seek for themselves private retiring places such as country villages, the seashore, mountains; yea thou thyself art wont to long much after such places. But this thou must know proceeds from simplicity in the highest degree.

At what time soever thou wilt, it is in thy power to retire into thyself and to be at rest and free from all businesses. A man cannot any whither retire better than to his own soul; he especially who is beforehand provided of such things within, which whensoever he doth withdraw himself to look in, may presently afford unto him perfect ease and tranquillity.

Let these precepts be brief and fundamental, which as soon as thou dost call them to mind, may suffice to purge thy soul thoroughly and to send thee away well pleased with those things whatsoever they be which now again thou dost return unto.

Among other things, let these two be most obvious and at hand: One, that things or objects themselves reach not unto the soul, but stand without, and that it is from the opinion only which is within that all the tumult and all the trouble doth proceed.

The next, that all these things which now thou seest, shall within a very little while be changed and be no more: and ever call to mind how many changes and alterations in the world thou hast already been an eyewitness of in thy time. This world is mere change, and this life, opinion. *IV. iii.*

WHENSOEVER by some present hard occurrences thou hast been constrained to be in some sort troubled and vexed, return unto thyself as soon as may be, and be not out of tune longer than thou must needs.

For so shalt thou be the better able to keep thy part another time, and to maintain the harmony, if thou dost use thyself to this continually; once out, presently to have recourse unto it, and to begin again. *VI. ix.*

THESE two rules thou must always have in a readiness. First do nothing at all, but what reason proceeding from that regal and supreme part shall for the good and benefit of men suggest unto thee. And secondly, if any man that is present shall be able to rectify thee or to turn thee from some erroneous persuasion, that thou be always ready to change thy mind. *IV. x.*

HE is a true fugitive that flies from reason by which men are sociable. He blind, who cannot see with the eyes of the understanding. He poor that stands in need of another, and hath not in himself all things needful for this life. *IV. xxiv.*

THY evil cannot subsist in any distemper of the natural constitution of the body, which is but as it were the coat or cottage of thy soul. Wherein then, but in that part of thee wherein the conceit and apprehension of any misery can subsist?

Though thy body either be cut or burnt, yet let that part to which it belongs to judge of these things be still at rest; let it judge this that equally may happen to a wicked man and a good man to be neither good nor evil. *IV. xxxii.*

THUS must thou according to truth and nature thoroughly consider how man's life is but for a very moment of time, and so depart meek and contented; even as if a ripe olive falling should praise the ground that bare her, and give thanks to the tree that begat her. *IV. xxxix.*

THOU must be like a promontory of the sea, against which though the waves beat continually, yet it both itself stands, and about it are those swelling waves stilled and quieted. *IV. xi.*

IN the morning when thou findest thyself unwilling to rise, consider with thyself presently; It is to go about a man's work that I am stirred up. Am I then unwilling to go about that for which I was born and brought into this world? Or was I made for this, to lay me down and make much of myself in a warm bed?

Seest thou not how all things in the world besides, how every tree and plant, how sparrows and ants, spiders and bees, how all in their kind are intent to perform whatsoever naturally doth become and belong unto them?

And wilt not thou do that which belongs unto a man to
do? Wilt thou not run to do that which thy nature doth
require?   *V. i.*

THE Pythagoreans [2] were wont betimes in the morning
to look up into the heavens, to put themselves in mind
of them who constantly and invariably did perform their
task; as also to put themselves in mind of orderliness
and of purity and of naked simplicity. For no star or
plant hath any cover before it.   *XI. xxv.*

SUCH there be, who when they have done a good turn
to any, are ready to set them on the score for it and to
require retaliation.

Others there be, who though they stand not upon retaliation to require any, yet they think with themselves never-
theless that such a one is their debtor.

Others again there be, who when they have done any
such thing, do not so much as know what they have done;
but are like unto the vine, which beareth her grapes,
and when once she hath borne her proper fruit, is contented and seeks for no further recompense.   *V. vi.*

WHAT is the use that now at this present I make of my
soul? What is now that part of mine which they call the
rational mistress part employed about? Whose soul do I
now properly possess? A child's? A youth's? A tyrant's?
Or some wild beast's soul?   *V. xi.*

SUCH as thy thoughts and ordinary cogitations are, such
will thy mind be in time. For the soul doth as it were receive its tincture from the fancies and imaginations.
                                                    V. xv.

---

[2] "There is a philosophy of which Pythagoras was the first representative.
And he in his studies of nature mingled astronomy and geometry and music
and arithmetic. And he asserted that God is a monad, and examining the
nature of number with especial care, he said that the universe produces
melody and is put together with harmony, and he first proved the motion
of the seven stars to be rhythm and melody." *Hippolyti Philosophumena.*

As the worth is of those things which a man doth affect, so is in very deed every man's worth more or less.

VII. iii.

Live with the Gods! And he doth live with the Gods who at all times affords unto them the spectacle of a soul both contented and well pleased with whatever is allotted unto her; and performing whatsoever is pleasing to that Spirit, whom (being part of himself) Jove hath appointed to every man as his overseer and governor.

V. xxi.

Thou mayst always speed if thou wilt but make choice of the right way; if in the course both of thine opinions and actions, thou wilt observe a true method.

These two things be common to the souls, as of God, so of men, and of every reasonable creature; first that in their own proper work they cannot be hindered by anything; and secondly, that their happiness doth consist in a disposition to and in the practice of righteousness; and that in these their desire is terminated. *V. xxviii.*

A happy lot and portion is, good inclinations of the soul, good desires, good actions. *V. xxx.*

Let this be thy only joy, and thy only comfort, from one sociable kind action without intermission to pass unto another, God being ever in thy mind. *VI. vi.*

Look in, let not either the proper quality or the true worth of anything pass thee, before thou hast fully apprehended it. *VI. iii.*

Do not ever conceive anything impossible to man, which by thee cannot, or without much difficulty be effected; but whatsoever in general thou canst conceive possible and proper unto any man, think that very possible unto thee also. *VI. xviii.*

Stir up thy mind, and recall thy wits again from thy natural dreams and visions; and when thou art perfectly awoken, and canst perceive that they were but dreams that troubled thee, as one newly awakened out of sleep

look upon these worldly things with the same mind as
thou didst upon those that thou sawest in thy sleep.
VI. xxix.

Fɪᴛ and accommodate thyself to that estate and to those
occurrences which by the destinies have been annexed
unto thee; and love those men whom thy fate it is to live
with; but love them truly. *VI. xxxv.*

Wʜᴇɴ thou wilt comfort and cheer thyself, call to mind
the several gifts and virtues of them whom thou dost
daily converse with; as for example, the industry of the
one; the modesty of another; the liberality of a third.

For nothing can so much rejoice thee as a lively image
of the several virtues, visible and eminent in the dispositions of those who live with thee. *VI. xliii.*

Tʜᴏᴜ shalt use thyself often to say to thyself, I am a
member of the mass and body of reasonable substances.
But if thou shalt say a *part,* thou dost not yet love men
from thy heart. *VII. x.*

Iғ ever thou sawest either a hand or a foot or a head
lying by itself, as cut off from the rest of the body, such
must thou conceive him to make himself that either is
offended at anything that is happened, or that commits
anything against the natural law of mutual correspondence and society among men; or he that commits any
act of uncharitableness.

Thou wert born indeed a part, but now thou hast cut
thyself off. However, herein is matter of joy and exultation, that thou mayst be united again. God hath not
granted it to any other part that once separated and
cut off it might be reunited and come together again.
But, behold, that Goodness how great and immense it is
which hath so esteemed Man! *VIII. xxxii.*

To grow together like fellow branches in matter of good
correspondence and affection; but not in matter of
opinions. They that shall oppose thee in thy right courses,
as it is not in their power to divert thee from thy good

action, so neither let it be to divert thee from thy good affection toward them.

But be it thy care to keep thyself constant in both; both in a right judgment and action, and in true meekness towards them. For either in the one to give over for fear, or in the other to forsake thy natural affection towards him who by nature is both thy friend and kinsman, is equally base, and much savouring of the disposition of a cowardly fugitive soldier. *XI. viii.*

Not only now henceforth to have a common breath with that air that compasseth us about; but to have a common mind also with that rational substance which compasseth all things.

For that also is of itself, and of its own nature (if a man can but draw it in as he should) everywhere diffused; and passeth through all things no less than air doth, if a man can but suck it in. *VIII. lii.*

There is but one light of the sun though it be intercepted by walls and mountains and other thousand objects. There is but one common substance of the whole world, though it be concluded and restrained into several different bodies, in number infinite.

There is but one common soul, though divided into innumerable particular essences and natures. So is there but one common intellectual soul, though it seem to be divided. *XII. xxiii.*

No man can hinder thee to live as thy nature doth require. Nothing can happen unto thee but what the common good of nature doth require. *VI. liii.*

Whatsoever any man either doth or saith, thou must be good; not for any man's sake, but for thine own nature's sake; as if either gold or the emerald, or purple, should ever be saying to themselves, Whatsoever any man either doth or saith, I must still be an emerald, and I must keep my colour. *VII. xii.*

WIPE off all opinion. *VII. xxi.*

IF therefore thou dost truly understand what it is that is of moment indeed, as for thy fame and credit, take no thought for that: let it suffice thee if all the rest of thy life, be it more or less, thou shalt live as thy nature requireth, or according to the true and natural end of thy making. *VIII. i.*

LABOUR not as one to whom it is appointed to be wretched, nor as one that either would be pitied or admired; but let this be thine only care and desire; so always and in all things to prosecute or to forbear, as the law of charity or mutual society doth require. *IX. x.*

WHEREAS thou shouldst in all things so join action and contemplation that thou mightest both at the same time attend all present occasions to perform everything duly and carefully; and yet so intend the contemplative part too that no part of that delight and pleasure which the contemplative knowledge of everything according to its true nature doth of itself afford, might be lost. *X. ix.*

WHAT use is there of suspicion at all? or why should thoughts of mistrust and suspicion concerning that which is future trouble thy mind at all? What now is to be done, if thou mayst search and inquire into that, what needs thou care for more? And if thou art well able to perceive it alone, let no man divert thee from it. *X. xiii.*

MAKE it not any longer a matter of dispute or discourse what are the signs and proprieties of a good man, but really and actually be such! *X. xviii.*

To live happily is an inward power of the soul when she is affected with indifferency towards those things that are by their nature indifferent.

To be thus affected she must consider all worldly objects both divided and whole; remembering withal that no object can of itself beget any opinion in us, but stands without still and quiet; but that we ourselves beget, and as it were print in ourselves opinions concerning them.

Now it is in our power not to print them; and if they creep and lurk in some corner, it is in our power to wipe them off. *XI. xv.*

I⊤ will suffice thee to remember as concerning pain, that that which is intolerable is soon ended by death; and that which holds long must needs be tolerable; and that the mind in the meantime may by stopping all manner of commerce and sympathy with the body, still retain its own tranquillity. *VII. xxii.*

Death is a cessation from the impression of the senses, the tyranny of the passions, the errors of the mind, and the servitude of the body. *VI. xxvi.*

Th⊤t which is not good for the beehive, cannot be good for the bee. *VI. xlix.*

Whatsoever it be that lieth upon thee to effect, thou must propose it unto thyself as the scaling of walls is unto a soldier. *VII. v.*

As one who had lived, and were now to die by right, whatsoever is yet remaining, bestow that wholly as a gracious overplus upon a virtuous life. *VII. xxxi*

Then hath a man attained to the estate of perfection in his life and conversation when he so spends every day as if it were his last: never hot and vehement in his affections, nor yet so cold and stupid as one that had no sense; and free from all manner of dissimulation. *VII. xl.*

How many such as Chrysippus,[3] how many such as Socrates, how many such as Epictetus, hath the age of the world long since swallowed up and devoured! The time when thou shalt have forgotten all things is at hand. And that time also is at hand, when thou thyself

[3] Chrysippus (died 207 B. C.) organised Stoicism into a system.

shalt be forgotten by all. Whilst thou art, apply thyself to that especially which unto man as he is a man is most proper and agreeable, and that is, for a man to love them that transgress against him.

This shall be, if at the same time that any such thing doth happen, thou call to mind that they are thy kinsmen; that it is through ignorance and against their will that they sin; and that within a very short while after both thou and they shall be no more.

But above all things, that they have not done thee any hurt; for that by them thy mind and understanding is not made worse or more vile than it was before. *VII. xvi.*

WHENSOEVER any man doth trespass against thee, presently consider with thyself what it was that he did suppose to be good, what to be evil, when he did trespass. For this when thou knowest, thou wilt pity him; thou wilt have no occasion either to wonder, or to be angry.

For either thou thyself dost yet live in that error and ignorance, as that thou dost suppose either that very thing that he doth to be good; and so thou art bound to pardon him if he have done that which thou in like case would have done thyself.

Or if so be that thou dost not any more suppose the same things to be good or evil that he doth; how canst thou but be gentle unto him that is in an error? *VII. xix.*

To them that ask, Where hast thou seen the Gods, or how knowest thou certainly that there be Gods, that thou art so devout in their worship? I answer; Neither have I ever seen mine own soul, and yet I respect and honour it.

So then for the Gods, by the daily experience that I have of their providence towards myself and others, I know certainly that they are, and therefore worship them. *XII. xxi.*

THOU hast taken ship, thou hast made the voyage, thou art come to shore; go out, if to another life, there also thou shalt find Gods, who are everywhere.[4]   *III. iii.*

[4] The above quotations from Marcus Aurelius are after the translation by Meric Casaubon (1634), except for III. iii; III. v, vi; III. xiii; and IV. xix, which are partly borrowed from the version by George Long (1862).

THE BOOK OF MOHAMMED

BEING SELECTIONS FROM THE KORAN

Now on the night that the Lord was minded to be gracious to him, Gabriel appeared to Mohammed in the cave, and holding a writing up before him, said Recite! He answered, I cannot. Whereupon the angel did tightly gripe him and cried, Recite! the second time. Mohammed said, What shall I recite? Gabriel said:

> *Recite thou, in the name of thy Lord who hath created man; recite thou, by thy most beneficent Lord who hath taught the use of the pen to record revelation!*

By Allah! If they brought the sun to my right hand and the moon to my left to force me from my undertaking, I would not desist from it until the Lord made manifest my cause, or I perished in the attempt!

Mohammed.

Oh Lord, I beseech Thee, assist me in the agonies of death! (and, in broken whispers) *Lord, pardon my sins . . . eternity in Paradise . . . pardon, yes! I come . . . the blessed companionship on high!*

Mohammed's dying words.

Abu Bekr drew aside the curtain, entered, and stooping down kissed the face of his departed friend: Sweet wast thou in life, he said, and sweet thou art in death, dearer than father or mother to me!

THE BOOK OF MOHAMMED

Mohammed, the Apostle of God and the Seal of the Prophets, the builder of a mighty empire and the founder of Islam which for thirteen hundred years has been the law of life for about one ninth of the human race, was born at Mecca in 570 A.D. and died in 632. At his death his utterances were collected from palm-leaves, skins, the shoulder-blades of sheep, and the hearts of men upon which they were inscribed, and it is from the resulting text, the Koran (Reading or Recitation), that these selections have been made.

In the Name of the Merciful and Compassionate God!

A revelation from the Merciful, the Compassionate; a Book whose signs are detailed; an Arabic Koran for a people who do know; a herald of glad tidings and a warning! *XLI. i.*

By the star when it setteth, your comrade Mohammed erreth not, nor is he deluded! Neither doth he speak of his own will. It is no other than a revelation inspired! One mighty in power, endued with wisdom, taught him, and appeared in the highest horizon.

Then drew he near and hovered over until he was at two bows' length or nearer still. Then he inspired his servant what he inspired him; his heart belieth not what he saw. *LIII. 1-10.*

They say, why is not a sign sent down upon him from his Lord? Answer,[1] The unseen is known only to God; wait, therefore; verily I with you will be one of those who wait.

---

[1] The commands: *Answer!* or *Say!* introducing sentences of the Koran intimate that the words are put into the mouth of the Prophet by Gabriel of whom Mohammed had had a vision during one of his seasons of retirement for devotion and meditation in his fortieth year.

Do they say, He hath devised it? Answer, Then bring a
verse like it, and call on whom ye can beside God, if ye
speak the truth!   *X, 21, 39.*

In the Name of the Merciful and Compassionate God!

Praise be to God, the Lord of the worlds, the merciful,
the compassionate, the Ruler of the day of judgment!
Thee we serve, and to Thee we cry for aid. Direct us in
the right way, the way of those to whom Thou art gracious; not of those with whom Thou art wroth, nor of
those who go astray.   *I.*

God's is the east and the west; and whithersoever ye turn
yourselves to pray, there is God's face! Verily God doth
comprehend and know.

Praise be to Him! His is what is in the heavens and the
earth, Him all things obey. Sole Maker of the heavens
and earth, when He decreeth a matter, He doth but say
to it, Be, and it is.   *II. 109, 110.*

Your God is one God, there is no God but Him, the Merciful, the Compassionate.

Verily in the creation of the heavens and the earth, and
the alternation of night and day, and in the ship that
runneth in the sea with that which is profitable to man,
and in the rain which God sendeth down from heaven to
quicken the dead earth, and in the shifting of the winds,
and in the clouds that are pressed into service betwixt
heaven and earth, are signs to men of understanding.

Yet there are some amongst mankind who take to them
idols along with God, and love them with the love due to
God. O that they could only see that power is altogether
God's!   *II. 159, 160.*

In the Name of the Merciful and Compassionate God!

Righteousness is not that ye turn your faces towards the
east or towards the west, but righteousness is to believe
in God, and the Last Day, and the angels and the Book,
and the prophets; and to give of your wealth for love

of God to kindred, to orphans, to the needy and to the son of the road, to beggars and those in captivity; and to be steadfast in prayer; and to be faithful to your covenant when ye have made a covenant; and patient in poverty and distress and in time of violence; these are they who are true, and these are they who fear the Lord! *II. 172.*

O ye who believe; expend in alms of what we have bestowed upon you before there cometh the day in which is no barter, nor friendship, nor intercession! *II. 255.*

The similitude of those who spend their wealth in God's way is as the likeness of a grain that groweth to seven ears, in every ear a hundred grains; for God will give twofold to whom He pleaseth!

(But) a kind speech with forgiveness is better than alms followed by injury.

The similitude of those who lay out their substance craving the good will of God and the establishing of their souls is as the likeness of a garden on a hill. A heavy shower falleth on it, and it bringeth forth twofold. God doth behold your actions. *II. 263-267.*

Ye shall never attain to goodness till ye give alms of what ye love; and whatever ye give, of a truth God knoweth it. *III. 86.*

In the name of the Merciful and Compassionate God!

God! There is no God but Him, the Living, the Eternal. Slumber taketh Him not nor sleep. To Him belongeth what is in the heavens and what is in the earth. Who shall intercede with Him save through His good pleasure?

He knoweth that which is past and that which is to come to men. His throne extendeth over heaven and earth, and it burdeneth Him not to maintain them both.[2]

---

[2] This is the famous ayatu 'l kursiy, *verse of the throne*, considered one of the finest passages in the Koran, and frequently inscribed in mosques.

Whoso believeth in God hath got firm hold of the handle that shall not be broken. God is the patron of them who believe; He bringeth them forth from darkness into light. *II. 255-257.*

His apostles say: We have heard and we obey: Thy pardon, Lord! for to Thee doth our journey tend! God will not burden any soul beyond its capacity. It shall enjoy the good which it hath acquired, and it shall bear the evil which it hath earned.

O our Lord! Catch us not up if we forget or make mistake! Lord, lay not on us a burden like that Thou hast laid on those who were before us. Thou art our Sovereign, then help us against the nations who believe not in Thee. *II. 287.*

It is not for any soul to die save by God's permission written down for an appointed time.[3] And whoso chooseth the reward of this world, we will give him of it; but whoso desireth the reward of the world to come, we will give him thereof, and we will certainly recompense the grateful. *III. 139.*

Every soul must taste of death; and ye shall only receive your recompense upon the day of resurrection. *III. 182.*

O Men! Fear your Lord, who hath created you from one soul! *IV. 1.*

Wheresoever ye be, death will overtake you, though it were in lofty towers.

Whatever good betideth thee, it is from God; and whatever betideth thee of evil, it is from thyself.

Fight, then, in the way of God; impose not aught on any but thyself, and urge on the believers! *IV. 80, 81, 85.*

A soul shall be given up for that which it hath earned, nor hath it, beside God, patron or intercessor. *VI. 69.*

---

[3] Also translated: according to the Book that fixeth the time of life.

In the Name of the Merciful and Compassionate God!

He it is who hath created the heavens and the earth in truth; and on the day when He saith to a thing, Be; then it is. His word is truth; and His will be the kingdom on the day when the trumpets shall sound; the Knower alike of the unseen and the evident; He is wise and well-aware! *VI. 72, 73.*

VERILY, God it is who causeth the grain and the date-stone to put forth; He bringeth forth the living from the dead, and the dead from the living.

He it is who cleaveth out the morning, and ordaineth the night for repose, and the sun and the moon for reckonings; this is the disposition of the Mighty, the All-wise!

He it is who made for you the stars that ye might be guided thereby in the darkness of the land and of the sea. And He it is who sendeth down rain from heaven, whereby we produce the close-growing grain, and palm-trees with sheaths of clustering dates, and gardens of grapes and olives and pomegranates. Verily, here are signs for people who believe! *VI. 95-99.*

VERILY, my prayers and my devotion and my life and my death belong to God, the Lord of the worlds. He hath no associate. Other than God shall I crave for a Lord when He is Lord of all? *VI. 163, 164.*

WILL they associate with Him those who cannot create aught, but are themselves created? Which have no power to help them, and cannot even help themselves? *VII. 190.*

VERILY, God's is the kingdom of the heavens and the earth! He quickeneth and He doth kill. *IX. 117.*

HE it is who made the sun for a brightness, and the moon for a light, and decreed for it stations, that ye may know the number of the years and the reckoning. God only created that in truth. He maketh His signs clear to those who understand. *X. 5.*

Come, I will rehearse what your Lord hath made binding on you; that ye assign not any to Him as a partner; that ye be good to your parents; and that ye come not near to pollutions, outward or inward.

And come not near to the substance of the orphan, but to improve it, until he come of age; and use a full measure, and a just balance.

And when ye give judgment observe justice, though it concern a kinsman; and fulfil the covenant of God. This is My right way; follow it then!   *VI. 152-154.*

Turn away evil by what is better, and lo! he between whom and thyself was enmity shall be as though he were a warm friend.   *XLI. 34.*

And when the Koran is read, attend thereto and keep silence, that haply ye may obtain mercy. And meditate on thy Lord in thine own mind with lowliness and fear, and without loud speaking, at even and at morn; and be not one of the heedless!   *VII. 203, 204.*

Verily, those who believe and do what is right, their Lord shall direct them because of their faith; rivers shall flow at their feet in gardens of delight.

Their cry therein shall be, Glory be to Thee, O God! And their salutation therein, Peace! And the end of their cry shall be, Praise belongeth unto God, the Lord of the worlds!   *X. 9, 10.*

Seest thou not to what God likeneth a good word? A good word is like a good tree whose root is firmly fixed in earth, whose branches reach to heaven; it yieldeth its fruit at every season.   *XIV. 29.*

O our Lord! Verily, Thou knowest what we hide and what we bring to light, for naught in heaven or earth is hid from Thee.   *XIV. 41.*

In the Name of the Merciful and Compassionate God!

The sentence of the Lord will surely come to pass; seek not then to hasten it on.

By His behest will He cause the angels with the Spirit to descend upon whom He will of His servants, bidding them: Give warning that there is no God but Me; therefore fear Me!

He hath created the heavens and the earth to set forth His truth! High let Him be exalted above the gods they join with Him!

He created man from a clot! the cattle too; from them ye have warmth and profit, and in them there is beauty when ye fetch them home to rest and when ye drive them forth to pasture. And they bear your heavy burdens to lands which else ye could not reach, save with sore travail of your soul;—verily, your Lord is merciful and kind!

He createth also what ye know not of. God's it is to show the Way. He it is who sendeth down rain from Heaven whence ye have drink and whence grow the plants whereon ye feed your flocks.

He it is who hath subjected the seas to you, that ye may eat fresh flesh therefrom; and that ye may go in quest of His bounties, and haply give thanks.

And He hath cast the firm mountains on the earth; and rivers and roads for your guidance.

Shall He then who doth create be as he who createth not? Are ye then unmindful?

If ye would number the favours of God, ye shall not be able to compute them. Verily, God is forgiving, merciful! And those on whom ye call beside God cannot create aught, for they are themselves created. Dead are they, not living, nor can they perceive!   *XVI. 1-20.*

GOD's alone are the unseen things of the heavens and the earth; nor is the matter of the last hour but as the twinkling of an eye, or even less! Verily, God is mighty over all!   *XVI. 79.*

BE thou patient, then; for God is with those who fear Him, and with those who do well.   *XVI. 128.*

IN the Name of the Merciful and Compassionate God!

Set not up another god with God, lest thou sit despised and forsaken.

Thy Lord hath decreed that ye worship none but Him; and that ye show kindness to your parents, whether one or both of them attain old age with you.

And lower to them the wing of humility out of tender affection, and say: O Lord! have compassion on them both, even as they reared me when I was little!

Your Lord knoweth well what is in your souls whether ye be righteous; and verily, He is gracious to those who come back penitent.

And walk not proudly in the land; for thou canst not cleave the earth, neither shalt thou reach the mountains in stature.   *XVII. 23-27, 39.*

BE thou steadfast in prayer from the declining of the sun until the dusk of the night and the reading of the dawn, and watch unto it in the night.   *XVII. 80.*

BE ye then constant at prayer and give alms, and cleave fast to God; He is your excellent Sovereign and help!
          XXII. 76.

IN the Name of the Merciful and Compassionate God!

We hurl the truth against falsehood, and it crasheth into the same, and lo! it vanisheth.   *XXI. 18.*

GOD is the light of the heavens and the earth; His light is as a niche wherein is a lamp, and the lamp is in a glass, the glass as it were a glistening star; it is lit with the oil of a blessed tree, an olive neither of the east nor of the west, the oil of which would well-nigh give light though fire touched it not. Light upon light! God guideth to His light whom He will please; and He setteth forth parables for men; for God doth know all things.   *XXIV. 35.*

HE it is who sent His winds with glad tidings before His mercy. He it is who hath let loose the seas, this one sweet and fresh, the other bitter and pungent, and hath made between them a barrier that cannot be passed. *XXV. 50, 55.*

S<small>EE</small> they not that we have ordained the night that they may rest in it, and the day with its gift of light? Of a truth herein are signs to a people who believe. *XXVII. 88.*

L<small>OOK</small> then to the vestiges of God's mercy, how after its death He quickeneth the earth; surely, He is the quickener of the dead, and He is mighty over all!

God it is who created you in weakness, then after weakness hath given you strength; and after strength, weakness again and grey hairs. *XXX. 49, 53.*

A<small>ND</small> were all the trees upon the earth to become pens, and the sea with seven more seas to swell its tides as ink, the words of God would not be spent, for God is mighty, wise! *XXXI. 26.*

I<small>N</small> the Name of the Merciful and Compassionate God!

God is the Creator of all things, and over everything He is guardian; His are the keys of heaven and earth.

The whole earth shall be but His handful on the day of resurrection; and in His right hand shall the heavens be rolled together. Praise be to Him!

And the earth shall shine by the light of its Lord, and the Book shall be laid open, and the prophets and the martyrs shall be brought up as witnesses; and judgment shall be given between them with equity; and every soul shall receive as it shall have wrought, for He knoweth well men's actions. *XXXIX. 63-70.*

B<small>UT</small> wait thou patiently for the judgment of thy Lord, for thou art in Our eye. And celebrate the praises of thy Lord what time thou risest, and in the night-season, and at the setting of the stars! *LII. 48.*

W<small>HEREFORE</small> be patient with becoming patience; verily they see it as far off, but we see it nigh!

The day when the heavens shall become as molten brass, and the mountains shall be as flocks of wool; when friend shall not question friend though they gaze at one another; and the sinner would fain give as a ransom from the torment of that day his sons and his spouse and his brother and his kin who stand by him, and all who are in the earth, that he might be delivered!   *LXX. 5-14.*

HE asketh, When shall this day of resurrection be? But when the eye shall be dazzled, and the moon be darkened, and the sun and moon shall be in conjunction, on that day man shall cry: Where is a place of refuge?

But in vain,—there is no refuge! With thy Lord on that day shall be the sole asylum. On that day shall a man be told of all that he hath done first and last, yea, a man shall be a witness against himself.

On that day some faces shall beam with light, looking towards their Lord; and some faces on that day shall be dismal, as if they thought a great calamity would befall; aye, a man's soul shall come up into his throat, and there shall be a cry, Who hath a charm to recover him?

That hour is nearer to thee and nearer, it is ever nearer to thee and nearer still!   *LXXV. 6-35.*

WHEN the sun shall be folded up, and the stars do fall, and when the mountains are moved, and the seas shall boil, and when the leaves of the book shall be unrolled, and the heaven be stripped off like a skin and hell begin to blaze, and when Paradise shall be brought nigh, then shall every soul know what it hath wrought!   *LXXXI. 1-14.*

WHEN the heaven shall be cloven asunder, and the stars be scattered, and the seas shall surge together, and the tombs be turned upside down, then every soul shall recognize what it hath committed or omitted!

O man! what hath seduced thee against thy gracious Lord, who created thee, and fashioned thee, and gave thee symmetry, and in what form He pleased hath moulded thee? *LXXXII. 1-8.*

WHAT shall make thee to know what the last proof is? It is to ransom the captive, to feed in the day of famine the orphan near of kin, or the poor man who lieth in the dust; and beside this, to be of those who enjoin steadfastness on each other, and encourage each other to mercy,— these are the people of the right hand! *XC. 12-17.*

By the Sun and his noonday brightness! By the Moon when she followeth him! By the Day when it revealeth his glory! By the Night when it enshroudeth him! By the Heaven and Him who built it! By the Earth and Him who spread it forth! By the Soul, and Him who balanced it, inspiring into it the power of choosing its wickedness and piety, blessed now is he who hath purified the same! *XCI. 1-19.*

By the brightness of the morning; and by the night when it darkeneth; thy Lord hath not forsaken thee, neither hath He been displeased. And surely the life to come shall be better for thee than this present life, and thy Lord shall be bounteous to thee and thou be satisfied. Did He not find thee an orphan and give thee a home? [4] And found thee erring and guided thee, and found thee needy and enriched thee? Wherefore oppress not the orphan, and as to him that asketh of thee, chide him not away; but declare abroad the goodness of the Lord! *XCIII.*

SAY: He is God alone; the eternal God! He begetteth not, neither is He begotten; and there is none like unto Him! [5] *CXII.*

---

[4] The charge of the orphaned Mohammed was undertaken by his grandfather, and tradition relates the fondness with which the old man of fourscore years treated the child, spreading a rug for him under the shadow of the Kaaba, and protecting him from all harm.

[5] On the traditional authority of Mohammed himself, this verse, which constitutes Sura CXII, is said to be equivalent in value to two-thirds of the Koran. The above selections from the Koran have been adapted from renderings by Sale, Rodwell and Palmer.

THE ADZAN *(Call to Prayer)*

From a thousand minarets at early dawn and at four other times during the day, the Muezzin cries:

Allahu Akbar! God is great, God is great, God is great!
I bear witness that there is no god but God!
I bear witness that there is no god but God!
I bear witness that Mohammed is the apostle of God!
I bear witness that Mohammed is the apostle of God!
Come hither to prayers!
Come hither to prayers!
Come hither to salvation!
Come hither to salvation!
God is great! There is no other god but God!
Prayer is better than sleep!

It is related from Omar binu-l-Khuttab that: On a certain day when we were near the Prophet there appeared before us a man dressed in white apparel; no marks of travel could be seen upon him, and none of us recognized him. He sat down beside the Prophet and said: O Mohammed, teach me about Islam!

Mohammed replied: Islam is that thou bear witness that there is no God but Allah, and that thou observe prayer, and that thou give alms, and that thou keep the fast in the month Ramadan, and that thou make the pilgrimage to the Temple at Mecca, if thou art able to provide for the journey.

He said: Teach me about faith.

The Prophet replied: It is that thou believe in God and His angels and His books and His apostles and in the last day, and that thou believe in predestination, both of good and evil.

Then he said: Teach me concerning the best action.

He replied: It is that thou worship God as if thou didst see Him; for if thou dost not see Him, yet He seeth thee.

The man said: Teach me concerning the hour of resurrection.

He replied: Concerning this matter the questioned is no wiser than the questioner.

After that the man departed, and I remained sitting for some time. Then the Prophet said to me: O Omar, dost thou know who the questioner was? I said: God and His Apostle know best. He replied: It was Gabriel.

Muslim (died 882 A.D.*).*

BIBLIOGRAPHY

In the compilation of this volume the following works have been consulted and may prove useful to students desiring to go more intimately into the study of the various religions.

EGYPTIAN LITERATURE:

Development of Religion and Thought in Ancient Egypt, by James Henry Breasted; Lectures delivered on the Morse Foundation at Union Theological Seminary. Charles Scribner's Sons, New York, 1912.

The Literature of the Ancient Egyptians, by Sir E. A. Wallis Budge. E. P. Dutton & Co., New York, 1914.

The Teaching of Amen-em-apt, by Sir E. A. Wallis Budge. Egyptian hieroglyphic text and English translation, and with translations of the moral teachings of Egyptian kings and officials illustrating the development of religious philosophy in Egypt during a period of about 2000 yrs. M. Hopkinson & Co., London, 1924.

Ptah-hetep, trans. by Philippe Virey, Vol. III, *Records of the Past,* ed. by A. H. Sayce, 2nd Series, 1887.

La Religion de l'Ancienne Egypte, by Philippe Virey. Beauchesne & Cie., Paris, 1910.

Records of the Past, 1st Series, ed. by Archibald Henry Sayce, 1875.

The Literature of the Ancient Egyptians; Poems, Narratives and Manuals of Instruction from the third and second millennia B.C., by Adolf Erman, trans. into English by Aylward M. Blackman. Methuen & Co., Ltd., 36 Essex St., London, W.C. 2.

The Origin and Growth of Religion, as illustrated by the religion of ancient Egypt; Hibbert Lectures for 1879; by Peter Le Page Renouf.

The Life and Times of Akhnaton, Pharaoh of Egypt, by Arthur E. P. Weigall. G. P. Putnam's Sons, New York, 1923.

"Egyptian Literature," article in Vol. IX, *Library of the World's Best Literature,* by Frances Llewllyn Griffith and Kate Bradbury Griffith, 1897.

BRAHMANISM:

The Thirteen Principal Upanishads, trans. by Robert Ernest
Hume, M.A., Ph.D., with an outline of the philosophy of the
Upanishads and an annotated bibliography. Humphrey Mil-
ford, Oxford University Press, 1921.

The Upanishads, trans. by Max Müller, *Sacred Books of the East,*
Vols. I and XV, 1879-1884. Oxford, the Clarendon Press.

The Religion and Philosophy of the Upanishads, by A. B. Keith,
Harvard Oriental Series, Vols. 31 and 32. University Press,
1926.

Vedic Hymns, Sacred Books of the East, Vol. XXXII (trans. by
Max Müller), Vol. XLVI (trans. by Oldenberg), 1891-97.

Hymns of the Atharva-Veda, trans. by Maurice Bloomfield;
Sacred Books of the East, Vol. XLII, 1897.

*The Religion of the Veda, the ancient religion of India, from Rig-
veda to Upanishads,* by Maurice Bloomfield. G. P. Putnam's
Sons, 1908.

The Religion of the Rig-Veda, by Hervey Dewitt Griswold. H.
Milford, Oxford University Press, 1923.

The Hymns of the Rig-Veda, by Ralph T. H. Griffith, 1897; 2
vols. E. J. Lazarus & Co., Benares, 1896.

The Religions of India, by E. Washburn Hopkins, 1895. Ginn &
Co., Publishers, Boston and London.

"Indian Literature," art. by E. Washburn Hopkins, p. 7905,
Vol. XIV, *Library of the World's Best Literature,* ed. by Chas.
Dudley Warner, 1897, New York.

A History of Sanscrit Literature, by Arthur A. Macdonell. Wm.
Heinemann, London, 1900.

Hymns from the Rigveda. Selected and metrically translated by
A. A. Macdonell, Boden Professor of Sanskrit in the University of Oxford. Oxford University Press, 1923.

Indian Wisdom, by Sir Monier Williams, pub. 1876.

The Laws of Manu, trans. by George Bühler, *Sacred Books of the
East,* Vol. XXV, 1886.

The Bhagavad Gita, trans. by Kashinath Telang, M.A. *Sacred
Books of the East,* Vol. VIII, 1882.

The Bhagavatgita, trans. by Mohini M. Chatterji, 1887. With
Commentary and notes. Ticknor & Co., Boston.

The Bhagavat-Geeta, an excellent old-English version by Charles
Wilkins, 1867, Reprinted for Geo. P. Philes, New York University.

The Bhagavatgita, by Lionel D. Barnett, in *The Temple Classics,* London, 1920. J. M. Dent & Sons, Aldine House, Bedford St., W.C.

The Song Divine (Bhagavadgita), by C. C. Caleb, a metrical rendering with annotations. London, 1911. Luzac & Co., 46 Great Russell St.

Sanskrit and Its Kindred Literatures, by Laura Elizabeth Poor, Robert Bros., 1880.

Accadian and Babylonian Literature:

Records of the Past, ed. by Archibald Henry Sayce; Ist Series, in 12 vols. Samuel Bagster & Sons, London, 1875.

"Accadian-Babylonian and Assyrian Literature," art. by Crawford H. Toy, Prof. of Hebrew, Harvard University, 1896. Vol. I, *Library of the World's Best Literature.*

Babylonian Literature, Hibbert Lectures for 1887, on the origin and growth of religion of the ancient Babylonians. By Archibald Henry Sayce. Williams & Norgate, London.

Cuneiform Parallels to the Old Testament, trans. and ed. by Robert Williams Rogers, Ph.D., Litt.D., LL.D. Henry Frowde, Oxford University Press, 1912.

Sumerian and Babylonian Psalms, by Stephen Langdon, Ph.D.; comprehending nearly all the temple liturgy of the official Babylonian and Assyrian religion yet published. G. E. Stechert & Co., New York, 1909.

Tammuz and Ishtar, by Stephen Langdon, Clarendon Press, Oxford, 1914.

History of Assyria, by Albert TenEyck Olmstead, Prof. of History, Curator of Oriental Museum, University of Illinois. Charles Scribner's Sons, New York, 1923.

Zoroastrianism:

The Zend Avesta, trans. by James Darmesteter and L. H. Mills, Vols. IV, XXIII, XXXI, *Sacred Books of the East.* Clarendon Press, Oxford, 1880, 1883, 1887.

Zoroaster, the Prophet of Ancient Iran, by A. V. Williams Jackson, Prof. of Indo-Iranian Languages in Columbia University. The Macmillan Co., New York, 1899.

"The Avesta," art. by A. V. Williams Jackson, Vol. II, *Library of the World's Best Literature,* ed. by Chas. Dudley Warner, 1896.

410 *BIBLIOGRAPHY*

Essays on the Sacred Language, Writings, and Religion of the Parsis, by Martin Haug. R. S. Peale and J. A. Hill, New York, 1878. Trübner's Oriental Series, London.

CONFUCIANISM:

Yü-yen Tzu-erh Chi, A Progressive Course designed to assist the student of Colloquial Chinese, by Thomas Francis Wade. Trübner & Co., Paternoster Row, London. (The proper names in the selections from the Chinese Classics in *Tongues of Fire* follow Wade's system of transliteration, though for simplicity's sake most of the diacritical marks have been omitted.)

The Chinese Classics, by James Legge, in 7 vols. Oxford, the Clarendon Press. The 1895 edition gives both Chinese and English texts.

The Sacred Books of the East, ed. by Max Müller. Vol. III, *Shu King, Shi King, Hsiao King;* Vol. XVI, *Yi King;* Vols. XXVII, XXVIII, *Li Ki,* 1885. Trans. by James Legge.

The Shu King, trans. from the ancient text by Walter Gorn Old, M.R.A.S., 1904, without consulting the translation by Legge. J. Lane, New York.

"The Literature of China," by Robert Douglas, Vol. VI, *Library of the World's Best Literature,* ed. by Chas. Dudley Warner, 1896.

The Sayings of Confucius, a new translation of the greater part of the Confucian Analects with introduction and notes by Lionel Giles, Assistant in Dept. of Oriental Books and Manuscripts, British Museum. In *Wisdom of the East Series,* ed. by L. Cranmer-Byng and Dr. S. A. Kapadia. John Murray, Albemarle St., W., London, 1924. E. P. Dutton & Co., New York.

TAOISM:

The Sacred Books of the East, ed. by Max Müller, Vols. XXXIX and XL, The Tao Teh King and The Writings of Chuang Tzu. Trans. by James Legge.

Lao Tzu, by Lionel Giles, M. A. *Wisdom of the East Series.* John Murray, Albemarle St., W., London, 1922. E. P. Dutton & Co., New York.

Lao Tze's Tao Teh King, by Paul Carus. Chinese-English, with introduction, transliteration and notes. Open Court Publishing Co., 122 S. Michigan Ave., Chicago.

Buddhism:

Buddhism in Translations, by Henry Clarke Warren of Cambridge, Mass. Vol. III, *Harvard Oriental Series,* ed. by Chas. R. Lanman. Harvard University, 1896.

Dialogues of the Buddha, trans. by T. W. Rhys Davids, in *Sacred Books of the Buddhists Series,* 1895-1899; Henry Frowde, Oxford University Press Warehouse.

Sanjutta-Nikaya, Book of Kindred Sayings, trans. by Mrs. Rhys Davids, and Woodward, pub. by the Pali Text Society, Oxford University Press, Amen Corner, London.

Life and Legend of Gautama, trans. by Rev. P. Bigandet, from Malankara Watthu's work, written 2000 years after the death of Buddha, 1880.

Buddhist Suttas, including the Maha-parinibbana Suttanta, trans. by T. W. Rhys Davids, Vol. XI, *Sacred Books of the East.* Clarendon Press, Oxford, 1881.

Vinaya Texts, trans. by T. W. Rhys Davids and Oldenberg, Vols. XIII, XVII, XX, *Sacred Books of the East,* 1881-1885.

Sutta Nipata, a collection of discourses, trans. by V. Fausböll, Vol. X, *Sacred Books of the East,* 1881.

The Dhammapada, a collection of verses, trans. by F. Max Müller, Vol. X, *Sacred Books of the East,* 1881.

The Dhammapada, with accompanying narratives, trans. from the Chinese, in 1878, by Samuel Beal. K. Paul, Trench, Trübner & Co., Ltd., 1902.

The Dhammapada, trans. by Kenneth J. Saunders and W. D. C. Wagiswara, in *Wisdom of the East Series,* J. Murray, London, 1912. E. P. Dutton & Co., New York.

Hymns of the Faith (Dhammapada), trans. by Albert Edmunds. Open Court Publishing Co., Chicago, 1902.

The Gospel of Buddha, According to Old Records, by Paul Carus. Open Court Publishing Co., Chicago, 1921.

Therigatha, Psalms of the Sisters, trans. by Mrs. T. W. Rhys Davids, in *Psalms of the Early Buddhists;* pub. for the Pali Text Society, by Henry Frowde, Oxford University Press Warehouse, Amen Corner, London, 1909 and 1913.

Theragatha, Psalms of the Brethren, trans. by Mrs. T. W. Rhys Davids, same pub. etc., as above.

The Life of Buddha, by Hermann Oldenberg, 1882.

The Questions of King Milinda (Milindapañha), trans. by T. W. Rhys Davids, Vols. XXXV and XXXVI, *Sacred Books of the East,* 1890-1894.

Fo-Sho-Hing-Tsan-King, A Life of Buddha, by Asvaghosha Bodhisattva, trans. from Sanskrit into Chinese by Dharmaraksha, 420 A.D.; from Chinese into English by Samuel Beal, Vol. XIX, *Sacred Books of the East,* Oxford, 1883.

Mahayana Texts, trans. by E. B. Cowell (*The Buddha-Karita of Asvaghosha*) Vol. XLIX, *Sacred Books of the East,* 1894.

Lotuses of the Mahayana, ed. by K. J. Saunders, *Wisdom of the East Series,* Dutton and Co., 1924.

The Heart of Buddhism, an anthology of Buddhist verse, trans. and edited by K. J. Saunders. The Association Press, 1915.

Gotama Buddha, a biography based on the canonical books of the Therevadin, by K. J. Saunders, Association Press, New York, 1920.

Lalita Vistara, trans. by Rajendrabla Mitra, 1881-1886, Calcutta.

The Udana, by Maj. Gen. D. M. Strong, C.B. London, Luzac & Co., 1902.

Asoka, by Devadatta Ramakrishna Bhandarkar, Carmichael Professor of Ancient Indian History and Culture, Calcutta University. The Carmichael Lectures for 1923, Pub. by the University of Calcutta, 1925.

Asoka, the Buddhist Emperor of India, by Vincent Arthur Smith; Third Edition, revised and enlarged. Oxford, The Clarendon Press, 1920.

Asoka, by James M. Macphail. Calcutta, The Association Press; London, New York, etc., Oxford University Press, 1918.

Asoka, Text and Glossary, by Alfred C. Woolner, London, New York, Oxford University Press, 1924.

Inscriptions of Asoka, by Eugen Hultzsch, with 55 plates. New Edition. Oxford, printed for the Government of India at the Clarendon Press, 1925.

EARLY GREEK PHILOSOPHERS:

Early Greek Philosophy, by John Burnet, M.A., LL.D. With the Fragments that remain of Herakleitos, Parmenides, Empedokles, Anaxagoras, Leukippos, etc. London, Adam and Charles Black, 4-6 Soho Square, 1920.

The First Philosophers of Greece, by Arthur Fairbanks. With the remaining Fragments of the Pre-Socratic Philosophers in Greek and English, and a translation of the more important accounts of their opinions contained in the works of Plato, Aristotle and other early authors and compilers. Kegan Paul, Trench, Trübner & Co., London, 1898.

Source Book in Ancient Philosophy, by Charles M. Bakewell. Composed entirely of quotations from the philosophers from Thales to Plotinus and of accounts of their opinions from early authors, all in translation. Charles Scribner's Sons, 1907.

Ancient Philosophy from Thales to Cicero, by Joseph B. Mayor, M.A. A brief introduction to the formal history of philosophy. Cambridge, University Press, 1912.

Ancient European Philosophy, A History of Greek Philosophy Psychologically Treated, by Denton J. Snider, Litt.D. Sigma Publishing Co., 210 Pine St., St. Louis, Mo., 1903.

PLATONISM :

The Dialogues of Plato, 5 vols. with analyses and introductions, trans. by Benjamin Jowett, M.A., Master of Balliol College, Regius Professor of Greek at Oxford, 1871. Oxford University Press, 1924.

Article on "Plato," Vol. XX, *Library of the World's Best Literature*, by Paul Shorey.

Plato and Platonism, by Walter Pater. Macmillan & Co., 1893.

Article on "Plato," Vol. XIX, *Encyclopædia Britannica* by Lewis Campbell, LL.D., Prof. Greek, University of St. Andrews, 1890.

The Republic of Plato, trans. by Davies and Vaughan, 1866. Burt's Home Library, A. L. Burt Co., publishers.

The Republic of Plato, trans. by H. Spens, D.D., 1873. *Everyman's Library*, E. P. Dutton & Co., New York, 1927.

The Socratic Discourses by Plato and Xenophon and Five Dialogues of Plato on Poetic Inspiration. Everyman's Library, ed. by Ernest Rhys, E. P. Dutton & Co., New York.

PLOTINUS :

Plotinus, trans. by Stephen Mackenna (four volumes, covering six Enneads have appeared so far, 1917-1926; but Inge says he has "translated the whole into admirably clear and vigorous English"). The Library of Philosophical Translations. Philip Lee Warner, Publisher to the Medici Society, Limited, 7 Grafton St., London, W.I.; 113 W. 57th St., New York City.

Select Works of Plotinus, trans. from the Greek with an introduction containing the substance of Porphyry's Life of Plotinus, by Thomas Taylor, 1758-1835. New Edition with

Preface by G. R. S. Mead, Sec. of the Theosophical Society. London; G. Bell & Sons, Ltd., York House, Portugal St., 1912.

The Evolution of Theology in the Greek Philosophers, Gifford Lectures delivered in the University of Glasgow in 1900-1902, by Edward Caird, LL.D., D.C.L., D.Litt., James MacLehose and Sons, Glasgow, 1904. "Nothing more helpful . . . written in the loftiest spirit," says Mackenna.

The Philosophy of Plotinus, Gifford Lectures at St. Andrews, 1917-1918, by William Ralph Inge, C.V.O., D.D. Longmans, Green and Co., 39 Paternoster Row, London, E.C. 4, 1923. "A work fascinating in detail and henceforth the necessary foundation of all serious study of Plotinus," says Mackenna.

The Problem of Evil in Plotinus, by B. A. G. Fuller, University Press, Cambridge, 1912. "Includes translations of many cardinal passages and is written throughout in as lucid a style as has ever expounded a metaphysical system," says Mackenna.

Plotinos, Complete Works. In Chronological Order, Grouped in Four Periods, with Biography by Porphyry, Eunapius and Suidas, by Kenneth Sylvan Guthrie, Comparative Literature Press, Alpine, N. J., 1918.

STOICISM:

Seneca Ad Lucilium Epistulae Morales, Latin, with English translation by Richard M. Gummere, Ph.D., Head Master Wm. Penn Charter School, Philadelphia; Loeb Edition, 1923. G. P. Putnam's Sons, New York.

L. Annaeus Seneca, Minor Dialogues, trans. by Aubrey Stewart, M.A., Late Fellow of Trinity College; Cambridge, 1889. Geo. Bell & Sons, London.

The Discourses of Epictetus; with the Encheiridion and Fragments. Translated, with notes, a Life of Epictetus, and a View of his Philosophy, by George Long, London, George Bell & Sons, York Street, Covent Garden, 1890. Bohn Classical Library.

Epictetus: Selections from His Discourses as Reported by Arrian and from the Fragments contained in the Writings of Stobaeus and others, with the Enchiridion, ed. by Benjamin E. Smith. After the translation from the Greek by Elizabeth Carter. The Century Co., New York.

Golden Sayings of Epictetus, with the Hymn of Cleanthes, trans. and arranged by Hastings Crossley. London, 1912.

The Golden Book of Marcus Aurelius, trans. from the Greek by Meric Casaubon, 1634. With an introduction by W. H. D. Rouse. Everyman's Library, ed. by Ernest Rhys, New York, E. P. Dutton & Co.

The Meditations of the Emperor Marcus Aurelius Antoninus, trans. by George Long, 1862; with a biographical sketch and a view of the philosophy of Antoninus, by the translator. It includes also Canon Farrar's "Marcus Aurelius" from *Seekers After God.* A. L. Burt Co., New York.

Seekers After God, by Rev. F. W. Farrar, D.D., F.R.S., Canon of Westminster. Macmillan & Co., 1877. It treats of Seneca, Epictetus, Marcus Aurelius.

Marc-Aurèle, by Joseph Ernest Renan; 7th volume of his *History of the Origins of Christianity,* 1882; the most vital and interesting book to be had relating to the time of Marcus Aurelius.

Marius the Epicurean, Walter Pater, an outside commentary of service in re-creating the period in which Marcus Aurelius lived.

The Treatises of M. T. Cicero, on "The Nature of the Gods," "Divination," "Fate," etc., edited and partially translated by C. D. Yonge, B.A. Bohn's Classical Library. London, 1853.

MOHAMMEDISM:

The Qur'an, trans. by E. H. Palmer, Vols. VI and IX, *The Sacred Books of the East,* ed. by Max Müller.

The Koran, trans. by George Sale (1680-1736), with explanatory notes, 1801.

The Koran, trans. by Rev. J. M. Rodwell, M.A., 1861. Pub. recently as No. 380, Everyman's Library, E. P. Dutton & Co., New York. Approaches nearer to the Arabic than Sale's version, and the Suras are arranged in the probable chronological order, instead of in the haphazard sequence of the Arabic manuscripts which Sale and Palmer follow.

The Religion of the Koran, by Arthur N. Wollaston, K.C.I.E.; *Wisdom of the East Series,* pub. by John Murray, Albemarle St., London, 1917. The extracts from the Koran are taken from Palmer's translation in the *Sacred Books of the East.*

Selections from Muhammadan Traditions, by Rev. William Goldsack, 1923.

Mahomet and Islam, by Sir William Muir (1819-1905) Religious Tract Society, London.

INDIAN FOLK LORE:

The Indians' Book, an offering by the American Indians of
Indian lore and songs, recorded and edited by Mrs. Nathalie
Curtis Burlin: illustrations from photographs and from orig-
inal drawings by Indians. Harper and Bros., 1907.
The Path on the Rainbow, an anthology of songs and chants from
the Indians of North America, ed. by George W. Cronyn, with
introduction by Mary Austin. Boni and Liveright, New York,
1918.
Article by Alice C. Fletcher and Francis La Flesche, an Omaha
Indian, 27th annual report of the American Bureau of Eth-
nology.
Primitive Man as Philosopher, by Paul Radin. D. Appleton & Co.,
New York, 1927.
The Polynesian Race (in two volumes), by Judge A. Fornander.
Trübner & Co., London.

The World's Living Religions, by Robert Ernest Hume, Ph.D.,
Prof. of the History of Religions, Union Theological Seminary,
New York. Charles Scribner's Sons, 1924.

INDEX

(Numbers, both Roman and Arabic, refer to pages)

Printed in the United States
3908